ESSENTIALS
OF RENT REVIEW

AUSTRALIA
The Law Book Company
Brisbane ● Sydney ● Melbourne ● Perth

CANADA
Ottawa ● Toronto ● Calgary ● Montreal ● Vancouver

Agents:
Steimatsky's Agency Ltd., Tel Aviv;
N.M. Tripathi (Private) Ltd., Bombay;
Eastern Law House (Private) Ltd., Calcutta;
M.P.P. House, Bangalore;
Universal Book Traders, Delhi;
Aditya Books, Delhi;
MacMillan Shuppan KK, Tokyo;
Pakistan Law House, Karachi, Lahore

ESSENTIALS
OF RENT REVIEW

by
Ronald Bernstein, Q.C., F.C.I.Arb.,
Hon. Assoc. R.I.C.S., Hon. F.S.V.A.
A Bencher of the Middle Temple

and

Kirk Reynolds, Q.C.

Consultant on Valuation Matters:
David Yorke, C.B.E., FRICS
*A Past President of
The Royal Institution of Chartered Surveyors*

*Published in collaboration with
The Royal Institution of Chartered Surveyors*

LONDON
SWEET & MAXWELL
1995

Published in 1995 by
Sweet & Maxwell Limited of
South Quay Plaza, 183 Marsh Wall, London E14 9FT.
Computerset by York House Typographic Ltd, London W13 8NT.
Printed by Butler & Tanner, Frome & London.

British Library Cataloguing Data

A CIP catalogue record
for this book is
available from the
British Library.

ISBN 0–421–45550–0

FOREWORD

by

CLIVE LEWIS Hon. D. Litt. FRICS FSVA
President of The Royal Institution of Chartered Surveyors

The English system of rent review for commercial property is unique. Resting, as it does, on the twin foundations of an advanced system of law and a highly trained and respected body of professional valuers, it has now stood the test of repeated cycles highlighting eras of property value booms and busts. One hundred per cent satisfaction is too much to expect from any manmade system, but comparative studies of other systems have not shown a higher degree of satisfaction anywhere in the developed world.

Ronald Bernstein and Kirk Reynolds, now both Queen's Counsel, have been in the forefront of rent review law and practice from its earliest days. They have acted as draftsmen to the Institution for every edition of the "Guidance Notes for Surveyors acting as Arbitrators or Independent Experts in Rent Reviews"; the current edition forming an Appendix to this book. In this field, their *Handbook of Rent Review* is the standard work of reference, and no names are more highly respected. Their Consultant on valuation matters is my distinguished predecessor as President, David Yorke CBE FRICS. He adds current hands-on experience as a practising arbitrator and is the former senior partner of one of the country's leading firms of surveyors and valuers.

The task of explaining simply the essentials of a subject in which valuation and law and practice are so interlinked is a formidable one. The Institution, and its members, and the very many others needing to know how renting commercial premises works in England and Wales, are fortunate that three people with such a combined experience of law, valuation and professional training have been willing to undertake this work.

Having personally spent much of my own professional life undertaking Arbitration and Independent Expert appointment work, I know how important it is that surveyors and their clients understand fully all the ingredients and the consequences that flow therefrom when making submissions or attending Hearings as an Expert Witness.

I believe this will therefore be found valuable by many people inside and outside the professions, overseas as well as in the United Kingdom. I am pleased to commend it, and The Royal Institution of Chartered Surveyors are happy to be associated with Sweet and Maxwell Limited in this publication.

CLIVE LEWIS
The Royal Institution of Chartered Surveyors
President July 1993 – July 1994

Authors' Note

Rent Review is now an integral part of the commercial landholding system in the United Kingdom. But the ingenuity of lawyers, fuelled by the demands of their clients (tenants as well as landlords), has made it an ever more complex subject. Our *Handbook of Rent Review* was first published in 1981 as a relatively slim looseleaf work, with a Digest of about 80 cases. The Digest now includes over 300 cases, and the consequent bulk and price make the *Handbook* unsuitable as an introduction to the subject. Hence this book.

Our object has been to give an overview of the rent review process which will be intelligible alike to students, practitioners and business men — abroad as well as in the United Kingdom — who need to understand how our commercial leasing system works. Where necessary, we go into detail; but we indicate Parts that can be passed over on a first reading.

We give references to many cases, but those readers who do not have ready access to law reports can find a Digest of every case referred to, in strict alphabetical order, in the Digest of Cases in the Handbook of Rent Review.

We reproduce, as Appendix III, the current 'Guidance Notes for Surveyors acting as Arbitrators or Independent Experts in Rent Reviews' (Sixth edition, April 1993), published by the Royal Institution of Chartered Surveyors, and included by kind permission of the Institution. For the beginner we provide, as Appendix I to the book, a Glossary of frequently used terms.

Throughout our labours on this book, David Yorke CBE, Fellow and Past President of the RICS, has been our Consultant Editor and has given us inestimable support from his wide experience both in practice with Weatherall Green & Smith and within the R.I.C.S. Clive Lewis FRICS, as President of the R.I.C.S., has contributed a most generous Foreword. And our editors at Sweet & Maxwell (except one who objected to our beginning any sentence with "and"!) have been most patient with us. We are truly grateful to them all.

The law is stated as at May 1, 1995.

RONALD BERNSTEIN   Falcon Chambers
KIRK REYNOLDS   Temple, EC4

Contents

Chapter One: The Function of Rent Review Provisions

Chapter Two: The Place of Rent Review in the Structure of Leases

Chapter Three: The Structure of a Rent Review Clause

Chapter Four: Interpreting Rent Review Provisions

Chapter Five: Methods of Resolving a Dispute as to the Meaning of the Lease

Chapter Six: The President of the R.I.C.S. and his appointment procedure

Chapter Seven: The Remuneration of the Arbitrator or Expert

Chapter Eight: The Basis of Valuation

Chapter Nine: Determining the New Rent – the Choice of Procedures

Chapter 10: The Procedure for Determination by an Expert

Chapter 11: The Procedures for Determination by Arbitration

Chapter 12: Evidence in a Rent Review

Chapter 13: The Award or Determination

Chapter 14: Costs and Fees

Chapter 15: Control by the Court of Arbitration

Chapter 16: Control by the Court of the Determination of an Expert

Chapter 17: Consequence of the Review

Abbreviations

The 1954 Act	The Law of Property Act 1954
R.P.I.	Retail Price Index
R.I.C.S.	Royal Institution of Chartered Surveyors
I.S.V.A.	Incorporated Society of Valuers and Auctioneers

Table of Cases

Table of Statutes

Chapter One: The Function of Rent Review Provisions

1.1—The central importance of rent review in our landholding system

Rent[1] is money. Money in the hands of the landlord, who counts on its arrival every week or month or quarter. Money in the hands of the pension funds, whose capital values and payouts to their pensioners are underpinned by the incoming stream of rent. Money from the pockets of the commercial tenant, who must find it out of the profits of his business. Money from the treasuries of national or local government, who must pay out of taxation for the many rented properties that they occupy. For a high proportion of the land and buildings in England and Wales, from the smallest of corner shops to the largest of industrial estates—indeed almost every kind of property except residential—is occupied by rent-paying tenants rather than by freehold owners.

This book is about the arrangements commonly found in lettings of non-residential property for adjusting the rent to take account of inflation and of changes in its rental value. It is also about the part that valuers and other professional advisers play in the efficient operation of the rent adjustment procedures.

Most commercial leases are granted for a term of more than five years, and the inflation of the last few decades has conditioned landlords against committing themselves for more than five years or so to a rent fixed today. Moreover, we have also seen great fluctuations in property values in the last few decades quite apart from the effects of inflation. Incoming industries have led to sharp increases in the value of land and buildings in, for example the M4 corridor or towns like Bridgend or Derby. The influx of overseas financial institutions in the 1980s had the effect of catapulting rents in the City of London which then slumped just as dramatically in the following decade. The arrival of a new Marks and Spencer or Sainsbury's can transform almost overnight values of nearby shops. The Channel Tunnel may cause large increases in values of properties near it and the road and rail links to it. Landlords do not wish to shut themselves out for too long from the benefit of these increases in value. Unless tenants will agree to provide for rent

---

[1] This word, with many others, is defined in the Glossary—Appendix I, p. 123.

1

review, most landlords will not grant the long leases that many tenants need. Hence the central importance of rent review in the eyes of landlords.

1.2—What the tenant wants

1.2.1—*In times of rising prosperity and rising rents*

Until about 1989 the tenant wanted security of tenure for a relatively long period – 15 years or more. Particular circumstances causing him to want this would be where he:

(a) is taking the premises for the first time, and therefore wants a period long enough to fit out the premises, settle in and get on with his business without having to face the expense and trauma of relocating again;

(b) wants a long period over which to amortise his acquisition, fitting out and moving costs;

(c) is a retailer, or carries on any business in which his customers' or clients' familiarity with his premises is a benefit to him, and therefore wants a long period in which to nurture, and take advantage of, his customers' familiarity with the premises; or

(d) would like to have a lease which can be sold for a substantial capital sum if he decides to dispose of it before the term ends.

In an ideal world, therefore, the tenant would seek the right to stay for as long, or as short, a term as he likes, at a rent which is fixed at the outset and which does not change during the term. But it would be financially suicidal for a landlord to let premises on those terms, and tenants recognise that a landlord cannot reasonably be expected to grant a long lease without receiving in return either some provision for rent review, or an initial rent so high that it will impose a crushing burden on the tenant in the early years of the tenancy. For 25 years or more it has been almost unknown for a lease of non-residential premises to be granted for more than about five years without some provision for rent review. The tenant has had to make a further concession to the landlord in order to obtain the length of term that he has historically required in that most rent review provisions are one-way valves: they allow the rent to go up if the market rental value of the property goes up, but remain unchanged if the market rental value falls. Yet traditionally the tenant has had to accept these provisions.

1.2.2—*In times of recession or of uncertain future*

In times of recession, however, two factors combine to change the balance of bargaining power. First, the recession reduces the number of prospective tenants in the market looking for premises. Second, many more premises are vacant and to let on the market. So landlords are less inclined to stick to the "take it or leave it" attitude that they have so often taken in times of prosperity. Many tenants are able to negotiate the right to bring their leases to an end by giving notice, either on a specified date, or within a specified time after they know the result of a rent review. If the rent fixed on review is unacceptably high, the tenant can either vacate the premises or negotiate a lower rent under threat of vacating.

1.3—What the landlord wants

1.3.1—*Most landlords are concerned about their investment*

A majority of non-residential leases are granted by a landlord who holds the premises (whether he is the freeholder or is himself a lessee) as an investment. As an investor the landlord wants:

(a) security of capital in real terms;
(b) security of income in real terms; and
(c) freedom from the labour of administration.

Security of income and capital are interlinked: if the anticipated income stream from the property is not secure, the capital value will be reduced to take account of the insecurity. Moreover, if the income stream remains unchanged in times of inflation, its real value will decline, and with it the real capital value of the property.

Even where the landlord is not an investor, he is often a tenant holding under a lease himself and is accordingly concerned that the rent he receives fully covers the rent his investor–landlord requires him to pay.

1.3.2—*The ability to redevelop or refurbish the property*

With the passage of time, the income-producing capability of many properties falls as the property becomes outdated compared with its newer competitors. As the income-producing capacity of a property falls, the capital value falls. So a landlord does not want to shut out the possibility of modernising the property (whether by refurbishment or by demolition and reconstruction) when modernisation becomes economically desirable.

1.3.3—*Freedom from administration costs and hassle*

In a time of rising rents, a possible course for a landlord to take is to let the property for successive periods of (say) one year only, so that the income stream is at a level never more than one year out-of-date. But there are major objections to this:

(a) The Landlord and Tenant Act 1954 fetters the landlord's ability to refuse the grant of a new lease, and to require the tenant to pay what the landlord considers to be the new market rent. In most cases, the practical effect of granting the tenant a lease for one year is to give him a contract under which he has an indefinite number of options to renew, and on each occasion the tenant can go to court if he thinks the rent proposed by the landlord is too high.

(b) The administrative hassle of having to negotiate, every year, a new tenancy at a new rent, combined with the inevitable delay and expense if the matter has to go to court, would be unacceptable to both parties.

(c) If the tenant chooses to vacate—an option that the short tenancy gives him—the costs of reletting would be high in relation to the rent. So would the associated risk that the premises will be empty, and producing no rent, whilst a new tenant is found.

(d) Few tenants would take the property with so short a period of security of tenure and certainty of outgoings, and those who would take it will probably be willing to pay only a reduced rent.

(e) Because the income stream is so insecure, the market value of the landlord's interest, if he is selling to an investor, will be much reduced.

1.4—The balance between these conflicting requirements

1.4.1—*If the rent cannot be varied, the term will be short*

If the rent is to remain unchanged throughout the term, the landlord will be willing to grant only a short lease. To induce the landlord to grant a lease long enough to meet the criteria mentioned in paragraph 2.1 below, the tenant must accept some method of adjusting the rent to take account both of falls in the value of money, and of increases in the value of the property.

Theoretically a number of methods of varying the rent are open; most of them have been tried at some time.

1.4.2—*The progressive or "stepped" rent*

Under this method the parties try to predict future market rental values, and the prediction is translated into fixed increases from specified dates. This is both simple—it is certain, in that both parties know from the outset how much rent will be payable in each year of the term—and cost-effective because no costs are involved in varying the rent. Where the amount of rent involved is small in relation to the costs and trouble involved in more complicated methods, this may be a sensible method to adopt. However, its major disadvantage is that, even over a five-year period, accurate predictions of the value of the property are impossible. In practice, therefore, this method is hardly ever used except over the first few years of the lease (perhaps during the first five years) and then more often as a way of helping the tenant to afford the rent in the early years than as a genuine rent-review mechanism.

1.4.3—*Linking the rent to the retail price index (R.P.I.)*

This is an easily understood and easy to operate method of adjusting the rent to changes in the purchasing value of money. It can operate at any chosen interval, *e.g.* quarterly, or annually, or at three-year intervals. It can ensure that the purchasing value of the income stream from the property remains reasonably constant.

But this method takes no account of changes in the value of the property as distinct from changes in the value of money. Thus, in the period from 1974 to 1978, a rent linked to the R.P.I. would have risen sharply in a period when rental values generally were falling sharply, to the great disadvantage of the tenant. In the period from 1985 to 1989, a rent linked to the R.P.I. would have risen only slowly at a time when rental values were rising sharply—to the great disadvantage of the landlord. In the period from 1989 to 1993, many rental values have fallen at a time when the R.P.I. was still rising. It may be said that, in the long run, the variations between market rents and the R.P.I. would cancel out, so that what the tenant loses on the swings he gains on the roundabout. One answer to this is that a tenant who took a lease in 1973 at a rent linked to the R.P.I. might be bankrupted by the 1974–1978 swings, long before the 1985–1989 roundabout arrived. Likewise, if a landlord who had granted a long lease at an R.P.I.-linked rent had

had to sell his interest in 1988, he would have received a much lower price than if the lease had been a conventional one with periodic rent reviews.

1.4.4—*Turnover or income-stream rents*

This method of rent adjustment relates the rent that the tenant has to pay to the income that he receives. In a retail shop the rent may be expressed as a percentage of the tenant's gross turnover, whereas in an office building intended to be sub-let in parts, it can be related to the aggregate of the rents received (or receivable) under the sub-lettings. There is usually a fixed element of rent in addition to the variable element.

This form of lease, which is very common in shopping malls in the United States, has much to be said for it in relation to lettings of properties which are unique or nearly so, or where for other reasons there are great difficulties in assessing the market rental value of the property in question. Landlords and tenants alike prefer to avoid situations where reasonable estimates of rental value can vary by 100 per cent or more. But this method is rarely practicable except in leases of shops or of buildings intended to be sub-let in parts. One particular difficulty arises in situations where the landlord has reason to question the tenant's reliability in furnishing true accounts of his business, yet doubts the efficacy of the accounting procedures necessary for verifying the turnover.

1.5—The advantages of rent review clauses

The disadvantages of the variation provisions outlined above are elimi-nated if, at predetermined intervals, rent is revised to the then current open market rental value of the premises, either by agreement between landlord and tenant or, failing agreement, by the determination of some independent person. The inclusion in the lease of provisions of this kind assures the landlord that, as the value of money falls, or the market rental value of his property increases, his rent will rise accordingly. If such provisions are included in the lease, he is willing to grant a relatively long term—indeed, in many cases he prefers to do so. For his part, the tenant knows that any increase in rent that he has to pay when the rent review operates should not result in a rent higher than he would have to pay if he vacated the premises on that date and took other equivalent premises. Nor will it be higher, so far as one can foresee, than the rent that his competitors will have to pay if they take a lease of similar premises at the time his rent is being reviewed. Of course, the tenant would prefer a long term at an affordable rent which cannot be increased, or at least a short term with a secure option to renew. But he knows that for premises for which there is any significant demand the landlord will not be willing to grant a lease of this kind.

1.6—The disadvantages of rent review clauses

Although the market has clearly judged that open market rent review provisions are much to be preferred to rival forms of rent adjustment, it must be admitted that such provisions have undoubted disadvantages.

(a) Cost

Most landlords and tenants do not have sufficient knowledge of market rental values to be able to agree upon a new rent without consulting at least one professional valuer. In most cases each party consults a valuer to advise him, so that two valuers are involved from the outset. Each of these valuers has to be paid not only for his valuation—which may involve prolonged and time-consuming research into transactions in comparable premises—but also for negotiations with his opposite number which may also be lengthy and time-consuming. The machinery of review often contains pitfalls, and requires the services of a lawyer to initiate the review process. The application of the provisions of the lease to the circumstances of the case may raise legal difficulties, so the lawyer has to be called in again to advise on these. Then, if the respective lawyers disagree on the law, or the respective valuers cannot reach agreement on the valuation, a third party has to be brought in to resolve the issues—whether a judge or a valuer acting as arbitrator or as an independent expert. If the valuer is asked to resolve legal issues, he may need to take independent legal advice. The process is often expensive, sometimes horrifyingly so.

(b) Delay

Most parties who want the services of a professional want a good one. Good professional advisers are usually busy. Even if only two are involved the process can take a long time. If three, four or five are involved it can take many months. It is not unknown (although fortunately rare) for the review date for review number two to arrive before review number one has been concluded. However, most reviews are settled within a year.

(c) Management time

The rent review process is now such an established part of everyday commercial life that the amount of management time and effort involved can go unnoticed. It is, nevertheless, considerable. The landlord must institute a reminder procedure and follow it. Solicitors have to be chosen and instructed. A valuer has to be chosen and instructed and a fee agreed. His valuation has to be studied and discussed. Then his negotiations with the opposing valuer have to be followed and instructions given to him as required. If he fails to agree the new rent, the arbitration or determination procedure has to be followed, the various draft submissions and counter-submissions read, and appropriate instructions given. The aggregate time taken is substantial.

In contrast, an indexation procedure can be operated by the party without the assistance of solicitor or valuer. A simple reference to the index, followed by a single letter to the tenant, and appropriate action to change the rent demands or standing order, is all that is required.

With so many disadvantages, it can be said that the rent review system is a lousy system. But it can also be said that all the alternatives are worse. If, or when, this cannot be said of it, the rent review system will begin to die.

1.7—Conditions required for the effective operation of a rent review system

1.7.1—*A desire for protection against future inflation*

When prices generally, and property values in particular, were stable, rents could be fixed for a long time to come. For example, for decades before 1960, the most common length of a lease of commercial premises was 21 years at a fixed rent.

1.7.2—*A history of fluctuations in property values*

If all that is needed is adjustment in rent to take account of inflation (or deflation), a simple linkage to an index will be far simpler, quicker, and cheaper than a review to market values.

1.7.3—*An available body of competent and trustworthy valuers*

Any procedure which relies upon determination by a third party relies upon the availability of a sufficient number of people recognised as having both integrity and competence. The skills required for competence as a third-party determiner, whether as arbitrator or as an independent valuer, need to be instilled by training.

1.7.4—*An effective procedure for choosing and appointing a suitable valuer*

In many cases where parties cannot agree the new rent, they do not know of and/or cannot agree upon a suitably qualified third-party determiner. The existence of first, a body of people of proven professional skills, and second, a wholly unbiased procedure for appointing from among that body a person suitable for the particular dispute, is essential.

1.7.5—*A legal system that supports and encourages the resolution of disputes by arbitration*

The availability of information about market lettings is crucial to the functioning of rent review.[2] If effective means of obtaining such information, particularly from large landlords, are not available, the process becomes far less acceptable to tenants.

English law, like other common law systems, provides procedures for making a party disclose relevant information in his possession, and for compelling the attendance of witnesses. Such supports are not normally available in continental jurisdictions. It is doubtful whether a rent review system can be effective without them.

---

[2] See the illuminating judgment of Phillips J. in *Banque Bruxelles Lambert S.A. v. Eagle Star Insurance Co. Ltd* [1994] 2 E.G.L.R. 108.

Chapter Two: The Place of Rent Review in the Structure of a Lease

2.1—Characteristics of a lease in English law

2.1.1—*The concept of a tenancy is common to many systems of law*

Most, if not all, legal systems have some mechanism whereby the owner of land grants to someone else the right to use the land for a limited period, receiving in return a rent. The rent may be in money, or in some other form such as part of the produce of the land. The grantor (the "landlord" or "lessor") has rights in contract against the grantee (the "tenant" or "lessee") to ensure he receives his rent. He may also have rights to enter upon the land to enforce payment of it. The tenant has rights in contract (usually much less extensive) to enforce the right to occupy the land that the landlord has agreed to give him.

2.1.2—*Special characteristics of the English system*

The special characteristic of the English leasehold system is that the grant of the right to occupy can confer upon the tenant not merely personal rights against the landlord, but also an interest in land, or in a building on the land, which—apart from the limitation as to the duration of the interest—has most of the characteristics of a freehold. This interest can be enforced not only against the person who granted it but against all comers. In particular, the interest can be for any period of time that the parties wish—there are many leases for 999 years. Subject to any restrictions that the parties have incorporated in the lease, the interest of the lessee and that of the lessor can be assigned as readily as a freehold. The lessee's rights to protect his possession and occupation of the property against everyone including his landlord are as full as those of a freeholder. So long as the lessee performs the obligations under the lease, the law will protect his rights. Moreover, if the lease is of "business premises" (a term which in this context includes almost all premises other than purely residential premises or premises used for farming) the lessee has extensive statutory rights to a new lease when the old lease expires.

2.1.3—"Lease", "leasehold", "lessor", "landlord", "lessee", and "tenant".

The interest held by a tenant may be called a "leasehold interest" if granted by a lease, or a "tenancy" if granted by a lease or a tenancy agreement. The agreement creating a tenancy is called the "tenancy agreement". If the agreement is contained in formal documents sealed by the landlord and tenant respectively it is called a "lease". The interest retained by the grantor of a lease or a person who has created a tenancy is called a "reversion". The interest retained by a freeholder who has granted a lease or created a tenancy is called "the freehold reversion". "Lessor" and "lessee" have the same meaning as "landlord" and "tenant" respectively but, strictly speaking, are only appropriate when a formal lease has been granted.[1]

2.2—The leasehold interest: creation and disposability

2.2.1—*The creation of a leasehold interest*

The nature of the legal formalities which need to be observed in creating a leasehold interest fall outside the scope of this book, but, in principle, the following are the ways in which such an interest can be brought into existence:

   (a)   by a formal sealed document called a "lease";

   (b)   by any document signed by the parties—if it is not made under seal, the document is called a tenancy agreement;

   (c)   by an agreement made by word of mouth between two or more persons; or

   (d)   by conduct of the parties, where a person who has possession of premises allows another person to have possession of them in return for a periodic payment.

2.2.2—*Presumption in favour of freedom of disposition*

In cases (a), (b) or (c) above, the parties can, and usually do, agree terms of the tenancy dealing with such matters as the duration of the tenancy, the circumstances in which the landlord can bring the tenancy to an end before

---

[1] See the Glossary of Frequently used Terms at p. 123 below.

the end of the specified period (*e.g.* if the tenant fails to pay the rent), who is to repair and insure the premises, and many other matters which usually include restrictions upon disposability.

In case (d) above—where an agreement to create a tenancy is implied from the conduct of the parties—the law implies only the bare minimum of terms necessary to make the grant effective (see paragraph 2.2.5 below).

In general, unless at the time of creating the tenancy the parties agree that the terms of the tenancy shall include some restrictions on disposability, the tenant is free to dispose of his interest as he wishes. The tenant can therefore:

(a) assign it, *i.e.* he can dispose of the whole of the premises let to him for the entire duration of his interest;

(b) assign part of the premises for the whole duration of his interest;

(c) sub-let the whole of the premises for a period significantly shorter than that of his interest, retaining the right to resume possession at the end of that period;

(d) sub-let part of the premises for almost the whole of the duration of his interest, retaining possession of the remainder of the premises; and

(e) sub-let part of the premises to one sub-tenant, and the other parts to another or other sub-tenants, for substantially the whole of the duration of his interest, retaining none of the premises of which he is tenant.

2.2.3—*Freedom to pass on his own freedom*

Whatever freedom a tenant may have to assign or sub-let all or part of the interest granted to him, he can, in turn, grant to an assignee or sub-tenant. This freedom of disposal is inherent in the grant of each subordinate tenancy that is created, subject always to:

(a) any restrictions that have been imposed on the grantor by any grantor further up the chain, together with

(b) any restriction imposed by the lowest grantor.

2.2.4—*Most leases restrict freedom of disposition*

In practice, it is rare for a tenancy to be granted without some restriction upon the tenant's right to dispose of the interest being granted to him. A not uncommon term in a lease is that the tenant shall not assign, sub-let or part with possession of part only of the premises being let. Another restriction

13

commonly found in all but very long leases is that the tenant shall not assign, sub-let or part with possession of the premises or any part of them without the consent of the landlord (and the consent of every superior landlord if there are any). Where such a term is agreed, the Landlord and Tenant Act 1927 imports into it a proviso that the landlord may not unreasonably withhold his consent, and the Landlord and Tenant Act 1988 provides that the landlord may be liable in damages if he unreasonably refuses or delays the grant of consent.

2.2.5—*Terms implied by law*

If there is an agreement to let premises, with nothing more specified than the premises, the rent, and the intervals at which the rent is to be paid (*e.g.*, weekly, or monthly, or annually), there are a few, but only a few, obligations which the law will impose on the parties. They are, briefly these:

(a) The landlord's obligations are:
  (i) to give quiet enjoyment, *i.e.* that there will be no disturbance of the tenant's enjoyment of the property by the landlord, or by anyone claiming under the landlord; and
  (ii) not to derogate from his grant, meaning that the landlord will not do anything which will deny to the tenant the benefit of the tenancy agreement.
(b) The tenant's obligations are:
  (i) to pay the rent—agreeing a rent puts an obligation on the tenant to pay it; and
  (ii) not to commit waste, *i.e.* to use the premises in a way that an ordinary reasonable tenant would do, *e.g.* if the tenant goes away for the winter he should turn the water off and drain any pipes likely to burst; if a sink is blocked he should unblock it.

It should be noted that the law does *not* imply any term limiting the disposability of the leasehold interest.

2.2.6—*The lessee's liability continues after he has disposed of his leasehold interest*

In English law there are two overlaying relationships between a lessor and a lessee. The first is a matter of contract: under the terms of a normal lease the lessee contracts to pay the rent and perform all the obligations of the lessee *for the duration of the lease*. This relationship is called "privity of contract". The second arises, as a matter of law, between the grantor and the grantee of an interest in land (which for this purpose includes buildings and structures fixed to the land). This is called "privity of estate" and it continues only for so long as the relationship continues. Privity of estate ends when either party to it disposes of the whole of his estate (*i.e.* his interest) in the property. Privity of contract ends only when the contract is brought to an end, *i.e.* when it has run its specified duration, or has been brought to an end in some other way, *e.g.* by a notice exercising a right to bring it to an end in circumstances specified in the contract.

2.2.7—*Adverse consequences of this continuing liability*

In times of inflation or of sustained rises in rental values, the fact that his liability in contract continues after he has disposed of his interest rarely matters to a lessee, for if his assignee (or a subsequent assignee) fails to comply with the obligations under the lease, the landlord has effective remedies against the assignee who is in possession of the premises, and does not need to exercise his rights against the original lessee. But in times of recession, when rental values have fallen, the position is different. In these circumstances more assignees get into financial difficulties and default in paying rent, or in carrying out the other obligations under the lease. Or they become bankrupt or go into liquidation. The landlord cannot protect his interest by retaking possession and reletting, for he may be unable to find a new tenant except by accepting a lower rent—indeed, he may be unable to find a tenant at all. Moreover the defaulting tenant may have left the premises in poor repair and the landlord may incur expense in repairing them so as to attract a new tenant. The original lessee will then be called on to perform the obligations he entered into for the duration of the lease. It will be no answer to say: "But I assigned these premises many years ago."

In practice, the existence of this continuing liability may prevent any assignment. When the original lessee asks the lessor to consent to an assignment, the lessor will usually say: "I will give my consent, but only if your assignee contracts with me to remain liable to me for the rest of the original term, even if he reassigns to someone else in due course."

In a recession, the prospective assignee may prefer to take one of the many other premises which will be available to him on less burdensome terms.

2.2.8—*Methods of protecting the lessee against these burdens*

There are various ways in which an original lessee, or an assignee, can protect himself against being called on after he has assigned his interest. They include:

    (a)   In the original lease

    (i)   provision that the lessee is not to be liable after assignment;

    (ii)   provision that the lessor cannot enforce a covenant against the assignor until the lessor has taken all reasonable steps to enforce it against the assignee(s);

    (iii) provision that if the lessor enforces the covenant against the lessee he will assign to the lessee his rights against the assignee(s).

(b)   In the deed of assignment

    (i)   a charge on the lease to secure performance of the covenants for indemnity entered into by the assignee;

    (ii)   a covenant by the assignee to reassign the lease to the assignor if the assignee defaults and the assignor is called upon by the lessor to make good the default; or

    (iii) the reservation of a right for the assignor to take the premises back if the assignee defaults on his covenants.

But these protections are unusual, and are likely to be resisted by landlords or assignees or both. How far the original lessee, or an assignee from him, can achieve any of them depends upon his bargaining strength, which in turn will vary according to the state of the market. At the time of writing (July 1995) it seems likely that legislation will soon be passed modifying the strict application of the "privity of contract" principle, set out above. But it is probable that the changes will not affect existing leases.

2.3—The disposability of the landlord's interest

2.3.1—*Freedom if there are no provisions to the contrary*

If the terms of the tenancy do not impose on the landlord any fetter upon his right to dispose of or otherwise deal with his interest, the landlord has complete freedom of disposal of the interest that he retains after he has granted the tenancy. This interest is called his "reversion".

2.3.2—*Restrictions on the landlord's freedom are rare*

As we have seen, a landlord may be a freeholder, a head tenant, or an inferior tenant. If he is himself a tenant, the terms of the tenancy under which he holds may, and probably will, restrict his freedom to dispose of his interest. In other words, restraints often operate downwards. But it is very rare for a direct restriction to be imposed upwards, *i.e.* so that a tenant has power to restrict his landlord's dealings with his (the landlord's) interest.

A degree of restriction may be imposed indirectly, *e.g.* if the terms of the tenancy under which the landlord holds contains restrictions on the land-lord's freedom to dispose of his interest, and the landlord agrees with his tenant that he (the landlord) will observe all restrictions imposed by the lease under which he holds the premises.

2.4—The variety of interests that can exist

2.4.1—*The value of a particular interest can be infinitely variable*

Because the variety of interests that can exist is so wide, the value of a particular interest is almost infinitely variable. A freehold interest, with no existing lease carved out of it, may today be worth £1 million. If tomorrow or the next day I grant out of it a 999 year lease at the rent of one peppercorn per annum, and I charge a premium of £999,000 for it, my reversion—the right to take possession almost a thousand years hence, if the property still exists and if no legislation has been passed in the meantime interfering with my rights—is almost worthless or may have a negative value. But my lessee may grant an underlease of substantially the whole property for a period of 998 years which (depending upon the amount of rent reserved and the other obligations of the lease) may be worth only a little less than £999,000. So the position of an intermediate interest in the hierarchy of interests from freehold down to occupation lease is no guide to its value. A leasehold interest may be, and often is, much more valuable than the freehold or other reversion remaining after it has been granted.

2.4.2—*The relationship between duration, rent and value*

There is a close relationship between the duration of an interest, the rents payable to and by the holder of that interest, the frequency with which those rents may be reviewed, and the value of that interest. In times of inflation, if a reversioner has no right to increase the rent payable to him, the value of his interest will be greatly diminished as compared with a reversion to a reviewable rent. So a provision for rent review may be as critical an element of the value of a reversion as the duration of the lease, the duration of the reversion, or indeed the amount of the rent presently receivable. At a time of actual or anticipated inflation a freehold subject to a 35-year lease at a rent of £10,000 per annum may be worth £150,000 if the rent is reviewable every five years, but only £50,000 if the rent is not reviewable at all. A leasehold interest under which the rent payable exceeds the current market rental value of the property—a position all too familiar in times of recession—may have a substantial negative value in that the lessee will probably be unable to get anyone to take it off his hands without being paid a handsome reverse premium[2] for doing so.

2.5—Statutory protection of business tenants

2.5.1—*Part II of the Landlord and Tenant Act 1954*[3]

Part II of the Landlord and Tenant Act 1954 (the 1954 Act) gives comprehensive protection to tenants of business premises in England and Wales. "Business" is given a very wide definition so that the protection extends to most premises other than residential and agricultural premises. The protection operates:

(a)   to prevent a tenancy from coming to an end, even when the period for which it was granted expires, unless and until a notice in a form prescribed by the statute is served on, or by, the tenant;

(b)   to give the tenant, when such a notice has been served, the right to apply to the court for a new tenancy for a period of up to 14 years;

(c)   to require the court to grant a new tenancy save in certain specified circumstances;

(d)   to let the court decide the duration, rent and other terms of the new tenancy, if the parties cannot agree them.

With minor exceptions, the practical effect of these provisions is to give a tenant an automatic right to a new tenancy unless:

(a)   he has been, objectively considered, a "bad" tenant, *e.g.* he has been persistently late in paying his rent, or he has broken other terms of his tenancy;

(b)   the landlord intends to demolish or reconstruct the premises or a substantial part of them;

(c)   the landlord intends to occupy the premises for the purpose of a business to be carried on in them by the landlord himself or by a person for whom he is a trustee, or as a residence for himself, for his son or daughter, or for a person for whom he is a trustee.

If the parties cannot agree upon the rent to be paid under the new tenancy, the court will determine it by reference primarily to the rent at which, having regard to the terms of the new tenancy, the premises might reasonably be

---

[2] See glossary—Appendix I, page 126.
[3] As amended by the Law of Property Act 1969.

expected to be let in the open market by a willing lessor. Except in the circumstances set out in points (a), (b), or (c) above, the tenant can expect to get a new lease and the landlord can expect the new lease to provide for him (at least in theory) the same rent as he would get if the tenant had gone out and the landlord had offered the premises for letting in the open market.

2.5.2—*The 1954 Act provides the background against which parties negotiate*

With some minor amendments introduced by the Law of Property Act 1969, the 1954 Act has proved broadly acceptable to both landlords and tenants, and provides the context in which terms for a new tenancy are negotiated when an existing tenancy expires. In negotiating terms for a new tenancy the existing tenant and his landlord each know that there is a point beyond which the other party can say:

> "The terms that you propose are unacceptable; rather than agree to them I will go to court and take my chance on what terms the judge will order."

If negotiations break down, and either party takes this course, it will be for the judge to decide what should be the terms of the new lease. In practice, the judge will have regard to the terms of the existing lease. If those terms conform to the terms of leases currently being agreed between landlords and tenants in the open market, the judge will be disposed to order that those terms be repeated in the new tenancy. If either party wants to change the terms, *e.g.* because they provide for a rent review every three years, which was the norm when the old lease was granted but is no longer so, he can call evidence of the terms of rent review clauses currently being agreed in circumstances similar to the present case, and put forward any other relevant arguments as to why the rent review pattern should be different.

2.6—Comparison between the assessment of a rent under a rent review clause and under a new tenancy granted under the 1954 Act

In many cases an assessment of rent under a rent review clause in a continuing lease will produce much the same figure as an assessment of rent for the same premises on the grant to the tenant of a new tenancy under Part II of the 1954 Act. But there are differences in the procedure and in the basis of valuation, and these can sometimes be significant.

2.6.1—*The tribunal*

In a lease renewal under the 1954 Act this is the court, *i.e.* a judge.[4] Virtually all rent review disputes are determined by a valuer acting either as arbitrator or as independent expert who should be better qualified to assess rental value than a judge, who is, of course, trained as a lawyer.

2.6.2—*The procedure*

In assessing market rental value the court can act only on the evidence put before it; it will be rare for the judge to have any relevant opinions or market experience of his own. A valuer acting as an independent expert will have regard primarily to his own knowledge, experience and expert opinion. Even when he is acting as an arbitrator he will, at least to some extent, be entitled to rely upon his own knowledge and experience.[5]

2.6.3—*Date of valuation*

Most leases fix the valuation date for the review, so that the date of the hearing, or the determination without a hearing, is irrelevant.

In a renewal under the 1954 Act the commencement date of the new tenancy depends upon the date of the hearing of the application for it, and the valuation date depends on the date of the hearing.

2.6.4—*Choice of procedure*

In practice there is only one procedure available to resolve a dispute as to the rent payable tenancy renewed under the 1954 Act: by a hearing in court, with valuation evidence called and the case conducted by a solicitor or (more usually) a barrister or (exceptionally) by a party himself.

A reviewed rent under a rent review clause may be assessed:

(a) by a valuer acting as independent expert, with or without representations from the parties but with no oral hearing; or

(b) by a valuer acting as arbitrator and proceeding on written submissions from the parties but with no oral hearing; or

(c) by a valuer acting as arbitrator and proceeding to an oral hearing,

---

[4] Or a deputy judge—a high proportion of cases under the 1954 Act, both in the High Court and in the County Court, are heard by a practising barrister or solicitor sitting as a deputy judge.

[5] See para. 9.3.3 below; R.I.C.S. Guidance Notes para. 3.1.4 (Appendix III, page 166 below) and *Fisher v. PG. Wellfair Ltd* [1981] 2 Lloyd's Rep. 514; [1982] 263 E. G. 589, 657.

with written pleadings and/or submissions, and with each party's case presented by the party himself or (if he wishes) by a valuer, solicitor or counsel.

A valuer arbitrator may, if he and the parties so wish, be assisted by a legal assessor.

2.6.5—*Basis of valuation*

All lease renewals involve a valuation on the same basis, namely that set out in section 34 of the 1954 Act. Before making that valuation the judge has to decide what the duration and terms of the new tenancy are to be; he has considerable discretion about these, though he usually follows the terms of the existing lease.

An assessment of rent on review almost always has to be conducted on the basis of a hypothetical letting whose terms are fixed by the lease; the arbitrator or independent expert conducting the review has no discretion as to what they are to be. This is a situation that rarely occurs in real life, where the main terms of the letting, and the amount of the rent, are usually agreed as part of the same negotiation.

2.6.6—*Delay*

The time normally taken from the date of application to the President of the Royal Institution of Chartered Surveyors (R.I.C.S.) for appointment of a surveyor to act as arbitrator or independent expert, until the date of issue of an award or determination, is around 16 weeks. The usual time taken in proceedings for a new tenancy, from the date of issuing the proceedings to the date of judgment, is rarely less than 26 weeks and often exceeds a year. These periods are based on the assumption that at least one party wants the procedure completed without delay. There may be wide variations on these figures depending on the complexity of the case.

2.6.7—*Cost*

Proceedings in court to determine a rent will usually be cheaper than proceedings in a rent review arbitration with a hearing at which the parties are represented by a solicitor and counsel. But as indicated in paragraph 2.6.4 above, a rent review can be, and most of them are, conducted without the intervention of lawyers, and for this reason will usually be far less expensive.

Chapter Three: The Structure of a Rent Review Clause

3.1—Introduction

The wording in leases currently in existence varies widely, and the way in which the rent review provisions of a particular lease operate depends upon its terms. Over the years there have been many decided cases on whether the attempted initiation of a review has been effective. In many of these cases, the consequence for the landlord of a failure to initiate the review would be that the right to obtain an increase in rent for five or more years would be lost; one can therefore well understand his desire not to accept this consequence without a struggle.

Because these cases turn on fine distinctions of wording, this Chapter makes somewhat heavy reading. If desired the reader can pass to Chapter Four, and can return to Chapter Three as and when more detailed guidance is desired.

3.2—Initiating the review

Rent review clauses commonly provide for one or other of the parties (usually the landlord) to begin the rent review procedure by taking some formal step, such as the service of a notice. The kind of notice required, and whether it has to be served by a particular date, or between two specified dates, depend on the terms of the clause. If those terms result in a situation whereby failure to give notice by a particular date will mean that the right to increase the rent is lost, or significantly delayed, there is a fertile—and much ploughed—field for dispute as to whether the terms of the clause have been complied with.

3.3—Time limits

3.3.1—*Where a clause provides a latest date*

Where the rent review clause provides for a notice to be served, it will usually set out the earliest date and the latest date for service, *e.g.* by stating that it may be served "not earlier than 12 months nor later than 6 months before the relevant review date". Most problems in practice have concerned the "latest date" time limits. The question which has arisen is whether "time is of the essence" of the relevant time limit, that is to say: if no notice has been served by the relevant time limit, has the right to review been lost altogether?

3.3.2—"Time of the essence": the general rule.

In *United Scientific Holdings Limited v. Burnley Borough Council*[1] the House of Lords decided that, as a general rule, failure to serve a rent review notice by the date required by the lease did not result in the right to review being lost; in legal parlance, "time was not of the essence" of rent review provisions. The reasoning was that the provision for periodic rent reviews was such an important part of the original bargain between landlord and tenant that the parties cannot be supposed to have intended that the right should be lost altogether merely because of one party's failure to take a particular step in time. This general rule is, however, subject to exceptions, some of them expressly mentioned in the speeches in the *United Scientific* case, and others developed in later decisions.

From this general rule there are exceptions which can be grouped into four, or possibly five, categories:

3.3.3—Exceptions from the general rule

The first exception: where the parties have expressly stated that time should be of the essence. If the lease clearly and unambiguously states that time is to be of the essence in relation to the rent review provisions generally, or in relation to some particular step or steps to be taken under them, the courts will give effect to it.

The second exception: where the wording of the clause shows that the time limits were intended to be strict. Even when a rent review clause does not expressly state that time is to be of the essence, the words used may clearly indicate that the parties intend it to be so.[2]

---

[1] [1978] A.C. 904, H.L.
[2] Contrast *Drebbond v. Horsham District Council* (1978) 245 E.G. 1013 and *Norwich Union Life Assurance Society v. Sketchley* [1986] 2 E.G.L.R. 126 with *Touche Ross & Co. v. Secretary of State for the Environment* (1983) 265 E.G. 982.

The third exception: where the parties expressly provide for what is to happen if the time limit is not complied with. Where the parties state the consequences of non-compliance with a time-limit and thereby show their intention that a time limit should be strictly complied with.[3]

The fourth exception: where other provisions in the lease show that the parties intended a time limit to be strictly observed. For example, where another clause gives the tenant the right to serve a notice breaking the lease by a specified date which is the same as, or later than, the last date on which the landlord can serve a trigger notice implementing the review.[4]

A possible fifth exception: where unreasonable delay has caused or will cause prejudice to the other party. A possible further exception to the *United Scientific* principle may be where the "unreasonable delay" causes prejudice or hardship to the tenant in circumstances such that the landlord ought to be prevented from exercising the right to implement the review. However, whenever an argument of this kind has been put before a court it has failed.

3.3.4—*Making time of the essence, where the lease does not do so*

Even though the lease does not expressly or impliedly make time of the essence for complying with a time-limit in the review process, it is in some circumstances possible for a party to make it so. For example suppose a lease gives the landlord alone the right to serve a notice initiating the rent review and the landlord fails to do so by the specified date. The tenant is entitled to serve a notice "making time of the essence". If the landlord fails, within a reasonable time after receiving this notice, to serve his notice, his right to review will be lost.[5] But this will not be so if the party seeking to progress the review can himself initiate it. In *Factory Holdings Group v. Leboff International Limited*[6] the landlord had failed to apply for the appointment of an arbitrator, even though the tenant had served notice seeking to "make time of the essence". It was held that this notice was ineffective since the rent review clause gave the tenant the right himself to apply for an appointment. If he really wanted the rent review to proceed, he should have done so.

---

[3] See *Lewis v. Barnett* (1982) 264 E.G. 1079 and *Henry Smith's Charity Trustees v. AWADA Trading & Promotion Services Limited* (1984) 269 E.G. 729; and contrast *Mecca Leisure Limited v. Renown Investments (Holdings) Limited* (1984) 271 E.G. 989.
[4] For example *Metrolands Investments Ltd v. J.H. Dewhurst Ltd* [1985] 1 E.G.L.R. 105.
[5] *Phipps-Faire v. Malbern Construction Limited* [1987] 1 E.G.L.R. 129.
[6] [1987] 1 E.G.L.R. 135.

3.4—Contents of the notice

Most leases require that notices be in writing, and the rent review clause may contain other requirements as to what the notice should state. Whether these requirements as to the form or content of a notice are:

(a)   mandatory, *i.e.* if they are not strictly complied with the notice is invalid, or

(b)   directory, *i.e.* given for guidance only, so that failure to comply with them does not make the notice invalid

is obviously of crucial importance, since it is upon this question that the right to the particular review turns.

Thus in *Taylor Woodrow Property Company Limited v. Lonrho Textiles Limited*[7] the rent review clause provided for service of a notice by the landlord and stipulated that the notice should state the figure which the landlord proposed and certain other information, including the facts that the tenant had the right to serve a counter-notice and that if he did not do so he would be deemed to have agreed to the landlord's figure. In the course of his judgment considering whether time was of the essence for service of the tenant's counter-notice, the judge expressed the view that none of these requirements were mandatory, that is to say that a notice which did not contain this information could nevertheless have been valid.

This is to be distinguished from *Commission for the New Towns v. R. Levy & Co. Ltd*[8] where the lease provided that "a rent review notice given by the landlord under the terms hereof shall specify the yearly rent which the landlord proposes from the relevant date of review". The lease laid down a time for service of the notice, in respect of which time was expressly made of the essence. The landlord served a notice in time, but it did not specify the proposed rent. It was held that the requirement that the notice "shall specify" the landlord's proposed figure was mandatory and not merely directory and the absence of a figure from the notice rendered it invalid.

The fundamental distinction between these two cases is that, in the latter case, the rent review machinery was unable to function at all unless the landlord had initiated the rent review procedure by specifying a figure, whereas in the former case, the rent review notice could serve its intended

---

[7] [1985] 2 E.G.L.R. 120.
[8] (1990) 28 E.G. 119.

function without containing all the matters which it should, strictly speaking, have contained.

3.5—Tenants' counter-notices

3.5.1—*Where lease provides for notice and counter-notice*

Many rent review clauses require the landlord to specify the amount that the landlord proposes should be the rent from the review date, and then give the tenant a limited time in which to serve a counter-notice electing instead for the matter to be determined by a third party acting as an arbitrator or independent expert. In such clauses, time is often expressly made of the essence in relation to service of the tenant's counter-notice. But it is often difficult to tell whether a letter written by the tenant after the service of the landlord's notice is a counter-notice requiring third-party determination or is a mere negotiating letter. There are many reported cases in which this problem has arisen. Each case turns upon its own particular facts, especially the wording of the alleged counter-notice. The test to be applied is[9]: are the terms of the counter-notice sufficiently clear to bring home to an ordinary landlord that the tenant is exercising his rights under the relevant provisions?

3.5.2—*Power of the court to extend time*

If the effect of service of a counter-notice is to initiate the process leading up to the appointment of an arbitrator (but not an expert) the court has power, under section 27 of the Arbitration Act 1950, to extend the time for service of the counter-notice.[10] The power to extend time is in the discretion of the court and will only be exercised where not to do so would cause "undue hardship" to the tenant. It is particularly important to apply promptly in any case where it is claimed that the tenant has either served an invalid counter-notice or is out of time for serving one. Any avoidable delay in applying will make it less likely that the court will exercise its discretion in the tenant's favour. The criteria to be applied in deciding whether to extend time in any particular case are laid down by the House of Lords in *Comdel Commodities Limited v. Siporex Trade S.A.*[11]

There is no power to extend the time for initiating the process of appointing an independent expert.

[9] *Nunes v. Davies Laing Dick Limited* [1986] 1 E.G.L.R. 106. The cases are extensively discussed in the Handbook and digested in the Digest of Cases.
[10] *Pittalis v. Sherefettin* [1986] Q.B. 868 (C.A.).
[11] [1990] 3 W.L.R. 1.

3.6—The negotiating stage

3.6.1—*The prevalence of compromise*

Most rent reviews are, sooner or later, settled by agreement, and most rent review clauses recognise this by building into their machinery the possibility of agreement being reached at various stages in the rent review process. Even if the possibility of agreement is not expressly referred to in the rent review clause it is, of course, open to the parties to compromise their differences at any stage; the advantage of doing so sooner rather than later is the considerable saving in costs which can be achieved. Once the parties have reached a binding agreement, neither party can change its mind and opt instead to go to arbitration (or to determination by an expert). Similarly, neither party will be able afterwards to rely on the fact that a procedural requirement of the rent review clause has not been complied with, since both parties will be taken to have waived it — see *Esso Petroleum Company Limited v. Anthony Gibbs Financial Services Limited*.[12] It is therefore important to decide at what point a binding agreement has been reached.

3.6.2—*The distinction between "without prejudice" and "subject to contract"*

The parties to a pending rent review will often express their offers to be "without prejudice" or "subject to contract" or both. These labels are convenient. But they have very different meanings and effects, and it is important to distinguish between them.

3.6.3—*The meaning of "without prejudice"*

Where terms of settlement of a dispute are being offered or discussed, the use by either party of the expression "without prejudice" means that nothing said or written by either party in the course of those discussions may be referred to before any court or arbitrator or (probably) independent expert who later is asked to resolve the dispute. The purpose of this is to encourage parties to compromise their dispute by enabling them to make offers, and negotiating statements, knowing that no reference can be made to them later if the dispute is not compromised and has to be decided by a third party.

Even where the words "without prejudice" are not used, any offer to

---

[12] (1982) 262 E.G. 661.

compromise a rent review will be presumed to be made "without prejudice" unless there are circumstances negating such a presumption.[13]

3.6.4—*Exceptions to the "without prejudice" rule*

In the rent review context, there are three important exceptions to the privilege from disclosure which otherwise attaches to "without prejudice" documents and offers. First, it should be noted that the privilege can be waived by the agreement of both parties (or, if more than two parties are involved, of all of them). Many practitioners think that anyone who makes a "without prejudice" offer may unilaterally waive the privilege against disclosure of it. This is not so; the privilege is that of both (or all) parties and may only be waived if both (or all) consent.

Second, where the "without prejudice" discussions have resulted in a concluded agreement to compromise the dispute, the privilege conferred by the "without prejudice" label is removed, at least for the purpose of proving and enforcing the compromise agreement.

Third, the practice has grown up in rent review arbitrations, and in those determinations by an independent expert where the expert has been given power to award costs of making offers "without prejudice save as to costs". The effect of making an offer in this form is discussed in paragraph 14.3.1, below.

3.6.5—*Negotiations "subject to contract"*

"Subject to contract" has a very different meaning. The effect of these words is to indicate that no binding agreement is intended to come into existence until it has been reduced to writing either in a single document signed by or on behalf of both parties, or in two identical documents, one of which is signed by one party and the other signed by the other party, after which the documents are exchanged between the parties. In general, once the label "subject to contract" has been introduced by either party it will be assumed that all further negotiation and correspondence on the matter is entered into on that basis. Thus, even where there is apparently complete agreement on every matter being negotiated there will be no contract by correspondence in the absence of some signed document (or documents exchanged as above) embodying the parties' agreement. In the context of a disputed rent review the "contract" which the parties have in mind is probably a document recording the agreement and signed by both parties (or their representatives) or exchanged as above.

[13] *Chocoladefabriken Lindt & Sprungli A.G. v. The Nestle Co. Ltd* [1978] R.P.C. 287.

3.6.6—*What amounts to agreement?*

If the words "subject to contract" are not used and if there is no special requirement in the rent review clause (*e.g.* a requirement that any agreement should be in writing) a binding agreement is made as soon as all the terms (and not merely the figure) put forward by one party have been accepted by the other. Where negotiations are carried out between agents rather than between the parties themselves (as is often the case in rent reviews) the question can arise whether those agents have sufficient actual or apparent authority to bind their principals. Another practical problem, which is discussed in more detail in paragraph 17.3, is the effect of agreement upon the original tenant under the lease, or upon a guarantor either of that tenant or of a subsequent assignee of the lease.

3.6.7—*The effect of mistake*

In some circumstances, an agreement reached when either or both of the parties were labouring under a mistake will not be binding. It is a general principle of the law of contract that where a person purports to accept an offer which he knows, or ought to know, is made by mistake, there is no genuine agreement between the parties and no contract comes into existence.[14]

An example in a rent review context is *Centrovincial Estates PLC v. Merchant Investors Assurance Co. Ltd.*[15] There the landlords' solicitors, by mistake, invited the tenants to agree a rent at the figure of £65,000, a figure lower than the landlords had intended to quote and lower than the rent passing under the lease at the time. And this at a time when rents were rising steeply! On the facts, the court held that the tenants either knew or ought to have known that the lower figure was quoted by the landlord as the result of a mistake by them, and that accordingly the landlords were not bound by their figure and the apparent agreement.

3.7—The type of determiner

If the parties cannot agree what the new rent should be, the next stage of the rent review procedure is determination by an independent third party. This will almost always be a chartered surveyor appointed by agreement between the parties, or, where they have failed to agree, by the President of the R.I.C.S. The chartered surveyor may be appointed to act as an arbitrator, or as an independent expert.

[14] For the relevant principles see standard textbooks on the law of contract, *e.g.* Chitty on Contracts (27th ed., 1994).
[15] [1983] Com. L.R. 158.

3.7.1—*Differences between arbitrator and independent expert*

An arbitrator acts in a quasi judicial capacity, that is to say he resolves the dispute which has been referred to him in much the same way as he would if he were a judge sitting in court, but with two important differences. First, he may have personal knowledge of facts relevant to the issues that the parties have referred to him. He is fully entitled to use any such knowledge, provided he discloses it to the parties so as to give them an opportunity of commenting on it and, if they so wish, calling evidence to rebut it. Second, his expertise makes him better able to weigh the expert evidence put before him. Extensive powers and duties are given to him by the Arbitration Acts 1950 and 1979 and he is also bound in procedural matters by the rules of natural justice. Generally speaking, he is also bound by the ordinary rules as to the admissibility of evidence.[16] More detailed consideration of arbitration procedures are contained in Chapters Nine to Eleven below.

An expert, by contrast, acts in a way which is much more like the performance by a valuer of his ordinary duties. The only substantial difference in a disputed rent review is that he is not appointed to act by and for one party, but is rather appointed to act as a valuer by or on behalf of two parties, his valuation being binding upon both of them. Since he is not acting in a judicial capacity, he is not generally bound by the same rules of procedure and natural justice as those that bind an arbitrator, nor does he have the benefit of the considerable powers conferred upon arbitrators by the Arbitration Acts. Essentially, he is using his own knowledge and experience as a valuer to determine the rental value in accordance with the terms of the lease. But he must hold the scales evenly between the clients instructing him. Moreover, like a valuer acting for a single client, he may be sued by either of the parties for negligence if his figure can be shown to be outside the "bracket" of valuation figures that could be reached by an ordinarily competent valuer. By contrast, a valuer acting as arbitrator in a similar dispute would be immune from claims for damages by a party aggrieved by an allegedly negligent valuation.

3.7.2—*Lease should specify the capacity of valuer*

The rent review provisions of the lease should always specify in clear terms whether the third party is to act as an arbitrator or as an expert. Unfortunately, some clauses are silent or unclear on this. Sometimes confusion is created by apparently contradictory statements in the rent review clause

---

[16] This text was finalised in May 1995, at which time proposals were under discussion for a new Arbitration Act under which, *inter alia*, an arbitrator (a) would not be bound by the formal rules of evidence, and (b) would be expressly empowered to apply his own knowledge and experience, subject to safeguards to avoid breaches of the principles of natural justice.

itself; it is not unknown for the same clause to state in one part that the third party is to "act as an expert and not an arbitrator" but further on to state that "the said reference is to be conducted in accordance with the Arbitration Acts".

3.8—A comparison between the two types of determination

Each of the two types of determination has advantages and disadvantages. These may be summarised as follows.

3.8.1—*Cost*

The amount of the new rent is a matter of valuation. In theory it should cost less to have it decided by a valuer acting as such, than by a valuer acting as an arbitrator and therefore acting on evidence put before him. This would be true if the parties were content to appoint the expert and to leave the valuation to him, without even instructing their own valuers. In practice, at least in the larger cases, the parties wish to be advised by their own valuers and wish those valuers to make representations to the independent expert. Sometimes those representations are just as extensive as they would be if the third party were acting as an arbitrator conducting the arbitration on documents only. In such cases, the overall cost of conducting the rent review may equal that which would have been incurred in an arbitration; indeed, it may be higher, since it is usual for an independent expert to charge a higher fee than he would if acting as arbitrator to reflect the greater overall responsibility of his task.

3.8.2—*Speed*

Here, too, if the parties do not instruct their own valuers, the process of determination by an expert should take much less time than an arbitration, which involves the preparation and submission of evidence in every case, and in some cases an oral hearing. But if (as often happens) the parties' valuers prepare and submit evidence to the expert, possibly with counter-submissions as well, the saving of time as compared with arbitration is small, or, if the comparison is with an arbitration conducted on documents only without an oral hearing, non-existent.

3.8.3—*Clear rules of procedure*

The Arbitration Acts, and the court's power of control over arbitration proceedings, result in a reasonably clearly defined procedure. There are no statutory or other rules of procedure for determination by an expert, except perhaps the rules of "natural justice" which by their nature are ill-defined. Most valuers acting as independent experts also follow the procedure set out in Guidance Notes published by the R.I.C.S.,[17] though these are not of course binding. In most cases this causes no difficulty, but there can be problems where, *e.g.* the expert's determination involves a point of law.

3.8.4—*Thoroughness*

In an arbitration there is power to:

— compel a party to disclose all relevant documents in his possession;
— compel the attendance of witnesses;
— test—by cross-examination at an oral hearing—the evidence given by the opposing party;

and there is the right to make submissions with the object of ensuring that the arbitrator understands the party's case. All these factors will, or should, result in an arbitrator's award being based upon a more thorough examination of all the facts and issues than is possible in the case of a determination by an expert, whose procedure allows for none of this.

3.8.5—*Suitability for point of law*

As will be explained in Chapter Five below, there are a number of ways in which a disputed point of law can be dealt with where it arises in the course of a dispute which has been referred to arbitration. The court has power, in the case of arbitration, to correct errors of law and procedure, even though its powers to do so are limited.[18] The procedures for handling a similar point determined by an expert are more cumbersome, and the possibility of putting right any error of law are, in practice, much more limited.[19]

3.8.6—*Control of fees*

An arbitrator's fees can be "taxed" (*i.e.* assessed by the court) under the Arbitration Act 1950 unless they have been previously fixed by an agreement in writing. The court has no direct role in controlling fees charged by an

---

[17] They are reprinted at Appendix III, page 158 below.
[18] See Chapter 15, page 113 below.
[19] See Chapter 16, page 117 below.

expert. In practice this point is of minor importance since the parties nearly always agree the level of fees with the expert at an early stage of the procedure.

3.8.7—*Power to require reasons*

An arbitrator will normally give a reasoned award if so requested, even if no point of law is involved. An expert is under no obligation to give reasons, and in practice will not do so, except where a point of law is clearly involved; even in such cases, he would be entitled to refuse, unless the lease specifies that he is to give reasons. But this is rare.

3.8.8—*Use of own knowledge and experience*

As will be explained in more detail in Chapter Nine below, there are limits upon the extent to which the arbitrator can rely upon his own knowledge and experience, since in doing so he would often be "giving evidence to himself". By contrast, the reason behind the appointment of an expert is that he should have the necessary knowledge and experience to equip him to carry out the valuation; he is not merely entitled, but bound, to do his own investigations and research and to use his own knowledge and experience in reaching his conclusion. There is a strong belief amongst landlords and tenants generally that the determination of an expert is more likely to reflect current market conditions. If this is correct (and in the authors' belief it is not) whether this will favour the landlord or the tenant in any particular case depends, of course, upon whether the market is moving up or down.

3.9—Appointing an arbitrator or independent expert as determiner

The rent review clause itself will almost invariably contain some machinery by which an independent third-party determiner is appointed as arbitrator or expert. If no such machinery exists this will not prevent the review being implemented—the court can assume jurisdiction to determine the amount of the rent.[20] Often the machinery will provide for the parties to attempt to agree the identity of a suitable determiner. If they can do so this takes effect as what is known as a "private appointment" as opposed to an appointment by the president of the R.I.C.S. or some other independent body. A private appointment has the advantage that the parties are themselves able to choose as arbitrator or expert someone in whom they have

---

[20] *Brown v. Gould* [1972] Ch. 53.

confidence. In the absence of agreement the clause will usually allow the landlord (or either party, as the case may be) to apply to the President to make an appointment. The appointment procedure is discussed in detail in Chapter Six below.

3.10—The valuation assumptions

An important part of any rent review clause is the rent review formula, that is to say the basis on which the valuation is to be carried out and the assumptions to be made. These are dealt with in detail in Chapter Eight below.

3.11—The procedure for determining the new rent

Sometimes the rent review clause itself will give no further guide to the procedure to be adopted than to indicate whether determination is to be by an arbitrator or an expert. In other cases (especially where the reference is to an expert) the clause will give more detailed guidance as to the manner in which the valuation is to be carried out. For example, it may expressly stipulate that the expert is to receive submissions from the parties and is to consider (but not to be bound by) those submissions. Sometimes the clause will provide a time-limit by which the valuation is to be completed. The court has jurisdiction to extend such a time-limit in the case of an arbitration under section 13 of the Arbitration Act 1950; no such jurisdiction exists in the case of an expert and the wisdom of including such a time-limit is doubtful.

3.12—Ancillary matters

The rent review provisions will often provide for other matters which might arise in the course of a reference, such as:

— the death or inability to act of the arbitrator or expert;
— what is to happen if a statutory "rent freeze" is to be imposed as happened in 1973;
— the payment of "back rent";
— the payment of interest on back rent;
— the evidencing of the review by a formal memorandum (see Chapter Seventeen below.).

Chapter Four: Interpreting Rent Review Provisions

4.1—The layman's and the lawyer's approach

There are few subjects on which the attitude of the lawyer to a problem differs more from that of the business man or other non-lawyer than that of interpreting a written document. The non-lawyer cannot understand why there should be any need to exclude from consideration letters or discussions that preceded the signing of the document. Moreover, the non-lawyer who has signed a contract says: "I know perfectly well what I intended by these words; why can't I tell the judge what I meant them to mean and what I understood them to mean?"

4.2—The lawyer's approach

The lawyer's answer is to be found in the classic statement of the principle on which all questions of interpretation of a written document should be approached. The question to be answered is always: "What is the meaning of what the parties have said?" not "What did the parties mean to say?" it being a presumption (of law), to rebut which no evidence is allowed, that the parties intended to say that which they have said.[1]

It follows from this statement of principle that evidence of discussions and negotiations leading up to the execution of the document cannot be given, save for the purpose of showing the factual background known to the parties at or before the date of the contract, including evidence of the "genesis" and—objectively—the "aim" of the transaction.

4.3—Why exclude evidence of negotiations?

The reason for excluding evidence of these pre-document discussions or exchanges is not a technical one, or even mainly one of convenience.

> "It is simply that such evidence is unhelpful. By the nature of things, where negotiations are difficult, the parties' positions, with each

[1] This passage from *Norton on Deeds* was cited with approval by Lord Simon of Glaisdale in *Wickman Tools Ltd v. Schuler A.G.* [1974] A.C. 235 at p.263.

passing letter, are changing and until the final agreement, though converging, are still divergent. It is only the final document that records a consensus. If the previous documents use different expressions, how does interpretation of those expressions, itself a doubtful process, help on the interpretation of the contractual words? If the same expressions are used, nothing is gained by looking back; indeed something may be lost since the relevant surrounding circumstances may be different. And at this stage there is no consensus of the parties to appeal to."[2]

4.4—Why not let the parties explain what they intended?

There are several reasons for refusing to allow the person who negotiated an agreement to explain what he intended his words to mean, or what he understood them to mean:

(a) No one could safely sign a contract or other document if the meaning that it bears on its face could be changed by evidence of what some other party to the document intended it to mean. If you have signed a contract to buy 1,000 cases of Black Label whisky, you would be very cross if the seller was allowed to say: "I understood the word 'Black' to mean 'White', and I am willing to supply only 'White Label'."

(b) In many cases the parties adopt a form of words as a compromise, each of them knowing that the other party understands the words to have a different meaning, but neither being willing to accept the other's meaning.

(c) The rights under many contracts (and particularly rights under leases) are capable of being assigned, and assignments are commonplace. It is important that assignees, and prospective assignees, whether of the term or of the reversion[3], be entitled to know the meaning by reading the document itself, free from the possibility that extraneous evidence, *e.g.* by a party who signed the original, may give it a different meaning.

4.5—What is the commercial purpose?

The general purpose of a provision for rent review is to enable the landlord to obtain, from time-to-time, the market rental which the premises would command if let on the same terms in the open market at the review dates.

---

[2] Per Lord Wilberforce in *Prenn v. Simmonds* [1971] 1 W.L.R. 1381.
[3] For an explanation of these expressions see Glossary, page 123 *below*.

Thereby the rent will be adjusted from time to time to reflect changes in the value of money and real increases in the value of the property during a long term. Such being the purpose, in the absence of special circumstances it would be wrong to impute to the parties an intention that the landlord should receive a rent which was additionally inflated by a factor which has no reference either to changes in the value of money or to the value of the premises as between the actual landlord and the actual tenant. Of course, the lease may be expressed in words so clear that there is no room for giving effect to such an underlying purpose. Again, there may be special surrounding circumstances which indicate that the parties did intend to reach such an unusual bargain. But in the absence of such clear words or surrounding circumstances the lease should be interpreted so as to give effect to the basic purpose of a rent review clause.[4]

This is an application to the particular nature of rent review of the words of Lord Diplock in *The Antaios*[5]:

> "If a detailed semantic and syntactical analysis of words in a commercial contract is going to lead to a conclusion that flouts business common sense, it must be made to yield to business common sense."

4.6—What if plain words conflict with business common sense?

The courts cannot remake a contract for the parties.[6] If the market price of White Label whisky is £25 a case, and the market price of Black Label whisky is £60 a case, and I enter into a contract to buy 1,000 cases of White Label whisky at £60 a case, I cannot escape from my obligations by asking the court to read "White" as meaning "Black"; the words are too plain. I may be able to escape from the bargain in some other way, *e.g.* by showing that I intended to buy Black Label, and the seller knew this when he and I signed the contract. But that is to set aside the contract, or (perhaps) to rectify it. So long as the contract stands, its terms allow only one meaning.

---

[4] Sir Nicholas Browne-Wilkinson V.-C. in *British Gas Corporation v. Universities Superannuation Scheme Ltd* [1986] 1 E.G.L.R. 120 and see also *Basingstoke & Deane B.C. v. The Host Group* [1988] 1 W.L.R. 348.

[5] [1985] A.C.191.

[6] This has been pointed out most recently by Hoffmann L.J. in *Co-Operative Wholesale Society Ltd. v. National Westminster Bank plc* [1995] 01 E.G. 111 where the commercial purpose of rent review compelled decisions in favour of the tenants in three of the cases being considered, but where the words were too plain to allow such a result in the fourth case under appeal, which was decided in favour of the landlord.

Chapter Five: Methods of Resolving a Dispute as to the Meaning of the Lease

Lord Diplock pointed out in *The Nema*[1] that Continental legal systems regard a dispute as to the meaning of a contract or other document as one of fact. Because of the influence of the jury system on the development of English law, the common law regards such a dispute as one to be decided not by the jury but by the judge, and therefore one of law. The capacity of those drafting leases to create new problems of interpretation greatly exceeds the capacity of the courts to find time to solve them. So in a relatively high proportion of rent reviews, a dispute about the meaning of the lease surfaces at an early stage in the review process.

5.1—Formulating the issue

In many cases, what appears to be a dispute between the parties as to the meaning of the lease disappears when their respective views are clearly formulated. So the first step should always be for each party to state clearly and in writing what he asserts to be: (a) the meaning, and (b) the effect, of the particular words used in the lease. A discussion of the two formulations often ends the dispute.

5.2—Possible ways of deciding the issue

If after this exercise there remains a dispute as to the meaning of the lease, the following possible procedures are available to the parties for resolving it:

(a)   submitting a joint case for the opinion of a barrister or solicitor, to be agreed between them or, failing agreement, to be nominated by the President of an appointing body such as the R.I.C.S., the Incorporated Society of Valuers and Auctioneers (I.S.V.A), the Law Society or the Chartered Institute of Arbitrators; the parties agreeing to be bound by his opinion;

[1] [1982] A.C.724.

(b) proceeding to arbitration by a valuer, and raising the point to be determined by the arbitrator as a preliminary issue (with or without a right of appeal to the court);

(c) as (b), but the arbitrator to determine the point with the assistance of a legal assessor who, failing agreement, shall be appointed by the arbitrator;

(d) proceeding to arbitration and leaving the point for argument at an appropriate stage of the hearing, to be determined by the arbitrator as part of his award, and with no right of appeal;

(e) as (d), but the arbitrator to determine the point with the assistance of a legal assessor as in (c);

(f) leaving the point for argument at an appropriate stage of the hearing, on the footing that the arbitrator will determine it as part of his award but will also make an alternative award in case, on appeal, the court reverses the arbitrator's decision on the point of law. This course cannot be adopted if the parties have excluded or propose to exclude the right of appeal to the court, see paragraph 15.3.1;

(g) as (f), but the arbitrator to determine the point with a legal assessor as in (c) above;

(h) remitting the point to be decided by the court as a preliminary point of law under section 2 of the Arbitration Act 1979. This can always be done if both parties consent, or even where one party objects but an arbitration has been commenced and the arbitrator consents. In the latter case the party applying for the determination has to satisfy the court that it is a proper case to be brought.

5.3—Originating summons in the High Court

Another possible course—not open without consent if an arbitration has been commenced and has reached an advanced stage or if the point is within the exclusive jurisdiction of a valuer who is to act as an expert—is to apply to the High Court by originating summons for the determination of a point of law.

5.4—Appointing a legally qualified chairman or umpire

In commodity or shipping disputes it is quite common for the arbitration tribunal to comprise two arbitrators with a chairman to be appointed by them, or two arbitrators and an umpire. This is so only in rare cases in rent review disputes, but in such a case the choice of a chairman or umpire who is legally qualified and experienced in the field of rent review will usually make it unnecessary to adopt any of the above courses.

Chapter Six: The President of the R.I.C.S. and his Appointment Procedure

6.1—The application for appointment

Most rent review clauses, having stated whether the third-party determiner is to act as arbitrator or as expert, simply provide that in the absence of agreement application may be made to the President of the R.I.C.S. to make an appointment.

Paragraph 2.1.1 of the R.I.C.S. Guidance Notes states:

> "Application to the President for the appointment of an arbitrator or Independent Expert should be in writing and preferably made on the form obtainable on application to the R.I.C.S."

Paragraph 2.1.2 goes on to state:

> "The application will not be processed until the appropriate non-refundable fee, currently £ ....[1] has been received together with a copy of the lease or other document conferring on the President power to make the appointment."

In *Staines Warehousing Co. Ltd. v. Montagu Executor and Trustee Company Limited*[2] the Court of Appeal had to consider the question whether a valid application for an appointment had been made within a strict time-limit contained in the rent review clause. The valuer acting for the landlord had simply written to the President informing him of the details of the lease, that in default of agreement an independent expert was to be appointed by the President, and that negotiations were continuing. The latter stated that he was making "an in time only application" for an appointment. The tenant was not informed that this application had been made, and no fee was sent at this stage to the President. Nonetheless the court, referring to the passages from the Guidance Notes just quoted, held that wherever a lease provided for an application to be to a specified appointing body such as the R.I.C.S.,

---

[1] At the time of writing (September 1995) the fee is £160 including VAT.
[2] [1987] 2 E.G.L.R. 130.

43

it was to be interpreted as requiring that any such application should be made in accordance with the current procedures of the appointing body. Since the landlord's valuer's letter conformed to the R.I.C.S. requirements for a valid appointment (albeit one that would not be processed until the fee was received) it was valid and effective.

Sometimes, when one party has applied to the President for an appointment, the other party will object that for some reason the power to appoint has not yet arisen or that for some other reason an appointment cannot be validly made. This was done in *United Co-operatives Limited v. Sun Alliance and London Assurance Company Limited*.[3] There, the President rejected the objection, on the grounds that it was not his policy to determine any legal questions which might arise as to the validity of any application made to him. The aggrieved party went to court to seek an injunction preventing an appointment. The injunction was refused on the ground that the President owed no duty to either party to make or not to make an appointment and the aggrieved party had no cause of action against him; in any event, it was more sensible to allow the question of whether or not jurisdiction existed to be decided by the independent expert, once he had been appointed.

6.2—The President's procedures

The President receives many thousands of applications for appointments every year, and the R.I.C.S. has a fully staffed unit to administer these applications. The President clearly sees his role as the main appointor of independent third parties in rent review disputes as one of great importance to landlords and tenants generally as well as to his members, and he accordingly makes considerable efforts to select a person who is suitable for appointment.

6.3—Qualifications and disqualifications

Sometimes the rent review clause itself will set out expressly qualifications which must be fulfilled by the person to be appointed as arbitrator or independent expert. Normally it will be stipulated that he should be a chartered surveyor and sometimes his standing in the profession, number of years' experience, his particular subject area, and the geographical location of his practice will also be defined. Clearly these express qualifications must be

---

[3] [1987] 1 E.G.L.R. 126.

complied with, unless both parties agree to waive or modify them. But in all cases, the President will be concerned to ensure, so far as practicable, that the intended appointee is equipped by intellect, judgment and experience to fulfil his task properly. In relation to arbitrations, the President is increasingly tending to select surveyors who have attended the intensive training courses in arbitration practice organised from time-to-time by the R.I.C.S. (and have thereafter complied with the professional development recommendations of the R.I.C.S.)

6.3.1—*Procedure in normal cases*

The arbitrations officer will write to the prospective appointee asking him to confirm (*inter alia*):

(a) that the matter falls within the scope of his own normal professional practice;

(b) that he would be able to undertake the task with reasonable expedition; and

(c) that there is no other reason why he should not accept the appointment.

It is important that the prospective appointee should satisfy himself, and if necessary the President, that there exists no conflict of interest which would prevent him being truly independent in deciding the dispute. In broad terms the appointee should disqualify himself if he has any pecuniary interest in the outcome of the dispute, or if, for any other reason, a reasonably minded person knowing the facts might think that there was a real possibility that he might be biased in favour of one party or the other. The most frequently encountered sources of an apparent conflict of interest are previous connections that the prospective appointee, or a member of his firm, has had:

(a) with one of the parties to the dispute;

(b) with the property in question; or

(c) with other properties in the locality.

In borderline cases, the appointee will not disqualify himself but will disclose to the parties through the President the matter which might be of concern, to see whether they have any objection to his appointment.

Once these enquiries have been satisfactorily completed, the President will make the appointment, by signing a formal notice of appointment which is then sent to the appointee, with copies to the parties.

When the appointment has been made, the President will normally have discharged his legal functions and will cease to have any further role in the arbitration or independent expert determination.

6.4—Challenges and Waiver

6.4.1—*Time for challenge*

A party who wishes to object to the appointment of a particular person as arbitrator or independent expert should do so as soon as he becomes aware both of the appointment, and of the facts on the basis of which he wishes to object. If, with knowledge of the grounds of objection, he takes any step which is inconsistent with the right to object, *e.g.* lodges a statement of his case on the substantive dispute (as distinct from a statement of his objection) he will thereby waive his right to object. A party who becomes aware of facts which entitle him to apply for the removal of the person appointed should act promptly to raise his objection. If no appointment has yet been made, he should ask the President to appoint someone else. If someone has already been appointed, only the Court can remove him.

6.5—Responses to challenge

6.5.1—*Response of the appointing authority*

A party who wishes to delay the making of an effective award against him sometimes makes representations to the President of the R.I.C.S. as to who should or should not be appointed, in the hope of causing the application for appointment to be stood over for further investigations.[4] The President is well aware of this tactic, and significant delay is rarely caused.

6.5.2—*Response by the arbitrator or independent expert*

In many cases the easiest course for the person being challenged is to accept the challenge and withdraw, even though he considers the grounds of objection to be wholly unjustified. This may do a great disservice to the non-challenging party. The person appointed should resist taking this easy option unless: (a) he considers the grounds of objection to be at least strongly arguable, or (b) the non-challenging party also wishes him to withdraw.

---

[4] This problem arose so frequently that the President of the R.I.C.S. issued a Policy Statement in 1987. It is reproduced in the Handbook, Commentary on the Guidance Notes para. G.2.1.7.

6.5.3—*Responses by the non-challenging party*

An arbitrator or independent expert will consider himself duty-bound to resign if both parties agree that he should; though he may, of course, require payment of any fees due to him to date as a condition of clearing the way for a new appointment. So a party faced with an objection to a proposed appointment, or a demand from the opposing party that a person already appointed be removed, should first consider whether it will be better to agree to the request rather than to oppose it. This will, in turn, raise the question of how quickly a replacement can be appointed. If agreement can quickly be reached on an alternative appointee it may be much better to concur and to ask the current appointee to withdraw.

6.5.4—*Resignation without challenge*

If, after appointment, an arbitrator or independent expert becomes aware of facts which are not known to the parties but which, had he known them before appointment, would have made him doubtful about accepting the appointment, he should notify the parties of the facts, and either resign or offer to resign.

For example, if he discovers that a company party is a subsidiary of his most regular client. Recent Presidents of the R.I.C.S. have attached much importance to the exercise of this self-discipline by arbitrators.

6.5.5—*Waiver and "without prejudice" objection*

A party who becomes aware of facts which ground an objection to the arbitrator's appointment and who does not raise the objection may be barred from objecting at a later stage. It may be open to him to raise the objection, and state that his continuing to take part in the arbitration is without prejudice to his right to raise the objection later, but there is at least an argument that a party acting in this way has waived the right to object.

6.6—Retirement and removal of arbitrator

6.6.1—*No general right of an arbitrator to retire*

An arbitrator is (save for statutory arbitration) appointed in pursuance of a contract, namely the arbitration agreement. Whether the appointment itself creates a second contract, namely a contract between him and the parties to the arbitration agreement, is a matter of some doubt.[5] The powers

---

[5] See Mustill & Boyd, *Commercial Arbitration* (2nd ed., 1989), p.186 *et seq*.

of the court to remove an arbitrator are discussed below,[6] but the Arbitration Acts do not confer any express power on the arbitrator to retire, once he has accepted appointment. It is difficult to imagine a contract of appointment under which the arbitrator or independent expert has a right to retire at any time and for any reason—retirement can involve the parties in great delay and expense, and if at the outset the arbitrator had stipulated an unlimited right to retire, the parties might well have gone elsewhere. However, it is equally difficult to find a way of interpreting the acceptance of appointment as arbitrator or independent expert as amounting to an unconditional promise that he will complete his task and issue an award or determination.

6.6.2—*Limited duty to complete*

For practical purposes it is suggested that these questions can be avoided by assuming that there is a duty on the appointee to proceed with reasonable diligence to the conclusion of the review, and a corresponding duty not to retire after appointment, where one or both parties wish him to continue, save on reasonable grounds. What are reasonable grounds will always be impossible to define precisely.

6.6.3—*Removal of arbitrator by the court: for delay*

By section 13 (3) of the Arbitration Act 1950, the High Court may on the application of any party remove an arbitrator or umpire who fails to use all reasonable despatch in entering on and proceeding with the reference and making an award. What is reasonable despatch must, of course, vary according to the circumstances. But it is the circumstances relating to the parties, rather than the circumstances of the arbitrator, that are relevant. The fact that the delay is due to the illness of the arbitrator, or to his unexpectedly being involved in other work that prevents his giving attention to the arbitration, will be of little relevance if the delay is unreasonable from the point of view of the party seeking to remove him.

There is no corresponding power in respect of an independent expert, but difficulties rarely arise in this context in practice.

6.6.4—*Removal of arbitrator by the court: for misconduct*

By section 23 (1) and (2) of the Arbitration Act 1950, where an arbitrator has misconducted himself or the proceedings, or an arbitration or award has been improperly procured, the High Court may remove the arbitrator and/or may set the award aside.

[6] Paragraph 6.6.3 and 6.6.4 and see p. 113 below.

These powers have been held[7] to give the High Court power to remove an arbitrator for "misconduct" in three situations:

(a) where actual bias is proved;

(b) where the relationship between the arbitrator and the parties, or between the arbitrator and the subject matter of the dispute, is such as to create an evident risk that the arbitrator has been or will be incapable of acting impartially;

(c) where the conduct of the arbitrator has been such that, quite apart from partiality, it is shown that he is—through lack of experience, expertise or diligence—incapable of conducting the reference in a manner which the parties are entitled to expect.

There is no corresponding statutory power to remove an expert, but it is thought possible that similar principles might be applied under the inherent jurisdiction of the High Court, at any rate in cases within (a) or (b) above.

6.7—Action on appointment

6.7.1—*Checking jurisdiction and powers*

Immediately upon appointment, the arbitrator or independent expert should call for all relevant documents, in particular the document(s) out of which his appointment arises. If he has been appointed by a third party, he should ensure that the terms of the appointment conform with the terms of the arbitration agreement.

Next, he should look to see whether the lease, or any special terms of appointment, in any way widen or narrow the powers conferred on him by the general law, *e.g.*, it may narrow his powers by specifying that any dispute is to be decided on documents only without a hearing.

---

[7] See *Bremer Handelsgesellschaft v. Ets Soules* [1985] 2 Lloyd's Rep.199.

Chapter Seven: The Remuneration of the Arbitrator or Expert

7.1—The arbitrator's implied right to remuneration

7.1.1—*The relationship between the arbitrator and the parties*

A person who accepts appointment as an arbitrator, with or without provision as to payment, thereby enters into a three-way relationship with the parties. By it the arbitrator assumes the status of a judicial adjudicator, and consequently accepts certain duties and disabilities. One of them is a duty to act in a way that not only *is* fair but *is seen to be* fair. So he cannot enter into an agreement with one party to which the other party objects, for that might well be thought to make him—consciously or subconsciously—favour the one party to the disadvantage of the other.

7.1.2—*The implied right to remuneration*

If a party to a dispute requests someone to act as an arbitrator in resolving it, a promise to pay a reasonable sum for the services supplied will be implied unless there are surrounding circumstances negating such an implication. The implication is stronger if the request is made to someone who is known to act professionally as an arbitrator, and is weaker if there is a relationship between the parties from which one might expect services of the kind requested to be given gratuitously, *e.g.* if the parties to the dispute, and the person asked to arbitrate, are members of the same religious congregation. What is a reasonable fee can be decided by the court in proceedings brought by the arbitrator.

7.1.3—*Remuneration for cancelled hearings*

This implied right is a right to be remunerated for services provided. This probably confers on the arbitrator a right to reasonable compensation if he sets aside time for a hearing that is cancelled at short notice, and he thereby suffers loss; there will usually be room for argument as to what is reasonable. Likewise there is room for argument if he does work that, through no fault of his, is of no benefit to the parties, *e.g.* if, when he has finished writing his award and it is being typed, the parties settle their dispute. It is preferable that before he is appointed, or if this is not practicable then immediately after being appointed, the arbitrator agrees with both parties the amount of his fee, or the basis on which it is to be calculated. The agreement should cover eventualities such as those just mentioned.

7.2—Express contract for remuneration of the arbitrator or expert

In rent review arbitrations or determinations by an expert it is well recognised that the arbitrator or expert is to be paid for his services. But there is no established scale for such services and so it is highly desirable for him to make an express agreement in writing with the parties as to his remuneration. Ideally, this should be done before he accepts the appointment, and he should always do this where he is appointed by agreement of the parties. In such cases there is little difficulty in ascertaining the sums in issue and the magnitude of the task involved. In the interests of speed the R.I.C.S. appointment procedure does not provide for agreement as to fees before the President makes the appointment. In practice he usually accepts appointment and leaves the subject of fees to be dealt with at or shortly after the preliminary meeting. In theory this can create difficulties, but in practice it does not; the arbitrator or expert negotiates a fee basis immediately after appointment, and failure to agree is relatively rare.

7.3—Contents of the express contract for remuneration

A lump sum payment will be appropriate only in the most straightforward cases; and even so a case that seems straightforward when the basis of remuneration is being decided often turns into something for which the agreed lump sum is wholly inappropriate. Moreover, an amount that would be appropriate for a completed determination would be inappropriate for the common situation where the parties agree on the new rent shortly after appointment. Some alternatives are:

(a) a percentage of the mean of the rival figures;
(b) a single rate per hour or day spent;
(c) one rate per hour or day spent in a hearing and another (usually lower) for time spent out of the hearing (*e.g.* on reading, or writing the award);

(d)   some combination of the above.

The decision as to which basis to adopt will vary according to the weight and complication of the case, the likely duration of a hearing, the effect of a possible over-run of the hearing, the effect of the commitment upon other earning capabilities, and the likelihood of compromise.

7.4—What is a reasonable fee?

In deciding what is a reasonable fee for the services rendered the court would have regard to such matters as:

(a)   what other people of the qualifications and standing of the arbitrator usually charge for acting as arbitrator;

(b)   what the arbitrator concerned is generally known to charge;

(c)   what other members of the same primary profession as the arbitrator (*e.g.* chartered accountant, valuation surveyor, or barrister) commonly charge for services in that profession.

These criteria will likewise be applied to a claim for remuneration for partial services, where the dispute has been ended, *e.g.* by compromise.

7.5—Remuneration for cancelled hearings

Most arbitrators take the view that the amount it is reasonable to charge when a hearing is cancelled depends upon a number of factors, and particularly the number of days set aside for the hearing, and the length of notice of cancellation. A hearing estimated to last two months cancelled because the dispute is compromised on the first day of the hearing creates a wholly different situation from a hearing estimated to last one week compromised six months beforehand.

7.6—Time when remuneration is payable

The usual, and accepted, practice is that the agreed fee is payable upon delivery of the completed award or determination. This does not deal with the position where the services of the arbitrator are discontinued before award or determination. If this position is not provided for in an express contract with the parties, the remuneration will be due as soon as the services of the arbitrator or expert are expressly or impliedly dispensed with.

As will be seen in paragraph 13.1.5 below, an award is "published" when letters notifying the parties that it is has been signed have been given to the parties. The time for lodging an appeal to the High Court or an application to set aside for misconduct arising out of the award—which is only 21 days—begins to run when the award is published. There is, therefore, some incentive for one or both parties to pay the fees and take up the award. If this is not done within a few days after the award is published, a letter to the parties reminding them of the position usually leads to some action; it is also a safeguard against the original letter having gone astray.

7.7—Enforcing the right to payment

7.7.1—*Payment on delivery*

The most common method of publishing an award is to enclose a note of fees and disbursements with the letters notifying the parties that the award is ready for collection, and to say that the award may be collected on payment of the amount specified.[1] If the award places ultimate liability on the opposing party, the party who has paid the fees may recover them from the opposing party.

7.7.2—*Payment into court*

If there is no agreement in writing fixing the amount of the fee, a party who wishes to take up the award but to challenge the amount of the fee demanded may apply to the High Court under Section 19 of the Arbitration Act 1950, for an order that the arbitrator deliver the award on payment into court of the amount demanded, and that thereafter the amount of the fees payable be "taxed", *i.e.* be assessed by a taxing master of the High Court.

Apart from the possibility that the fees allowed may be much lower than the amount that the arbitrator has claimed, the procedure under section 19 has the following disadvantages:

(a) the arbitrator may be put to the trouble of justifying his charges in the minutest detail;

(b) payment to him may be delayed for months whilst an appointment for the taxation is awaited;

(c) if the amount awarded is substantially less than he has claimed he may be liable for the costs of the taxation;

(d) he—a person appointed to resolve disputes—has succeeded in involving the parties, or one of them, in a fresh dispute.

Hence the importance, to the arbitrator and to a lesser extent to the

---

[1] See the example at Appendix II, p. 148 below.

parties, of ensuring that the amount or basis of calculation of the fees payable is regulated by a prior written agreement.

There is no corresponding provision for challenging the fees demanded by an independent expert.

7.7.3—*Security for fees*

The plainest obligation to pay fees will not avail if the debtor cannot or will not pay. In many cases the arbitrator or independent expert is willing to rely upon the standing of the parties as a sufficient security that his fees will be paid. But where he has no indication of the standing of the parties it will often be wise for him to obtain some security other than a mere promise.

Various methods are available, for example:

(a) a deposit with the administering institution of the estimated fees, see, *e.g.* the International Chamber of Commerce's Arbitration Rules Article 9. The deposits are intended to be paid in equal shares by the claimant and the respondent but if either refuses to pay his share the other may pay it[2];

(b) a deposit with the arbitrator or expert;

(c) a personal undertaking from a director or other officer of a company party;

(d) an undertaking by a solicitor to be responsible for the fees might be appropriate. It should, however, be noted that a solicitor who makes an appointment does not become personally liable for fees due from the client unless he gives a personal undertaking to be responsible, and not merely an undertaking on behalf of his client.

7.8—Remuneration of a valuer appointed as independent expert

7.8.1—*When appointed by the parties*

A valuer asked by the parties to determine the new rent under a rent review clause is in the same position as one invited by only one of the parties. He can negotiate the terms on which he is to act, including not only the amount of his fees but also such matters as, *e.g.* whether it is to be inclusive or exclusive of disbursements, the date of payment(s), whether interest is to be payable if the fee is not paid on the due date, and whether he requires security to be given for payment.

---

[2] The RICS does not operate such a system.

7.8.2—*When appointed by the President*

For the reasons given in paragraph 7.2 above, the procedure for appointing an independent valuer does not provide for fees to be agreed before the President makes the appointment. It is as important for the independent surveyor as it is for an arbitrator that the fees, or the fee basis, be agreed immediately on being appointed. There is no express procedure for his fees to be assessed by the court, and failure to agree them speedily after appointment could lead to much dispute between and with the parties.

Chapter Eight: The Basis of Valuation

8.1—Introduction

With the exception of Chapter three above we have hitherto tried to avoid technicalities. But when dealing with the basis of valuation for rent review it is impossible to avoid them. Any process of valuation must begin by identifying what has to be valued. A lease or tenancy is a bundle of rights. What it would fetch if offered for sale in the market must depend on what rights are, and are not, included in the bundle. A lease for 999 years may be worth £1 or £1 million, depending on its terms. The terms are expressed in words, and the value of the lease may vary with nuances of meaning of those words. So some degree of "detailed semantic and syntactical analysis" is unavoidable, and this Chapter tackles such issues. The non-technical reader can, if desired, pass directly to Chapter Nine and return to this Chapter at leisure.

8.2—The need for a hypothetical basis

8.2.1—*The central valuation hypothesis*

Almost all rent reviews (at least those whose purpose is to assess a market rental value as opposed to a ground rent) take as their basis a hypothetical situation, namely a letting of the subject premises on the rent review date by a hypothetical willing landlord to a hypothetical willing tenant upon certain terms, incorporating certain assumptions and disregarding certain matters which would otherwise have an effect on value. Once the nature of this hypothetical exercise has been fully defined, it is then for the parties to try to agree what rent would, in fact, be achieved if this notional scenario were actually to happen. If they cannot agree, the question is then put to an independent third party who must answer it by applying his valuation skills to the material before him. Clearly, therefore, the valuation hypothesis is at the centre of any rent review. Over the past 30 years or so, in hundreds of reported decisions,[1] the courts have examined and interpreted the various components of the hypothesis.

[1] As at December 1994, the Digest of Cases in the Handbook of Rent Review contains over 300 reported cases, the majority of which concern the basis of valuation.

8.2.2—*The art of valuation*

In his judgment in *Banque Bruxelles Lambert .S.A. v. Eagle Star Insurance Co. Limited*[2] Phillips J. said:

> "In order to estimate the value of a commercial property on the basis of comparable rental values and yields a valuer needs a substantial volume of information much of which is not in the public domain. Some of this information will be available within the valuer's own company as a result of other transactions with which the company has been concerned. Some can be obtained from specialist publications or information services. Much of the information will be available only on a hearsay basis, either directly or indirectly, from those concerned with the transactions in question. It became apparent from the expert witnesses, who in this respect at least were in entire agreement, that there has grown up between valuers and surveyors a practice of reciprocal provision of information in relation to transactions in which they are or have been involved. It is plain that there is available to valuers in this way a mass of market information, the source of which may not always be clear nor the reliability certain. The art of valuation includes the maintenance of a good intelligence network and skill in evaluating the information received. The complexity of the task of producing a valuation by a process of comparison tends to conceal a simple fact. A valuation is no more than the opinion of the valuer of the price that the property is likely to realise if sold on the open market. Forming this opinion on the basis of comparables is not a precise science. Different competent valuers will produce different opinions. The experts agreed that when valuations are based on comparables, one competent valuation may differ from another by as much as 20%."

8.3—Words describing the rent to be assessed

Most review provisions require the assessment of a market rent. Often some words such as "open", "rack", "fair", "reasonable", "best", or "highest" are added. In a few cases the reference is to a "fair rent" or a "reasonable rent" without reference to market. From time-to-time a party has argued that the addition of one or more of these adjectives has an effect on value. Most of these attempts have failed in that judges have declined to find any difference between an "open market rent" and a "market rent", and have held that the words "market rent" are not by themselves apt to refer to a rent fixed within a closed or circumscribed market to which only certain bidders are

---

[2] [1994] 2 E.G.L.R. 108.

admitted.[3] Again, it has been held that where the rent is to be "a reasonable rent for the demised premises" it is to be assessed as an open market rent as opposed to a rent which would be fair and reasonable as between the particular landlord and the particular tenant. In summary therefore, it will be unusual for words descriptive of the rent to be assessed to have any valuation significance.

8.4—The physical premises

8.4.1—*At what date do you identify the physical premises?*

Sometimes the rent review clause will be specific as to what is to be valued—see, *e.g. Standard Life Assurance Company v. Oxoid Limited*[4] where a specification of notional "standard" premises was given as the subject of the valuation. More often, the rent review clause requires a valuation of "the premises" or "the demised premises". The valuer has to consider the premises which are demised by the lease as they are on the review date. To decide whether buildings, erected after the lease was granted, have become part of "the demised premises" under normal principles of land law, you have to read the lease as a whole in order to decide whether they are intended to be valued for rent review purposes.[5] In the absence of special circumstances, and in the absence of the usual direction that improvements carried out by the tenant are to be disregarded, new buildings would be included in the premises to be valued.[6] If part of the premises originally demised has been surrendered (*i.e.* given back to the landlord) before the review date, only the remaining part would on that date be "the demised premises". If by a subsequent grant, additional premises had been deemed to be included in the original demise, the additional premises would, on the review date, form part of "the demised premises". (This would not, of course, apply if the second grant was intended to take effect as a wholly separate and independent demise). The first task, therefore, is to look at the lease and any other relevant documents in order to decide exactly what, for rent review purposes, is meant by "the demised premises".

Again, under normal principles of English property law, the expression "premises" will, unless there are indications to the contrary, include all easements such as rights of way, rights of light, or rights of support which

---

[3] See, *e.g. Sterling Land Office Developments Limited v. Lloyds Bank plc* (1984) 271 E.G. 894, a decision of Harman J. Similarly Peter Gibson J. attached no particular significance to the word "full" in the expression "full current market rack rental value" in *Royal Exchange Assurance v. Bryant Samuel Properties* [1985] 1 E.G.L.R. 84 or to the word "highest" in "highest market rent" *Daejan Investments Limited v. Cornwall Coast Country Club* [1985] 1 E.G.L.R. 77.

[4] [1987] 2 E.G.L.R. 140.

[5] See *Ipswich Town Football Club Company Limited v. Ipswich Borough Council* (1988) 32 E.G. 49.

[6] *Ponsford v. HMS Aerosols Limited* [1979] A.C. 63.

are either expressly granted by the lease or are implied into the grant by section 62 of the Law of Property Act 1925.

8.4.2—*What fixtures and fittings are to be included in the valuation?*

Almost every tenant brings on to the premises, or makes in them, things that he wants to use for the purposes of his occupation. Some of them are used without being attached to the premises in any way, *e.g.* a desk, a chair, a filing cabinet. Others are attached to the premises, but only minimally; for example a picture hook hammered into the wall to hold a picture or a wall chart. Yet others are so much attached to the premises that they cannot be removed without much structural work, *e.g.* a new fireplace put in the living room of a house, an air-conditioning system installed in the office, or a bar and servery in a restaurant.

It can be of considerable valuation importance to know what (if any) of the fixtures and fittings with which the demised premises are equipped at the review date are to be taken into account as part of the subject-matter being offered to the hypothetical tenant. In English law anything which is built on land, *e.g.* a building, becomes part of the land. Unhappily however English law as to what a tenant who during his tenancy fixes something to the land or to a building on the land may remove, when his tenancy ends and he vacates the premises, is complicated.[7] It is suggested that the question be approached in stages.

The first stage. is to eliminate those alleged "fixtures and fittings" which are not fixtures at all, because they are in no way fixed to the land or buildings demised. Examples are books, desks, filing cabinets, and partitions which are merely resting on the floor and can be picked up and moved around without unfixing them. These are not to be valued as part of the demised premises. If the article is in some way attached to the land or building the second stage should be approached.

The second stage is to ask whether the article was there at the commencement of the demise under which the tenant holds the premises. If it was, unless there is some express agreement to the contrary, the tenant will never acquire the right to remove it, and the premises must be valued with the article attached to them. (This can sometimes decrease, rather than increase, the value, *e.g.* if the premises were let with an old and outmoded electrical

---

[7] An instructive modern case on the subject is *Young v. Dalgety plc* [1987] 1 E.G.L.R. 116 (C.A.).

generating plant which any incoming tenant would want to remove and the removal would be expensive.)

If the article in question has not been eliminated by these stages the third stage should be considered.

The third stage is to ask whether the degree of fixing to the premises is minimal. For example, a fitted carpet merely tacked to the floor round the edges of a room, though in a sense "fixed", is minimally so and does not become part of the land or building. Likewise a half-height partition screwed to the floor of an office, and removable by unscrewing two screws. On the other hand breeze-block partitions on a concrete foundation are so far fixed as to become part of the building, and the tenant does not have the right to remove them at the end of his tenancy.

In cases lying between these extremes there is the fourth stage.

The fourth stage is to look at the nature of the item which has been introduced into the premises and the degree to which it has been physically attached to the structure or to the land, and to consider whether it was so attached with the purpose of making it part of the demised premises, or whether it was put there by the tenant for the greater enjoyment or convenience of his occupation.

Having applied these tests, the valuation should be made on the assumption that the actual tenant has, before vacating the premises, removed everything that he was entitled to remove.

8.5—State of repair and compliance with covenants

8.5.1—*Dilapidated premises are usually worth less in the market*

The state of repair of premises often has a considerable effect on their letting value, since if premises are so dilapidated that a prospective tenant would have to spend a great deal of money before or soon after moving in, he will require either a rent-free period or a substantial discount in the amount of the rent payable, to compensate him both for the money he will have to spend and for either the delay in being able to move in, or the disruption he will suffer if he does the work after moving in, or both.

This does not by any means apply in all cases. For example, if the premises are in a prime position in a busy high street, attractive to the kind of trader who has many branches all fitted out in a "house" style, the fact that the premises need re-wiring, new floor-covering and redecorating might be no deterrent at all.

61

8.5.2—*Absence of an assumption as to repair may be irrelevant*

Often the rent review provisions of the lease will contain an express assumption that the tenant has complied with all his covenants under the lease. If the tenant has covenanted in the lease to keep the premises in full repair they are accordingly to be valued as if they were in a state of full repair. The court has held that this is the case even where there is no express assumption contained in the review clause; to allow the tenant to argue otherwise would be to allow him to rely upon his own wrong.[8] But if the disrepair is not due to any breach of the tenant's obligations, there is no room for implying that the obligation has been performed.

8.5.3—*Assumption that all covenants have been performed*

Sometimes the rent review clause will expressly require an assumption that all covenants as to repair have been performed (*i.e.* including the landlord's). From the landlord's point of view this assumption may be justified on the basis that it avoids the issue of disrepair being raised during the course of review and so avoids involving the arbitrator or expert in the potentially difficult task of deciding which existing defects were the responsibility of the landlord and which were those of the tenant. But where the landlord has covenanted to repair, and has failed to do so, the assumption that the covenant has been performed will be unfair to the tenant. His primary concern will be for beneficial occupation of the premises and it will be small comfort for him to be told that he has a claim in damages against his landlord because of the disrepair (including presumably an amount to compensate him for paying more than the premises were worth because of the assumption in the rent review clause.)[9]

8.6—The different kinds of restriction on use

A lease may restrict the use of the demised premises, and most leases do. It may do so positively, *i.e.* by stating that the premises shall be used for a specified purpose or purposes, or negatively, *i.e.* by stating that the premises shall not be used for a specified purpose or purposes. In either case, the restrictions may for rent review purposes be divided into one of three, or possibly four, categories. These are:

---

[8] See *Family Management v. Gray* (1980) 253 E.G. 369 and *Harmsworth Trustees v. Charringtons Industrial Holdings Limited* [1985] 1 E.G.L.R. 97.
[9] See *Clarke v. Findon Developments Limited* (1984) 270 E.G. 426.

8.6.1—*Where the lease restricts the use, with no mention of consent to a change of use*

Where the clause simply states that the tenant is only entitled to carry on some particular use or uses, or that he is prohibited from carrying on certain types of use, without any mention of the landlord's consent, the restriction is said to be absolute. The landlord has an absolute right in law to insist that the restriction is complied with, and may arbitrarily refuse any request by the tenant for permission to use the premises for a purpose outside those permitted by the lease. Alternatively, the landlord may demand a payment for consenting to the request. No matter how unreasonable his attitude may be, the court cannot interfere with it. In the context of rent review, the right of the hypothetical landlord strictly to control the use to which the premises may be put may have a very depressing effect on the rent obtainable on a letting. Thus in *Plinth Properties v. Mott Hay & Anderson*[10] the tenants had covenanted "not to use the demised premises . . . otherwise than as offices . . . in connection with the lessee's business of Consulting Engineers". The arbitrator made a deduction of one-third from the rent which he would otherwise have assessed, because of this restriction. On appeal the High Court and the Court of Appeal rejected the landlord's argument that the arbitrator should have considered the possibility of the hypothetical landlord giving consent.

This important case is often misunderstood. *The court's decision*, set out above is binding in law. *The arbitrator's decision* to award a discount, and the amount of it, is not binding in law because it depended upon the particular circumstances of the case. Thus an absolute restriction on a user which might appear to be every bit as restrictive as that in the *Plinth Properties* case might have little or no effect on value, *e.g.* a covenant in a lease of ground-floor premises in London's Chinatown restricting the use of the premises to that of a Chinese restaurant.

8.6.2—*Where the words "without consent" are added*

The position is somewhat different where the words "without consent", or similar words, appear in the clause. In such a case, the effect of Section 19(3) of the Landlord & Tenant Act 1927 is to import a term that no money payment may be required by the landlord in return for permission to a change of use, provided no structural alteration of the premises is involved. The landlord may, however, require the tenant to pay the costs of the licence

[10] (1978) 249 E.G. 1167.

and a reasonable sum to compensate for any diminution in value of the premises or neighbouring premises. Whether the presence of these words significantly reduces the depressing effect of the restriction on use is doubtful; although the landlord is deprived of his right to demand money for giving his consent, he retains his absolute right to refuse consent. Indeed, it may be argued that he is more likely to refuse if he is forbidden by law from receiving a financial benefit for giving it. Attempts by landlords to argue that the presence of the words "without consent" necessarily implied that such consent would not be unreasonably withheld have failed.[11]

8.6.3—*Where the lease prohibits change of use "without consent, such consent not to be unreasonably withheld"*

If the landlord has imposed only a qualified restriction of this kind the valuer is fully entitled to value the premises on the basis of the most profitable use thereof for which consent could not be reasonably withheld. The reason for this is that a prospective tenant, in the market for the premises, who wished to change to some more profitable use, being a use which a reasonable landlord would not oppose, would know that he would merely have to apply for consent to change the use, and that the landlord would be bound in law to give it. Indeed, in most cases the landlord would have a sound commercial motive for giving consent, since the rent which would be paid by the tenant seeking the most profitable use would be the highest rent.

8.6.4—*A possible fourth category*

In *Forte & Company Limited v. General Accident Life Assurance Limited*[12] the lease required the premises to be used only for certain specified purposes "or for such other purpose or purposes as may be authorised ... by the Superior Landlords".

Although there was no obligation in law on the superior landlords not unreasonably to withhold their consent, the judge held that the valuer could take into account the fact that the superior landlords might authorise some other forms of use. It was a matter for the valuer to decide whether this was a factor he could evaluate and, if so, what weight he should give to it. It is difficult to reconcile this decision with that of the Court of Appeal in the

[11] See, for example *Pearl Assurance v. Shaw* [1985] 1 E.G.L.R. 92.
[12] [1986] 2 E.G.L.R. 115.

Plinth Property case.[13] It is, therefore, doubtful whether this category exists.

8.7—Interpreting restrictions on use

To decide the effect of a restriction on use upon the value of premises one must first look at the lease to decide exactly what the tenant can and cannot do. In doing so one must distinguish between positive and negative user covenants. Most covenants in a lease are negative, that is to say they restrict the use to which the premises may be put; they do not oblige the tenant to carry on any particular use. But sometimes the covenant will impose a positive obligation, so that it will be a breach of covenant if the tenant does not use the premises at all but merely keeps them empty. Such covenants are particularly common in shopping centres where it may be important to the landlord that all the shops are open for business, particularly those such as supermarkets which are thought to attract custom to the centre. In several rent reviews of supermarket premises the presence of a positive covenant to keep the premises open and trading has been considered by the valuer to have a depressing effect on rental value.

8.7.1—*User restricted to the purposes of the lessee's business*

The result of the arbitration in the *Plinth Property* case shows how the restriction to use of premises for the purposes of the lessee's particular specified business may dramatically depress the rental value. The court will not, however, allow this argument to be pressed so far as to negate the whole object of rent review, which is to assess an open market valuation. In *Law Land Company Limited v. Consumers Association Limited*[14] the user provisions in the lease required the tenant to use the premises as offices of the Consumers Association and its associated organisations. The tenants argued that for rent review purposes the presence of this clause meant that there would be only one hypothetical tenant in the market, namely the Consumers Association. This argument was rejected by the Court of Appeal which held that references in the rent review provisions of the lease to "market rent", "the open market" and "vacant possession" precluded the argument that there would have been no competition for the lease. Accordingly, it was necessary in the rent review valuation to read the user clause as if the reference to the Consumers Association was deleted and the name of the

---

[13] *Plinth Property Investments Ltd v. Mott, Hay & Anderson* (1978) 249 E.G. 1167 (CA).
[14] (1980) 255 E.G. 617.

hypothetical tenant (whoever that might be) was to be inserted once his identity was known.

8.7.2—*Statutory restrictions on use*

In deciding whether, and how much, to bid for premises the hypothetical tenant will consider not merely what restrictions on use are contained in the lease being offered to him but also whether any restrictions or limitations are imposed by statute. Many such statutory restrictions exist, but by far the most important are those imposed by the Town & Country Planning Acts. Most leases contain a covenant by the tenant to comply with planning legislation, and consequently statutory requirements can be enforced by the landlord as well as by the relevant planning authorities. In *Compton Group Limited v. Estates Gazette Limited*[15] the court rejected an argument that the valuer—for rent review purposes—might take into account the possibility of the hypothetical tenant taking the premises with a view to using them in breach of planning control, on the basis that it was unlikely to be enforced. This highlights the critical effect which planning restrictions may have upon the rental value of premises. However, where the valuer considers that an application to the planning authorities for permission to change the use of the premises has some hope of succeeding, and that the market will place some value upon this hope, the valuer may take this "hope value" into account.[16] This is not inconsistent with the decision in the *Plinth Property*[17] case because the right to grant or refuse planning permission is not arbitrary but is a statutory discretion which must be exercised by the planning authority according to law.

8.7.3—*Assumed planning permissions*

It is always open to the parties to agree expressly in the rent review clause that it is to be assumed that a particular use is permitted by law even if that is not in fact the case. For example in *Bovis Group Pension Fund Limited v. G. C. Flooring & Furnishing Limited*[18] the clause provided that the reviewed rent was to be that at which the demised premises "might reasonably be expected to be let for office purposes". The Court of Appeal held that for rent review purposes the valuer had to assume that planning permission for offices existed on the relevant review date even though, in reality, it did not.

[15] (1977) 244 E.G. 799.
[16] *6th Centre Limited v. Guildville Limited* [1989] 1 E.G.L.R. 260.
[17] Discussed in para. 8.6.1.
[18] (1984) 269 E.G. 1252.

8.8—The notional term

8.8.1—*How the period of the lease is relevant to value*

The period of the lease which is being granted to the hypothetical tenant is likely to have an effect on value. If it is too short, a prospective tenant may be reluctant to take on the burden of repairing the premises, moving into them, carrying out whatever works of improvement and fitting out he considers necessary, and then taking the risk of losing all his work, and the goodwill that he builds up by his trading, when the lease expires. Moreover, if the lease is short, the amount that he will be able to realise by selling the business and assigning the lease with it will be reduced, perhaps to zero. On the other hand, if the lease is too long covenants such as the repairing covenants may be unduly onerous, and the prospect of being "locked in" to a lease of a particular building for a long period may be unattractive. What is "too short" or "too long" in any particular case must depend, of course, upon tenant preference in the market for buildings of the particular type in question.

8.8.2—*The rent review clause should define the period of the notional lease*

Most rent review clauses state the length of lease which is to be assumed for rent review purposes. The period commonly stated is the unexpired residue, at the review date, of the term granted by the lease. Some leases specify the period between reviews, or a fixed period which may or may not be the same number of years that was originally granted by the lease.

8.8.3—*Where the period is not clearly defined*

Where the length of the notional term is not clearly defined, the court will apply "the presumption in favour of reality"; see paragraph 4.5 above. The valuation should be made on the basis of a notional term equal to the residue unexpired at the review date of the term granted by the actual lease. For example, in *Ritz Hotel Limited v. Ritz Casino Limited*[19] the premises had originally been demised for a term of 21 years from July 1, 1977, so that on the second review, 11 years remained unexpired. The direction in the rent review clause was that the notional term should be "a term equivalent to the term hereby granted". The court held that this did not mean a term of 21 years starting on the relevant review date but the balance of the term which still subsisted at that date, namely 11 years.

[19] [1989] 2 E.G.L.R. 135.

8.8.4—*The possibility of statutory renewal of the lease*

Where the notional term is exceptionally short by market standards, the market will take into account the likelihood or otherwise of obtaining a new tenancy under the Landlord and Tenant Act 1954, and accordingly the valuer too must take this into account. For example, where what was to be valued was "a term not exceeding five years and one half of another year" the Court of Appeal held that the possible rights of renewal under the 1954 Act should be borne in mind, and upheld the arbitrator's higher figure awarded on that basis.[20] In assessing the value of the rights of renewal the valuer will, of course, have to take into account the likelihood of any application for a new tenancy under the 1954 Act being successfully opposed by the hypothetical landlord on the ground, *e.g.* of redevelopment. If renewal is unlikely, the existence of statutory rights will add little, if anything, to the value of the premises.

8.8.5—*Whether the notional lease contains provisions for rent review*

The amount of rent determined in a rent review can be dramatically affected by whether the hypothetical lease itself contains provision for periodic review during the term. Suppose that on the rent review date it is market practice to grant leases for terms of 15 years with upwards only reviews every five years. It follows that the comparable evidence will consist wholly or mainly of transactions effected on that basis. If the lease being valued for rent review purposes is a 15-year term with no rent reviews, and if the market considers that rental values are likely to rise over that period, such a lease will command a higher rent in the market, because the tenant will know that whatever rent is fixed at the beginning will not be subject to any increase for 15 years. The extra rent that a tenant is prepared to pay, over and above what he would pay for a similar lease containing provision for rent review every five years, is sometimes called "uplift" or "overage". The amount of such "uplift" will depend upon market conditions at the relevant review date. In the rising market up to 1989 many valuers used a rule of thumb of adding one per cent per annum to the rent for every year the rent was to remain unreviewed after the fifth year so that if the actual lease directed that the rent, on review, should be assessed on a hypothetical lease for 20 years with no rent review, the rent would be determined at 15 per cent above the rent that would be obtained on a letting for 20 years with reviews every five years. In the recessionary market conditions prevailing since 1990 such a "rule" can rarely operate.

There has been much litigation concerning rent review clauses which

[20] See *Pivot Properties Limited v. Secretary of State for the Environment* (1980) 256 E.G. 1176.

could be interpreted to mean that, although the rent under the actual lease was subject to review at five-yearly intervals, the terms of the hypothetical lease by reference to which the rent was to be reviewed contained no rent review provisions. After a period of uncertainty as to how the courts would approach the interpretation of such clauses the position was clarified by the decision of the High Court in *British Gas Corporation v. Universities Superannuation Scheme Limited*[21]. In accordance with the "presumption in favour of reality"[22] the courts will normally construe the rent review clause so as to incorporate into the notional term the same pattern of rent reviews as exist in the actual lease. Thus the argument about "uplift" will only apply either where the words of the lease clearly require the existence of rent reviews in the actual lease to be disregarded, or where the period for rent reviews in the actual lease is different from the period provided in leases prevailing in the market at the rent review date.

8.9—Unusually onerous obligations as to repair

The question of the assumed state of repair of the premises at the commencement of the hypothetical term has already been considered—see Section 8.5. The obligations of the landlord and tenant for the future repair of the premises will also, in most cases, have an effect on value. In many cases the tenant will have entered into a full repairing obligation or (if he is the occupier of part only of a building) have covenanted to re-imburse by way of service charge the cost of repairs carried out by the landlord. Assuming that all the comparables are let on a similar basis, there will be no need to make any adjustment in such cases. Where, however, for some reason, the terms of the lease are particularly favourable to the tenant, or particularly onerous compared with the comparables, an appropriate adjustment will need to be made to reflect this factor. For example, in *Norwich Union Life Insurance Society v. British Railways Board*[23] the lease of an office building for a term of 150 years contained a covenant by the lessee "to keep the demised premises in good and substantial repair and condition and where necessary to rebuild, reconstruct or replace the same and in such repair and condition to yield up the same at the expiration or sooner determination of the term".

The arbitrator held that this covenant was unusually onerous in that it required the tenant to rebuild the building completely if that should be necessary during the term. He deducted $27\frac{1}{2}$ per cent from the rent established by comparables where the leases had ordinary full repairing terms which would not have involved an obligation to rebuild or replace. The court

---

[21] [1986] 1 E.G.L.R. 120 as affirmed by the Court of Appeal in *Basingstoke and Deane D.C. v. Host Group Ltd* [1986] 2 E.G.L.R. 107.
[22] See para. 4.5 above.
[23] [1987] 2 E.G.L.R. 137.

dismissed an appeal against the arbitrator's interpretation of the repairing covenant.

As with the *Plinth Property*[24] case it would be a mistake to regard this case as an indication that the particular percentage deduction would be appropriate in other cases; the amount (if any) of a deduction would depend on a number of circumstances, including the age of the building and the likelihood of it requiring total rebuilding within the term of the lease.

8.10—Restrictions on assignment and sub-letting

The right of the tenant to dispose of all or part of the premises comprised in the lease can be of considerable practical importance, and the presence or absence of restrictions on disposal may accordingly have an important effect on value. As with restrictions on use, it is necessary to distinguish various kinds of restriction on alienation.

8.10.1—*The difference between assignment and sub-letting*

As we have seen in paragraph 2.2.2 above, the two main forms of alienation are:

(a) assignment, that is to say a transfer of the lease to an assignee who then becomes the direct tenant of the landlord; and

(b) underletting, that is to say the grant by the tenant to someone, (variously called a "sub-tenant", "under-tenant", "sub-lessee" or "under-lessee") of an interest less than that which the tenant himself holds, either because it is of part only of the premises or because, though it is of the entire premises, it is for part only of the unexpired term of the tenant's interest.

Under-letting does not involve a change in the identity of the person who is the tenant under the lease, but introduces into the hierarchy of ownership of the property a new party who is the tenant's tenant.

Assignment of part only of the premises is theoretically possible but most unusual because of the complications it introduces. Most leases absolutely forbid it. Under-letting, on the other hand, is often of part only of the demised premises. Sometimes the lease will contain an express restriction on the parts of the premises that may be under-let, *e.g.* a lease of an office building may permit under-letting complete floors of the building, but prohibit under-letting of part of a floor.

---

[24] Discussed in para. 8.6.1.

70

8.10.2—*Absolute and qualified covenants against assignment or sub-letting*

A covenant against assignment or sub-letting is said to be absolute if the prohibition does not use the words "without consent" (or similar words). The landlord has the absolute right to enforce such a restriction. It does not matter whether he is being reasonable or not. On the other hand, if the prohibition is qualified by the words "without consent" (or similar words), a term is imported by section 19 (1) of the Landlord and Tenant Act 1927 that the landlord will not unreasonably withhold his consent. Often the clause will expressly state that consent is not to be unreasonably withheld but this is, strictly speaking, unnecessary because of the statute. Some leases, especially those granted for long terms (*e.g.* 99 years) contain no restriction or minimal restriction upon assignments and sub-lettings, or only impose restrictions towards the end of the term. Accordingly, there is a wide variety of restrictions on assignment or sub-letting. The impact of such restrictions upon the mind of the hypothetical tenant, and his perception of the flexibility or inflexibility of the legal interest he is proposing to acquire, may have an important effect on the amount of rent he is willing to pay. This is likely to be particularly important where the premises are unusually large (so that there will be a limited number of tenants who could occupy them as a whole without sub-letting part) or where the term of the lease is unusually long (so that the likelihood of the lessee wishing to dispose of them before the end of the term is correspondingly increased).

8.11—Restrictions on alterations or improvements

Another covenant which may have an important effect on value is that which restricts the tenant as to the physical alteration of the demised premises so that the tenant can make them more suitable for his use, or for sub-letting parts of them if he wishes to do so. Once again it is necessary to distinguish between absolute covenants and those which are qualified.

If the words "without consent" do not appear, the hypothetical tenant must, in practical terms, comply strictly with the restrictions on alterations which means that he must take the premises as he finds them and use them in their existing state. He can ask the landlord to consent to proposed alterations, but the landlord has an absolute right to say "No".[25]

Where the covenant is not absolute, but is qualified by the words "without consent", statute once again intervenes. It is provided by section 19 (2) of the Landlord and Tenant Act 1927 that insofar as the works proposed are

---

[25] Even where an absolute prohibition is concerned there is available a complicated procedure under Part I of the Landlord and Tenant Act 1927 which enables the tenant to obtain the court's consent to "proper improvements". It is rarely of any practical use.

works of improvement, any covenants restricting the carrying out of those works without the landlord's consent are subject to a proviso that such consent may not be unreasonably withheld. The question of whether particular proposed works are or are not "improvements" is looked at from the tenant's point of view. In practice, this means that most works the tenant wishes to carry out are likely to come within the statutory provision.[26] Such works may even include a complete demolition of the existing buildings and their replacement with new structures of a different kind.[27] Thus, in practice such a covenant will only allow a landlord to withhold consent to works proposed by the tenant if the landlord would suffer some serious prejudice as a result of them being carried out, as, *e.g.* in a case where there would be a danger of damage to the structure of the building. What (if any) impact all this has on the value of the premises will depend upon their nature and, in particular, their suitability to the trade or business which would attract the highest rent. If premises are obsolete in their design or specification a very restrictive covenant against improvements may have a very depressing effect on the rental value. On the other hand, if they are already ideally suited to the intended use, an inability to carry out works or alterations may have no effect at all on their value.

8.12—Matters to be disregarded

Many rent review clauses direct the valuer to disregard certain matters, because the parties have agreed that some factor which might increase or decrease the rent should not be taken into account. Common items directed to be disregarded are:

    (a)   the goodwill of the tenant's business;
    (b)   the fact that the tenant has been in occupation of the premises;
    (c)   certain categories of improvement carried out by the tenant.

The last-mentioned is the most important in practice, and is the only one which will be discussed here.

8.12.1—*Disregard of tenant's improvements*

The scope of the disregard depends upon the wording of the rent review clause but the following points are commonly encountered:

    (a)   The subject matter of the disregard is normally physical works carried out by the tenant. It is thus important for every tenant to

[26] See *F.W. Woolworth & Company Limited v. Lambert* [1937] Ch.37.
[27] See *National Electric Theatres v. Hugdell* [1939] Ch.553.

keep careful records showing what has been done, when, and at what cost.

(b) The disregard may be limited to works carried out by the tenant, or may extend to include works carried out by sub-tenants.

(c) The disregard may be limited to works carried out by the person who is tenant or sub-tenant at the date of review, or may extend to include work carried out by a predecessor in title.

(d) Normally it will be stipulated that works will only be disregarded if they were carried out otherwise than in pursuance of an obligation to the landlord. The obligation may have arise from the lease itself or from some other document such as an agreement for lease, or a licence.

(e) A licence permitting alterations does not usually impose any obligation upon the tenant to carry out the work if he should decide not to do so. But whether that is so in any particular case depends upon the wording of the licence.[28]

(f) Normally the improvements to be disregarded are those carried out during the term of the lease, but the wording of the clause may depart from the normal. For example, in *Brett v. Brett Essex Golf Club Limited*[29] the tenant carried out substantial improvements but then surrendered his lease and took a new lease of the premises together with additional premises. It was held that, on the wording of the disregard in the rent review clause of the new lease, the improvements carried out under the old lease were *not* to be disregarded. This demonstrates the need for care in the wording of the disregard.

(g) Once the relevant improvements to be disregarded have been identified, valuers vary in their approach to what deduction should be made from the rent which would have been assessed for the premises in their improved state, to give effect to the disregard. Some valuers assess the cost of carrying out the improvement at the rent review date and decapitalise[30] that cost over the entire term. Others decapitalise the cost over the period to the next review, which produces a higher discount. Yet others reject an approach based upon the capital cost of the works and simply attempt to identify how much of the total rent is fairly attributable to the existence of the improvement. The courts have persistently refused to endorse one method or the other as being correct, on the basis that the question is one of valuation not of law.

[28] See *Godbold v. Martin The Newsagents Limited* (1983) 268 E.G. 1202.
[29] [1986] 1 E.G.L.R. 154.
[30] See Glossary—Appendix I, page 124.

8.13—The market in which the premises are being offered

8.13.1—*The hypothetical willing landlord and willing tenant*

Most rent review clauses direct that the rent is to be assessed on the basis that the premises are being offered by a willing landlord to a willing tenant. Even if this is not expressly stated it will be implied, since the assessment of an open market rent necessarily involves a landlord willing to let the premises and a tenant willing to take them.[31] But the willing landlord and the willing tenant are hypothetical parties; they are not to be equated with the actual landlord and the actual tenant.[32]

8.13.2—*Where the premises would be unlettable in the actual market*

The assumption of a willing landlord and a willing tenant is particularly important where market conditions prevailing at the rent review date are such that if the premises had been offered on that date there would have been no takers. Even if that is the case in reality, the valuer is required to assess the rent on the basis that it would have been possible to let the premises, since a willing landlord and a willing tenant must both be assumed. However, the assumption does not prevent the valuer from deciding that the rent which would be paid even by a willing tenant would be low, or even nominal, if that is what the evidence of market conditions indicates.[33]

---

[31] *Dennis & Robinson v. Kiossos* [1987] 1 E.G.L.R. 133.
[32] See *F.R. Evans of Leeds Limited v. English Electric* (1978) 36 P. & C.R. 185.
[33] See *Dennis V. Robinson v. Kiossos*, above.

Chapter Nine:
Determining the New Rent
—the Choice of Procedures

9.1—The need for third-party determination

A high proportion of rent reviews are settled by negotiation between the parties and/or their valuers, without outside intervention. The exact proportion is unknown, but it probably exceeds 95 per cent. But this still leaves many thousands of reviews every year where—after attempts to agree the reviewed rent have failed—the parties, either themselves or through the R.I.C.S. appointments procedure discussed in Chapter Six above, seek the appointment of some outside person to decide the new rent. Since it is impossible to predict which reviews will and which will not be settled without invoking outside assistance, every review clause should provide some procedure if the parties cannot otherwise decide what the new rent is to be.

9.2—The choice of procedures available

As mentioned in paragraph 2.6.4 above, the rent review provisions in a lease may provide for the new rent to be assessed:

(a) by a valuer acting as independent expert, with or without representations from the parties;

(b) by a valuer acting as arbitrator and proceeding on written submissions from the parties but with no oral hearing; or

(c) by a valuer acting as arbitrator and proceeding to an oral hearing, with written pleadings and/or submissions, and with each party's case presented by the party himself or (if he wishes) by a valuer, solicitor or counsel.

A valuer arbitrator may, if he or the parties so wish, be assisted by a legal assessor.

9.3—The differences between these procedures

9.3.1—*Essential difference between arbitration and determination by an expert*

The essential difference is:

(a)   arbitration is the decision of a dispute by a person who decides it by reference to evidence and submissions put before him by the parties, and who must therefore give the parties a fair opportunity to put evidence and submissions before him;

(b)   determination by an expert is the decision of a question (whether or not the parties have attempted to agree upon the answer, and therefore whether or not there is any dispute between the parties) by a person who answers it by reference to his own knowledge and experience; he may or may not invite the parties to put evidence and/or submissions before him, and in rent review he nearly always does.

9.3.2—*Specific ways in which the procedures differ*

These essential differences affect the procedure for determining the reviewed rent in respect of:

(a)   the need for each party to formulate a case rather than leave everything to the appointee;

(b)   the right of a party to obtain an oral hearing at which he can present his own case and test that of his opponent;

(c)   the time taken to determine the new rent and (often) the time at which the tenant has to pay it;

(d)   the existence or otherwise of clear rules of procedure;

(e)   the thoroughness of the investigations which precede the determination;

(f)   the adaptability of the procedure to dealing with questions of law (usually, of interpretation of the lease) which often arise in rent reviews;

(g)   the powers of the court to assist in the procedure;

(h)   the power of the parties to control the fees charged by a determiner appointed by an appointing institution;

(i)   the cost to the parties;

(j)   the extent to which the parties can require the determiner to give reasons for his determination;

(k)   the liability of the determiner for negligence.

9.3.3—*To what extent can an arbitrator apply his own knowledge and experience?*

With few exceptions, the arbitrator in a rent review arbitration will be a valuer. The parties have agreed—directly by appointing him, or indirectly by agreeing to arbitration by someone to be appointed by the President of a professional association of valuers—that they want their dispute decided by a valuer. It would be absurd if when the valuer has been appointed they were then to say to him: "But in deciding our dispute you must not apply the knowledge and experience that you have gained in the field of valuation." Nor do they.

The problem is one of reconciling the parties' choice of a valuer as arbitrator with the fundamental principle of English justice that a party to litigation or arbitration is entitled to a fair opportunity not merely to present his case to the tribunal but also to meet the case made by the other party. Where the tribunal is in effect itself making a case in opposition to a party's case, the party is entitled to know what that case is, and to an opportunity to meet it. Thus in *Fox v. Wellfair*[1] Dunn L.J. said: "An expert should not in effect give evidence to himself without disclosing it to the parties."

So the solution to the problem is that an arbitrator who is minded to take into account material from his own knowledge and experience may do so provided that he first discloses it to the parties, and then gives each of them a fair opportunity of challenging, rebutting or commenting on it.

There is no corresponding duty upon a person appointed to determine the reviewed rent as independent expert.

---

[1] [1981] 2 Lloyd's Rep. 514.

Chapter Ten: The Procedure for Determination by an Expert

10.1—Determination by an expert

The differences between determination by an expert and determination by an arbitrator have been explained in Chapter Nine above. As regards procedure, the essential characteristics of an expert determination are that it is not quasi judicial, no set procedures are laid down, and the expert generally has no procedural powers. It is simply his job to make his own investigations and then to decide on the basis of his own skills, knowledge and experience what rent should be assessed in accordance with the rent review provisions. In practice, the expert will invite submissions from the parties or their advisers, since they will often have relevant information which he might not otherwise discover. For example, it might be virtually impossible for the expert to decide how to give effect to the disregard of improvements without access to information from the tenant as to exactly what work had been done and when. Similarly, even in an expert determination, the parties will often wish to bring to his attention certain matters, including comparable evidence, which they are afraid he might otherwise overlook. In addition, there may be arguments of law which the parties may wish to put before the expert. It is therefore in many ways as important for each party to present its case adequately to the expert as it is in the case of an arbitration.

10.2—How a valuer appointed by a party prepares for a determination by an expert

Where the new rent is being decided by an expert, a party-appointed valuer is not as concerned to "make a case" as he would before an arbitrator. He should, nevertheless, be concerned to ensure that the expert has a comprehensible statement of his client's case in relation to the rent review, and, more importantly, that the expert has before him such relevant material as would incline him to decide upon a figure favourable to the client. So in many ways the task is similar to that of presenting a case to an arbitrator.

The following matters are of particular importance.

10.2.1—*Identifying issues of law*

The expert determination procedure is particularly ill-adapted to deal with difficult points of interpretation arising out of the rent review clause or other parts of the lease, because the expert, being a valuer, may not even appreciate the legal difficulty and, if he does, may not have sufficient legal expertise to reach a correct decision. He does not have the benefit of formal pleadings, nor of the procedures which help an arbitrator to identify, and then to decide, an issue of law. He is unlikely to seek legal assistance unless one or both parties specifically ask him to do so. So it is particularly important that issues of law should be identified and suggestions made to the expert as to how he should decide them.

Unless a party or his valuer is confident that the issue is well within the competence of the expert, it would be as well to suggest that he should take legal advice from a solicitor or barrister experienced in the field of rent review. Since his decision will, for all practical purposes, be binding and there is no right of appeal from it, the expert should be asked to consult with the parties as to the identity of the barrister or solicitor whom he intends to instruct. Issues of law can be disposed of in an efficient and acceptable way if both parties have full confidence in the person who is deciding them. If the point of law is of particular importance, it may be that the matter should be decided by the High Court.[1] In such a case, the expert should—with the concurrence of both parties—consult a solicitor or barrister (in the latter case taking advantage of Direct Professional Access to the Bar).

10.2.2—*Submitting statements of agreed facts*

Although it is for the valuer to satisfy himself as to factual matters, there will be many facts which can usefully be agreed by the parties or the valuers acting for them. These include floor measurements, specifications, a statement of the permitted planning uses, and other matters which may be easily available to the valuers for the parties but only discoverable by the expert after long and costly research. It is in all parties' interest to give the expert every assistance and to reach agreement whenever possible. If the expert is left to decide such things for himself, he may make mistakes which are incapable of remedy.

---

[1] For all practical purposes this can only be done with the consent of both parties. The courts will not normally accept jurisdiction to decide an issue—even an issue of law—which is within the terms of reference of the expert, see *Norwich Union Life Insurance Society v. P. & O. Holdings Limited* [1993] 1 E.G.L.R. 164.

10.2.3—*Information peculiarly within a party's knowledge*

Special attention should be given to matters which are within a client's knowledge. A good example is what improvements are to be disregarded for rent review purposes. In many cases, it may be impossible for the expert, without the assistance of the parties, to ascertain what work was done, by whom, and in what circumstances, so as to qualify as tenants' improvements. Since the onus is on the tenant to establish that the disregard of improvements applies, it is particularly for the tenant's valuer to provide the expert with all the information and documentation that he needs.

10.2.4—*Obtaining full copies of the relevant documents*

The valuer should take steps to obtain copies of all relevant documents. This will include not merely the lease, but also deeds of variation, licences and other documents which may be relevant to the rental valuation.

10.2.5—*Inviting parties to submit information as to comparables*

It is often helpful for an expert to receive details of comparables which one party or the other thinks are relevant to the valuation. Although the expert is not bound by the rules of evidence, those rules often have a sound practical basis in common-sense. It is therefore a good working rule that, as far as practicable, the presentation of material to an expert should be in a form which complies with the basic rules of evidence, giving full details, certified by a valuer involved in the relevant transaction, and with certified copies of supporting documentation.

10.2.6—*Following the rules of natural justice*

How far, or even whether, an expert is bound by the rules of natural justice is doubtful. But the basis of those rules is fairness to both parties, and common-sense dictates that many of the procedures which arbitrators are required to follow in order to ensure that the parties are dealt with fairly, will apply equally to the expert. It is therefore reasonable to ask the expert to ensure that each party has a fair opportunity of meeting the case put by the other party. Some experts do not, as a matter of course, send to each party a copy of the other party's representations and case. Few experts would refuse to do so if requested, and such a request should always be made at the outset of the determination process.

10.2.7—*Should the expert hold a meeting with the parties or their valuers?*

It is possible, but virtually unknown, for a rent review clause to direct the valuer to hold a meeting with the parties or their representatives before coming to his decision. In the absence of such a direction there is no obligation upon the expert to hold such a meeting, and few experts do so. Yet there are many cases where such a meeting will be helpful—in clarifying issues and avoiding actual and potential misunderstandings—to the expert and to the valuers instructed by the parties. Moreover, holding a meeting demonstrates to the parties that the independent expert is giving them a fair opportunity to present their views to him.

10.2.8—*Expert's powers as regards costs*

Few rent review clauses confer upon an independent expert any discretion as to the parties' costs, so that it is rarely appropriate for the valuer to make any *Calderbank* offer as would normally be the case in an arbitration (see paragraph 14.3 below).

10.3—How a solicitor prepares for determination by an expert

A solicitor is much less likely to become involved in a determination by an expert than he is in an arbitration. The reason is that, as has already been explained, there are no formal procedures and the issue is often merely one of valuation which the client's valuer will deal with himself. The solicitor is accordingly likely to be brought in to cases where some issue of law or other legal dispute arises. It is important to identify any issue of law, to explain to the expert how it arises, and to advise him how he should respond. In some cases it will be appropriate for the expert to act upon legal advice. Unless the legal issue is a very simple one the solicitor should furnish a concise statement of the client's case in relation to the issue, supporting it with arguments and authority, where appropriate. A formal Opinion from counsel will often carry considerable weight with the expert.

10.4—A suggested structure for a written submission

The form and contents of the written submissions are not greatly different from those of a proof of evidence to be exchanged in an arbitration where there is to be an oral hearing, nor indeed from an ordinary formal valuation report to a client. But the expert will usually have given directions of some kind, and these must be studied before drafting the report.

The following paragraphs are suggested:

(a) the identity of the author, his qualifications and relevant experience;

(b) location of the subject premises with references to annexed maps or plans;

(c) physical description of the subject premises, with floor areas and other relevant dimensions;

(d) tenant's improvements if any and whether they should be disregarded;

(e) the town planning situation and any statutory restrictions on use or alteration of the subject premises;

(f) the basis of rental valuation to be adopted, specifying all valuation assumptions being made, and referring to any words in the lease requiring them to be made, and support being relied upon, e.g. from statutes or of counsel's opinion;

(g) the evidence upon which the valuation is based, referring to any schedule of comparable transactions annexed or agreed;

(h) the valuer's analysis of the evidence;

(i) other points relevant to the valuation;

(j) the rental valuation;

(k) alternative valuations, if any, and the basis on which each is made; and

(l) the valuer's final opinion of rental value;

(m) the date of the submission.

10.5—Counter-submissions

Experts do not always provide for, or welcome, counter-submissions but if they do, their directions usually direct that counter-submissions should be confined to matters arising out of the other side's written submissions. Fresh material may be included only insofar as may be necessary to rebut a point made by the other party. It is often convenient to photocopy the opposing party's written submissions and to reply to them on a facing page.

Chapter Eleven: The Procedures for Determination by Arbitration[*]

11.1—The decision whether to request a hearing

Where a rent review clause provides that the new rent is to be determined by arbitration, it rarely specifies that the arbitration is to be on documents only, *i.e.* without a hearing. And even if it does specify this, the circumstances of a particular review may make a hearing desirable in the opinion of both parties. So at the outset of the review, each party should consider with his valuer whether to request a hearing. Moreover, facts may emerge for the first time during the course of the arbitration making a hearing desirable. For example, a tenant's written submission may assert that some alterations which have clearly increased the rental value should be disregarded because they were carried out by the tenant. If the landlord wishes to contest the assertion, he can request a hearing so that the issue can be decided.

11.2—Arbitration on documents only

11.2.1—*Structure of a written submission*

The suggested structure of a written submission to an expert set out in paragraph 10.4 above is suitable for a submission to an arbitrator who is to decide on documents only, but with the following modifications:

(a) An arbitrator will always give directions about the lodging of submissions, and these must be studied at the outset.

(b) It is usually safe to assume that the valuer appointed as an expert has *some* relevant information about the subject premises or some premises comparable with them. No such assumption should ever be made about an arbitrator. *All* material that a party

---

[*] At the time of writing (September 1995) it is likely that a new Arbitration Act will be passed in the 1995-6 Session of Parliament. If passed in its present draft form, it will have little effect on rent review arbitration, except perhaps as regards the admission of evidence of determinations of rent in other arbitration or court proceedings, as to which see Chap. 12, n.4 below. A new Arbitration Act would be closely followed by a new edition of the RICS Guidance Notes, to which reference should then be made.

considers supports his case should be included in a submission to an arbitrator.

(c)   An expert can be expected to make such checks of the reliability of the information put before him as he considers necessary. An arbitrator is never expected to make any inquiries of his own. So, for example, if a letter giving information about a comparable transaction, on which a party wishes to rely, is imprecise on an important matter, the party wishing to rely on it should clarify the point so that the information included in the submission is precise.

(d)   An arbitrator usually has power to make an order for costs and so the submission should deal with this, possibly by asking the arbitrator to make an interim award as to all matters other than costs, leaving the parties to make submissions about costs later if they so wish.

(e)   If a reasoned award is desired, a request for it should be made in the submission.

11.2.2—*When a solicitor is likely to be instructed*

A solicitor is likely to become involved in a documents-only rent review arbitration either where legal advice is required or where his legal expertise (*e.g.* in the assembly and analysis of the relevant documents) may be useful. Where counsel is likely to be instructed either in relation to legal issues or upon the presentation of the case generally, the valuer will often wish to leave the task of liaison with counsel to the solicitor rather than using the Direct Professional Access procedure to instruct counsel directly. When instructed, the solicitor and valuer should agree who does what. The valuer will be responsible for the collection and analysis of comparables and their analysis. He will usually undertake negotiations and discussions with the other party's valuer, certainly as to agreeing the facts and sometimes also as to settlement. Legal argument, instructing counsel, procedural applications to the arbitrator, discovery, and the collation of documents will usually be dealt with by the solicitor.

11.2.3—*Preparation for an arbitration on documents only*

The following is how a solicitor should prepare for an arbitration on documents only:

(a)   read the lease;

(b)   check that the notices (including counter-notices if any) comply with the requirements of the lease as to both form and contents;

(c) read any advice that has hitherto been given by the client's valuer;

(d) if no valuation advice has been taken, discuss with the client the need for it and the choice of valuer;

(e) check that insofar as any valuation advice expressly or impliedly takes any view as to the law, that view is correct;

(f) identify the issues between the parties;

(g) discuss with the client's valuer whether any attempt should be made to agree the issues with the other side;

(h) if the law is doubtful, advise the client on it. If appropriate discuss with the client whether an opinion should be taken from counsel;

(i) if no arbitrator has yet been appointed, discuss with the client the choice of arbitrator;

(j) if the client has the right to apply for the appointment of an arbitrator, discuss with the client when application should be made and whether the application should contain any request for the appointment of an arbitrator with particular qualifications, *e.g.* in out-of-town superstores;

(k) if directions have not been issued, discuss them with the valuer; if directions have been issued, consider whether any amendment to them is desirable and, if so, discuss this with the valuer; thereafter seek to agree the amendments with the opposing solicitor;

(l) attempt to agree, or cause the valuers to agree, the comparables and the way in which the comparables are to be put before the arbitrator;

(m) get the valuer to draft a submission to the arbitrator, and finalise it with him and with the client;

(n) obtain the valuer's comments on the other side's submission, discuss them with him and with the client, and discuss with the valuer the gist of the counter-submission to be lodged; and

(o) obtain the draft counter-submission from the valuer, discuss it with him and the client, finalise the counter-submission, get the client's approval, and deliver it to the arbitrator.

11.2.4—*The division of functions between solicitor and surveyor*

The solicitor has a particularly important part to play:

(a) in checking the lease and any notices that have been served to see if any points of law arise;

(b) in advising upon, and then drafting and serving, the notice or counter-notice and any other documents required; and

(c) in advising on the form (as distinct from the valuation contents) of the submissions or counter-submissions, and on legal matters to be included in those documents.

He is also likely to be consulted on questions of discovery, both as to what can be sought from the other side, and as to what documents in the possession, power or control of his client are privileged from discovery. If agreed bundles of documents or other correspondence are to be put before the arbitrator these are best prepared by the solicitors, unless they have little litigation experience.

11.2.5—*Changing the review procedure*

When solicitors are involved they should consider whether to recommend to their client that an attempt be made to change the documents-only procedure into the procedure for an arbitration with an oral hearing. This is because the involvement of solicitors itself suggests that there may be some point of law or fact central to the dispute which may not be easy to resolve without oral evidence. Or there may be issues of fact which cannot satisfactorily be resolved without a hearing.

Conversely, where there are no complications, it may be desirable to seek to change an arbitration with a hearing to one on documents only.

11.3—The procedure for arbitration with a hearing

The R.I.C.S. Guidance Notes, printed in Appendix III, though addressed primarily to valuers acting as arbitrators or independent experts, give valuable help to parties and their advisers in the preparation and presentation of a case for a hearing. Conversely, though the following Chapter is addressed primarily to the parties and their advisers, it will be helpful to arbitrators.

11.3.1—*The decision to hold a hearing*

Unless the lease otherwise provides, or the parties have otherwise agreed, a party to an arbitration has an absolute right to a hearing. But a hearing is not essential to an arbitration; the great majority of arbitrations are conducted without one. So the decision whether to hold a hearing does not have to be made at the outset of the arbitration; it can be deferred until the submissions and counter-submissions have been lodged. At that stage the issues will have been identified, and the parties and the arbitrator can make an informed decision as to whether a hearing is desirable.

Factors making a hearing desirable include the following:

(a) there is an important issue of fact (*e.g.* whether an improvement was or was not carried out by and at the expense of the tenant). To resolve an issue of pure fact against a party without hearing him, even if the decision is "right", is likely to leave the losing party with an understandable sense of grievance;

(b) there is a difficult point of law, on which a substantial amount turns, and on which the arbitrator would like to be assisted by legal argument; or

(c) a party (or each party) believes that the other party's valuer is exaggerating or even lying, and would like an opportunity to cross-examine him.

So the arbitrator and the parties should consider at the preliminary meeting whether either party requires a hearing. If not, the arbitrator should consider whether the issues, as they then appear, can be satisfactorily resolved without a hearing. Whatever he decides at that stage, he can be asked at any stage of the arbitration to reconsider any provisional decision he has made. So, *e.g.* if he has decided to hold a hearing because there appeared to be a substantial issue of fact, and later some agreement of the parties disposes of that issue, they can ask him to reverse his decision and to proceed on documents only.

11.3.2—*The right to representation*

Where there is a hearing, each party has a right not only to be present, but to be represented by an advocate (lay or professional) of his choice unless that right has been excluded by agreement or by rules under which the arbitration is being conducted. There are no such rules applicable to rent review and so a party can conduct his case himself, or instruct a solicitor or valuer to represent him; or he can, through solicitors or valuers, instruct a barrister.

11.3.3—*Identifying the issues*

A primary function of an advocate, of any profession or none, is to identify the issues between the parties. The process of identifying them often leads to their being disposed of before the hearing. If the process is neglected, much time and costs may be wasted; in an extreme case the hearing may even have to be adjourned or abandoned.

11.3.4—*Dealing with a point of law*

This is discussed in Chapter Five above.

11.4—The conduct of the hearing

11.4.1—*Order of events at the hearing*

The following is a run-down of the order of events at the hearing:

- (a) opening statement for the claimant—if the issues have been properly identified, this should be short;
- (b) evidence in chief of the claimant's first witness;
- (c) cross-examination of the claimant's first witness;
- (d) re-examination of the claimant's first witness;
  ((b), (c) and (d) are repeated for each successive witness)
- (e) opening statement (if any) for the respondent (in some cases it is convenient to make this statement, or a summary of it, immediately after the claimant's opening);
- (f) evidence in chief of respondent's first witness;
- (g) cross-examination of respondent's first witness;
- (h) re-examination of respondent's first witness;
  ((f), (g) and (h) are repeated for each successive witness)
- (i) closing submissions for the respondent; and
- (j) closing submissions for the claimant.

11.4.2—*Taking evidence on oath*

An arbitrator has power to take evidence on oath or affirmation, and he should normally do so where there is or may be an issue of fact between the witnesses. In practice, if either party so requests, the arbitrator will require the evidence to be given on oath or affirmation.

11.4.3—*Evidence in chief*

The object of evidence in chief is to obtain from the witness an unprompted statement of what he knows about the issues to which his evidence is directed and, to the extent that the form of question itself suggests the answer, it is a "leading question". Some prompting is unavoidable. But the more leading the question, the less weight can be attached to the answer. "Did you see cracks in the flank wall?" is a leading question. "What did you see?" is not.

11.4.4—*Putting in written statements of evidence in chief*

In most cases a witness' evidence can conveniently be given by putting in a written statement (called a "proof") rather than by oral question and answer.

11.4.5—*Cross-examination*

Cross-examination has, or may have, three objects:

(a) to put before the opposing party's witness (or the appropriate witness, if he is calling more than one) the substance of the cross-examining party's case insofar as it conflicts with the evidence given by that witness;

(b) to elicit from the witness facts favourable to the cross-examining party's case; and

(c) where the evidence that the witness has given in chief is disputed, to elicit facts relevant to the credibility of the witness, so as to show that he should not be believed.

Object (a) does not apply where the witness has already had an opportunity to dispute or comment upon the cross-examining party's case, *e.g.* because proofs of evidence have been exchanged, or because the witness has been present in the hearing while an earlier witness gave evidence that conflicts with his evidence. Questions put to the witness under heads (a) or (b) must be relevant to some issue in the arbitration. Cross-examination as to credibility is not limited in this way.

In the absence of any agreement to the contrary, or of any provision of arbitration rules which the parties have agreed to adopt, arbitration in England and Wales operates on an adversarial system of justice. It is fundamental to that system that each party shall be entitled not only to put forward his own evidence but also to probe, by cross-examination, the accuracy or otherwise or the completeness or otherwise of the evidence that has been given by the opposing party.

11.4.6—*Re-examination*

The object of re-examination is to enable the advocate who called the witness to give the witness the opportunity to explain, supplement, or qualify answers that the witness has given in cross-examination. The credibility of a witness whose evidence seems to have been badly shaken in cross-examination can sometimes—albeit rarely—be restored by re-examination. The points put to the witness must arise out of the cross-examination; unlike cross-examination, which is unlimited save in the respects indicated above.

11.4.7—*Opening statement for the respondent*

The advocate for the respondent should not make an opening statement unless he thinks it is really necessary. If a list of issues has been agreed before the hearing, and has not been significantly changed by the time the respondent's case begins, in many cases little or no opening statement will be necessary.

11.4.8—*Closing submissions*

The final submissions by the advocates are important for a number of reasons. First, the final submission is the first and only opportunity that each party has for putting before the arbitrator his comments upon the evidence taken as a whole, and upon the case finally presented by the opposing party. Second, it should help the arbitrator to see the shape of each case as finally presented. Third—though too few arbitrators take the opportunity—it enables the arbitrator to clarify his mind by a dialogue with each advocate in turn as to what the crucial issues really are, and as to how, if at all, any doubt that the arbitrator has about accepting a particular argument may be dispelled.

If an arbitrator intends to remain silent whilst final submissions are being made to him, there is little point in their being made orally; they can be made in writing, first on behalf of the respondent, then on behalf of the claimant.

11.5—How an arbitration hearing differs from a court hearing

11.5.1—*Depends on the arbitrator and the case*

The extent to which an arbitration hearing differs from a court hearing depends on the personality of the arbitrator and the nature of the case. The arbitrator *can* make the hearing almost as formal as a court hearing. In a major dispute involving witnesses of fact and expert witnesses, with the parties represented by counsel, it is difficult to stray far from the way in which a court hearing is conducted without leaving all concerned floundering as they try to guess what will happen next. But the normal pattern is for a valuer arbitrator to discuss with each party-appointed valuer in turn the various matters at issue. Their evidence will be contained in the written submissions each has lodged, and each can "cross-examine" his opposite number, that is, can put questions to him about statements he has made in his written submissions. The order of events may or may not follow that set out in paragraph 11.4.1 above.

11.5.2—*Representation by a valuer acting as both advocate and witness*

Representation by a lawyer—usually a barrister—is the norm in a court hearing. It is much less common in arbitration. Many valuers are wholly competent to conduct a hearing without legal assistance; this never happens in court.

11.6—How a solicitor prepares for an arbitration hearing

The following is a list of how a solicitor should prepare for an arbitration hearing:

(a) Read the lease.

(b) Check that the notices (including counter-notices if any) comply with the requirements of the lease as to both form and contents.

(c) Read any advice that has hitherto been given by the client's valuer.

(d) If no valuation advice has been taken, discuss with the client the need for it and the choice of valuer.

(e) Check that insofar as any valuation advice expressly or impliedly takes any view as to the law, that view is correct.

(f) Identify the issues between the parties.

(g) If the law is doubtful, discuss with the client whether an opinion should be taken from counsel.

(h) If no arbitrator has yet been appointed, discuss with the client and the valuer the choice of arbitrator, and try to agree it with the other party's representative.

(i) If the client has the right to apply for the appointment of an arbitrator or independent expert, discuss with the client when to apply and whether the application should contain any request for the appointment of an arbitrator with particular qualifications, *e.g.* in out-of-town superstores.

(j) Obtain the draft proof from the client's valuer, and take the client's instructions on it. If it has already been decided to instruct counsel on the hearing, send the draft proof to counsel and arrange a conference/consultation with the client, valuer and counsel's clerk.

(k) If directions have not been issued, discuss them with the valuer (and counsel if instructed or to be instructed). If directions have been issued, consider whether any amendment of them is desirable and if so discuss with the valuer (and counsel if instructed or to be instructed). Thereafter seek to agree the amendments with the opposing solicitor.

(l) Attempt to agree, or cause the valuers to agree, the comparables and the way in which the comparables are to be put before the arbitrator/expert.

(m) Finalise (with counsel if instructed) the proofs of the valuer and of any other witness if any, get the client's approval, and exchange with the other side.

(n) Peruse the other side's proofs, reconsider the issues between the parties, discuss with the client's valuer (and counsel if instructed or to be instructed), and decide whether any attempt should be made to agree the issues with the other side.

(o) Obtain the client's valuer's comments on the other side's proof(s). If counsel is instructed or to be instructed, send the comments to him.

(p) If any proofs or cross-representations are outstanding, arrange a conference with the client, valuer, any other expert witness, and with counsel if he is instructed, to finalise them.

(q) Exchange cross-representations and send copies to all concerned for comment.

(r) If counsel or other advocate is to be instructed, draft and deliver the brief. If you are yourself to conduct the client's case at the hearing, draft as detailed and orderly a brief as if you were instructing someone else.

11.7—How a valuer prepares for a hearing without lawyers

11.7.1—*Similar to a documents only arbitration*

The initial stages of preparation for an arbitration with a hearing differ little from those for an arbitration on documents only. Initial representations, containing the valuer's description of the property and its features, the comparables, and his valuation, are exchanged with the opposing valuer. Whether cross-representations are exchanged depends on the arbitrator's directions. Certainly, the representations should be exchanged to the point where the issues between the parties are identified and, if necessary, clarified.

But if there is to be a hearing a certain amount of clarifying the details can be dealt with during it.

11.7.2—*Analysing the issues*

The valuer should next analyse the issues appearing from the representations into:

    (a)   issues of law;
    (b)   issues of fact; and
    (c)   issues of expert opinion.

11.7.3—*Is a point of law involved?*

As to issues of law, the valuer should make a conscious decision that:

    (a)   he is satisfied that no point of law arises;
    (b)   he is not sure whether or not a point of law arises—in which case he should consult a lawyer, who may be a solicitor or barrister;
    (c)   a point of law arises, but that he is capable of dealing with it himself without legal assistance; or
    (d)   a point of law arises of such importance that he should advise his client to hand over the conduct of the arbitration to a solicitor or barrister, and thereafter act as expert witness only.

11.7.4—*Issues of fact*

It is only in simple cases that a valuer should undertake to continue to manage the case and thereby undertake to identify the issues, interview the appropriate witness(es), take statements, and lead each witness through examination/re-examination. These functions are pre-eminently those of a solicitor or barrister.

11.7.5—*Issues of expert opinion*

The main difference that a hearing makes to the valuer is that he must prepare himself for a rigorous inquiry into the basis, particularly the factual basis, for the opinions and valuations expressed in his submission and cross-submission, or implicit in them. He should check and re-check the statements of fact in his representations, and also check carefully the statements of fact expressed in or implied by his opponent's representation.

11.7.6—*Evidence of comparables*

A vital part of the valuer's preparation is to ensure that proper evidence of every transaction in a comparable on which his valuation is based is before the arbitrator. The usual way of putting such evidence before the arbitrator is to obtain a letter from a principal (landlord or tenant) engaged in the transaction or from a person who was personally engaged in it and who knows of all the factors affecting it (*e.g.* whether there were any side letters making the transaction different from what it seems to be). If efforts to persuade the opposing valuer to admit such a letter in evidence fail, the safe course is to call as a witness the writer of the letter. All that he need be asked in evidence in chief is whether, from his own knowledge, he can say that the statements made in the letter are true.

Chapter Twelve: Evidence in a Rent Review

12.1—What is evidence?

12.1.1—*The broad definition*

In the broadest sense, evidence is any material which is logically relevant to the correct determination of whatever question has to be answered. In this general sense, therefore, the availability and quality of the evidence is crucial at all stages of the rent review procedure. The landlord will need to consider the evidence before he can quote a figure, and the tenant will need to consider the evidence before he can agree it or make a counter-proposal.

In trying to agree a rent, the parties will be guided primarily by their respective views of the rental level the evidence supports. If the question has to be resolved by an independent expert he will need to seek out and analyse, with the benefit of his knowledge and experience, the evidence which tends to support a particular figure of rental value. If the matter goes to a hearing the arbitrator is bound to decide upon the evidence put before him.

There are strict rules as to what evidence is admissible in a court of law. Most of them are soundly based on principles of justice or common sense, and are therefore relevant, at least by analogy, at all stages of the rent review process, even if the final determination will be made not by an arbitrator but by an expert.

The rules are too detailed to be examined here.[1]

12.2—Kinds of evidence

In the context of an arbitration, evidence may be tendered in one of the following forms:

    (a) Documentary evidence.
        This may consist of leases, licences, planning permissions, or correspondence between the parties concerning matters relevant to the arbitration.

[1] They are discussed in section 7–4 of the Handbook of Rent Review; and in parts 3 and 8 of the Handbook of Arbitration Practice (Bernstein and Wood; 2nd ed. 1993).

(b) Evidence from witnesses of fact.

At a formal arbitration hearing this evidence would usually be given orally, often upon oath. Where the arbitration is by written representations the evidence might be in the form of statements signed by witnesses. Whatever the procedure, evidence can be given on oath in the form of a statutory declaration. If a hearing is to be held the arbitrator may direct that the person making the sworn statement should attend to be cross-examined upon its contents.

(c) Opinion evidence from expert witnesses.

The form of such evidence is the same as for witnesses of fact, although there are special rules which will be considered later.

(d) "Real" evidence, that is to say matters which are apparent upon an inspection or view, or are otherwise to be demonstrated by physical evidence (*e.g.* a sample of concrete from the building might be put before the arbitrator to illustrate the use of defective materials in its construction).

(e) Plans and photographs.

(f) Agreed or admitted facts.

In practice, in most rent review arbitrations the parties will have agreed most of the facts including, usually, the basic facts of the comparables relied upon by each party. The arbitrator is bound and entitled to accept facts which have been formally agreed for the purposes of the arbitration and need not enquire into them further.

12.3—Obtaining the evidence

12.3.1—*What is discovery?*

Discovery is a procedure whereby a party to an action or an arbitration may be ordered to disclose to the other party information or documents in his possession or control, relevant to the issues in the action or arbitration, which may help the other party in his case. The order may be for general discovery, *i.e.* all relevant documents, or for specific discovery, *i.e.* specified documents, or documents of a specified class.

12.3.2—*The power but not duty to order discovery*

An arbitrator has statutory power to order discovery.[2] But he is not obliged to do so. General discovery is rare in rent review arbitration. But specific discovery is often ordered.

---

[2] Under s. 12 of the Arbitration Act 1950.

12.3.3—*The procedure for obtaining discovery*

A party who knows, or believes, that the opposing party has or may have documents which will help his case can apply to the arbitrator for a direction that the opposing party should disclose either a specified document or documents, or a document or documents of a specified class. Thus in an arbitration about the rent of premises on an industrial estate, the tenant might apply for discovery of any documents relating to a particular letting, or he could ask for discovery of documents relating to any letting on the industrial estate in question which had taken place within, say, the previous two years.

12.3.4—*Privilege against disclosure*

Some documents in the possession of a party are said to be privileged; that is, the party cannot be compelled to disclose them.

12.4—Subpoena ad testificandum or duces tecum

A direction for discovery of documents can only be made against a party to the arbitration. Thus, it is of no assistance where the evidence to be put before the arbitrator is not in documentary form, or where there is documentary evidence which is in the possession of a third party. In either of these cases the party wishing to put in the evidence may apply to the High Court for a writ of subpoena. A *subpoena ad testificandum* requires the person named to attend to give evidence. A *subpoena duces tecum* requires the person to attend and to bring with him certain specified documents.

12.5—Expert evidence

Expert evidence is of crucial importance in rent review arbitrations; very often there is little or no dispute of fact and the only issue to be resolved by the arbitrator is the opinion of value which he should reach on the basis of those facts. Expert evidence is, accordingly, essentially opinion evidence, although the opinions expressed will be based upon a large number of facts, either agreed or put in evidence. Opinion evidence may only be given by experts, that is to say persons who, by virtue of their qualifications or experience, are able to express an opinion on the technical or valuation questions in issue.

In litigation in court, elaborate provision is made with regard to expert evidence. In most rent review arbitrations such complications are largely avoided by the standard directions issued by arbitrators, which provide for the exchange of written submissions or proofs of evidence and counter-submissions or replies, as well as statements of agreed facts and agreed schedules of comparables.

12.6—"Without prejudice" negotiations

The law recognises that it is in the public interest that parties to a dispute be encouraged to compromise their disputes. They will be less likely to offer to settle if what they say or write can be used against them in evidence if and when the dispute comes to be determined by a judge or arbitrator. For this reason, all negotiations, written or oral, which are made in the course of a genuine attempt to compromise a pending dispute are taken to be "without prejudice" to the position of the negotiating parties, with the result that neither party may use those negotiations as evidence in the case or arbitration. Often the parties will make it clear that they intend to invoke this privilege by expressly agreeing that a certain meeting is to take place on a "without prejudice" basis or by marking the relevant correspondence "without prejudice". This practice is desirable but not necessary. The "without prejudice" privilege can be waived, but only with the consent of both parties. This rule has led to the adoption of the "without prejudice save as to costs" (or *Calderbank*) procedure which is discussed in more detail in Chapter Fourteen. If the result of the "without prejudice" negotiations is that a final and binding agreement is reached, the dispute is at an end, and evidence of the "without prejudice" negotiations may be put before the court or arbitrator to show that a binding compromise has been reached.

12.7—Post-review date evidence

After much controversy as to the extent to which evidence of transactions taking place after the relevant review date could be put in evidence, several cases, in particular *Segama N.V. v. Penny le Roy Limited*[3] have clarified the position thus:

    (a)   Evidence of comparable transactions which took place before or after the review date is admissible in evidence, although the arbitrator must make adjustments to take account of any rise or fall in rental values between the rent review date and the date of the comparable in question, whether that took place earlier or later than the review date. The more distant in time from the review date, the less likely the comparable is to be a reliable guide

[3] (1984) 269 E.G. 322.

to value. The courts have not sought to draw any distinction between open-market lettings, and agreed rent reviews, in this regard, but arbitrators' awards, and (perhaps) experts' determinations will normally be inadmissible—see paragraph 12.8 below.

(b) By contrast, events (as opposed to transactions) which took place after the review date are to be ignored, because they are irrelevant. Thus, if the Chancellor of the Exchequer were to announce a major new tax on property one week after the relevant review date, the effect which that announcement had on rental values would be ignored, but not, of course, any effect which anticipation of that announcement might have had if the rent had been agreed on the review date.

However, to the extent that a transaction after the review date has been affected by an event after the review date, evidence of the event is admissible as part of the context of that particular transaction.

(c) Events such as that described in the example above taking place before the review date might, of course, have an effect on rental values, and it is for the arbitrator to assess what that impact would have been.

12.8—Use of arbitrators' awards as evidence

Until recently, awards of arbitrators in other rent review disputes were often used as comparable "transactions", although it was usual to give them much less weight than open market transactions or agreed rent review settlements. However, it has now been decided[4] that (partly because they infringe the rule against "hearsay" evidence) arbitrators' awards in other arbitrations are inadmissible and therefore cannot (without both parties' consent) be used as evidence in the subject arbitration. At the time of writing it is unclear how far this principle applies to experts' determinations in other reviews, but it is highly arguable that it applies both to them and also to rental awards by County Court Judges in Landlord and Tenant Act 1954 renewals.

---

[4] By Hoffmann J. in *Land Securities Plc v. Westminster City Council* [1992] 2 E.G.L.R. 15. The Civil Evidence Bill currently (September 1995) before Parliament proposes to abolish, in civil proceedings, the prohibition against "hearsay" evidence. If the Bill is enacted in its present form, the problem discussed in this paragraph is likely to become of little practical importance in rent review arbitrations. See also the proposal for a new Arbitration Act, mentioned in n. 73A above.

Chapter Thirteen: The Award or Determination

13.1—The arbitrator's award

13.1.1—*Form of the award*

A few leases contain some provision for the form of an award. In all other cases, there are no requirements as to form. But the award in a rent review arbitration may have effect for many years after it is made, and it may be or become important to many other people who are not parties to it. Examples are a mortgagee of the landlord's or tenant's interest, a purchaser of either interest, a purchaser's mortgagee, or a guarantor. The award should, therefore, be self-explanatory.

To achieve this:

    (a)   it should be in writing;
    (b)   it should identify clearly
        (i)   the arbitrator,
        (ii) the parties to the arbitration,
        (iii) the lease, under-lease or other document under which the arbitration took place, and
        (iv) the premises whose rent is being determined;
    (c)   it should briefly identify the circumstances in which the arbitrator came to be appointed, *e.g.* by agreement of the parties, or by the President of the R.I.C.S. or the I.S.V.A.;
    (d)   it should *always* be signed and dated.

It is often convenient if it also identifies the valuers (if any) who have submitted representations to the arbitrator.

13.1.2—*The award must be certain*

It is preferable, though it may not be legally essential, that the award be certain on the face of it. An award that "the rent payable as from June 24, 1995, be increased by 10 per cent over that previously payable" may be valid if there is no dispute as to what rent was previously payable. But it is much better to say: "I determine and award that the rent as from June 24, 1995, be £11,000 per annum."

13.1.3—*Interim or final*

The award should be final unless the arbitrator has decided to issue an interim award, in which case he should clearly state that the award is an interim one. As to making an interim award which is final as to all matters except costs, see paragraph 14.3.2 below.

13.1.4—*Reasons and other contents*

See the R.I.C.S. Guidance Notes, paragraphs 3.8.9 and 3.8.10 in Appendix III, page 190 below.

13.1.5—*Publication of the award*

The award is "published" when the arbitrator has informed both parties that it is available to be taken up. Time for appealing or seeking to have the award remitted or set aside for misconduct[1] runs from this date, not the date when the award is released to the parties.

13.2—The independent expert's determination

13.2.1—*Form of the determination*

What has been said in paragraph 13.1.1 above, about the form of the arbitrator's award, applies equally to the form of the determination of a valuer acting as an expert. In particular, he must bear in mind that the determination may affect persons who are not parties to the review, and should therefore be self-explanatory apart from the expert's reasons for arriving at his figure.

13.2.2—*Reasons or no reasons*

Unless the lease or some other agreement of the parties requires that he give reasons, a valuer acting as an independent expert is under no duty to give reasons for his determination, and normally he should not give them. This is, however, not an invariable rule. For example, where there is a difficult point of law which greatly affects the amount of his determination, he may think it desirable to state his decision on the point of law, and his reasons for deciding it as he has, leaving the disaffected party to pursue legal remedies if it thinks it has any.

---

[1] See Chapter Fifteen, generally.

13.2.3—*Dealing with points of law*

As to points of law arising in the course of a review by an independent expert, see the R.I.C.S. Guidance Notes paragraph 4.5.3 in Appendix III, page 207 below.

13.3—An independent expert's power to award costs

A valuer appointed as an independent expert has no power to make any order as to the costs incurred by the parties, or as to payment of his fees, save insofar as such power is expressly conferred upon him by the terms of the lease under which he is appointed, or by some other agreement of the parties. It follows that, in the process of determination of rent by an independent expert, there is no room for the *Calderbank* offer procedure often used in arbitration, see paragraph 14.3.2 below, unless the parties expressly agree that there should be.

Where the lease provides for determination by an independent expert, and does not give him power to award costs, it is often sensible for the parties to agree either that the valuer shall have such power, or that they should appoint him as an arbitrator. Before doing the latter they should bear in mind that a rent which is not determined by the procedure specified in the lease will not necessarily bind persons who have not agreed to change the review procedure.

Chapter Fourteen: Costs and Fees

14.1—The duty to deal with costs

An arbitrator has both the power and the duty to deal with the costs: both his own fees and the costs incurred by the parties.[1] He has not fully performed his duties until he has decided who should bear the cost of his fees and disbursements, and the costs incurred by the parties—how much is to be paid or how such a sum is to be assessed. However, the arbitrator can (and often does) make an interim award (final save as to costs) which, as its name suggests decides all matters except costs, leaving that to be dealt with in a subsequent award. Such an interim award decides finally the matters with which it deals.

14.2—Principles on which the discretion as to costs is to be exercised

By section 18 of the Arbitration Act 1950, costs are at the discretion of the arbitrator. Although the discretion is wide, it is a judicial discretion and must be exercised according to rules of reason and justice, not according to the private opinion of the arbitrator, or from notions of benevolence or of sympathy.[2]

14.3—The effect of a *Calderbank* offer

14.3.1—*What is a Calderbank offer?*

A *Calderbank* offer is a firm offer to settle the proceedings or part of them, made in terms having the effect "without prejudice except as to costs". It is so called after the name of the case in which the practice was first approved by the courts.[3]

---

[1] See the Arbitration Act 1950 s.18(1) and (4).
[2] See Section 7-10 of the Handbook, paras 3.10.4 of the Guidance Notes and section 25 of the Handbook of Arbitration Practice (2nd. ed.).
[3] *Calderbank v. Calderbank* [1975] 3 All E.R. 333. The views expressed *obiter* by Cairns L.J. were later approved by the Court of Appeal in *Cutts v. Head* [1984] 1 All E.R. 597.

14.3.2—*Payment into court, sealed offer, and Calderbank offer*

A defendant who wishes to protect himself against having to pay the costs of litigating a money claim against him is entitled to make a payment into court of the sum that he is willing to pay. If he does so, the issue between the parties becomes: is the plaintiff entitled to recover more than that sum?[4] Under the Rules of the Supreme Court, provided the payment in is made at least 21 days before the trial begins, the plaintiff may, without the leave of the court, accept the sum paid in, with any interest that has accrued on it, and may thereafter tax his costs up to the date of acceptance[5] and recover them from the defendant. So the mere fact of payment into court of a sum of money amounts to an offer to the plaintiff of:

(a)   the sum itself;
(b)   interest that may accrue on it; and
(c)   taxed costs up to the date of giving notice of acceptance.

If the plaintiff does not accept the payment, and the sum awarded to him (excluding interest and costs) is less than the amount paid in, then he will be ordered to pay the defendant's costs from the date of payment in, unless there are circumstances connected with the case that justify the making of some other order.

The judge who tries a case is not told that any payment into court has been made, until after he has decided all questions other than costs. It is not practicable in arbitration to conceal facts from the arbitrator in the same way. So the practice has grown, in arbitration, of making a *Calderbank* offer, that is, a letter of offer, whose existence and contents are to be concealed from the arbitrator until he has decided all matters except costs. To make this practice effective, an arbitrator should always ask the parties, before he makes his award, whether they would like him initially to make an interim award, final on all matters except costs.

14.3.3—*Where there is no Calderbank or open offer*

The present practice in rent review arbitration appears to be broadly thus:

(a)   if the amount awarded is that contended for by a party (a rare result) the arbitrator awards that party the costs;
(b)   if the amount of his award is very much nearer that contended for by one party he makes a fractional award of costs in favour of that party; and

---

[4] See *Findlay v. Railway Executive* [1950] 2 All E.R. 969, Somervell L.J. at p. 971.
[5] See Rules of the Supreme Court, Ord. 22.

(c) in all other cases he makes no order as to costs, save as to the
payment of his own fees and expenses.

14.4—Award of costs by an expert

14.4.1—*No power unless expressly conferred*

Many rent review clauses expressly provide that the expert shall determine
who shall bear the fees that he charges. Some go further, and give him power
to determine who shall bear the costs incurred by the parties. The powers of
an expert are limited to those conferred upon him by the parties. Unless the
lease, or some agreement outside the lease, gives him power to make an
award of costs, he has none—not even power to decide who shall bear the
costs of employing him. If after appointment he asks the parties whether
they wish to confer such power on him, they often agree to do so.

14.4.2—*Is the expert acting as arbitrator as to costs?*

Where an expert is given power to make an order as to costs, whether as to
his own fees only or as to his own fees and the costs incurred by the parties,
it is arguable that in deciding such questions he is acting as an arbitrator
rather than as an expert. Certainly it is prudent for him to assume that he has
some of the responsibilities of an arbitrator.

14.4.3—*Directions by an expert as to costs*

Since it is standard practice in determinations by an expert for the expert
to receive submissions from the parties, it is also standard practice for him to
indicate to the parties the procedure to be adopted, see the R.I.C.S. Guidance Notes paragraph 4.3.3.[6]

14.5—Assessing the amount of costs to be paid

14.5.1—*Carrying into effect the order for costs*

Although it is open to an arbitrator to award costs in the form of a money
sum, this is often inconvenient. First, it should rarely be done without giving
the parties an opportunity to make submissions as to the amount. Second,
the party who is to receive the costs often wants time to make a more or less

---

[6] Appendix III, p. 203 below.

detailed account of his costs. The more usual course, therefore, is for the arbitrator merely to award that party R. pay to party P. his costs (or a fraction of his costs) of the arbitration (or of a specified section of the arbitration proceedings, (*e.g.* the costs of an adjournment which in the arbitrator's opinion has been necessitated by the fault of party P.) and pay the arbitrator's fees and disbursements (or a fraction of them). The next stage is for party R. to formulate his claim for costs, and to invite party P. to agree it. Where solicitors are acting for both parties, they more often than not agree upon the amount. But if they cannot agree, there is a dispute which has to be resolved. In a heavy case the amount of issue as to costs can be substantial. The process of resolving this dispute is called "taxation of costs".

14.5.2—*Arbitrator determines method of taxation*

Section 18(1) of the Arbitration Act 1950 gives the arbitrator a discretion to direct not only who should make a payment to whom in respect of costs, but also how the amount is to be assessed. By S.I. 1986 No. 1632 there are now two possible bases of assessment: the standard basis and the indemnity basis. If the arbitrator makes an award of costs without indicating the basis of taxation, the standard basis will apply.

14.5.3—*Difference between the two bases*

In either case the receiving party is entitled to be paid "a reasonable amount in respect of all costs reasonably incurred".

On the standard basis, any doubts as to whether the costs were reasonably incurred or were reasonable in amount shall be resolved in favour of the paying party; whereas on the indemnity basis any such doubts shall be resolved in favour of the receiving party.[7] The usual practice in a rent review is to award costs on the standard basis unless there is a particular reason from departing from the usual practice.[8] Examples of such reasons are where:

(a) a party has been found guilty of fraud or gross impropriety either in the events out of which the proceedings arise or in the proceedings themselves;

(b) a party or his representative has, by dilatoriness, greatly increased the costs of the other party; or

(c) a hearing has to be adjourned through the inexcusable fault of a party or those acting for him.

[7] See R.S.C., Ord. 62 r.12.
[8] *Preston v. Preston* [1982] 1 All E.R. 41.

14.5.4—*Who should tax the costs—courses open to the arbitrator*

An arbitrator's order as to costs will not be enforceable until it specifies how the amount to be paid is to be "taxed", *i.e.* assessed. The most usual methods of assessment are by the arbitrator himself, or by the High Court. Where solicitors have been heavily involved, the latter method will usually be preferable. Otherwise taxation by the arbitrator will be quick, effective, and relatively cheap.

If the arbitrator does not direct some other form of taxation, the costs will be taxed in the High Court.

Chapter Fifteen: Control by the Court of Arbitrations

15.1—The two jurisdictions

The courts have powers to control arbitrations under two separate statutory jurisdictions. The first is the power to remit or set aside an award, or remove an arbitrator, under the Arbitration Act 1950. The second is the jurisdiction conferred by the Arbitration Act 1979 to hear an appeal on a question of law arising out of an award.

The courts have no power to interfere where the complaint is that the arbitrator has made an error of fact. Nor is it necessarily enough that he has made an error of law, for there is no right of appeal without leave, and leave will only be given in the limited class of cases indicated below. But the courts will, in appropriate cases, intervene where there has been an error of procedure (sometimes called "procedural mishap") which has led, or might have led, to an unjust result.

Control by the court of a determination by an expert is discussed in Chapter Sixteen below.

15.2—Control of arbitration awards under the Arbitration Act 1950

15.2.1—*Power to remit or set aside award*

Under section 22 of the Arbitration Act 1950, the court has a general power to remit any reference to arbitration to the reconsideration of the arbitrator. Under section 23 of the Arbitration Act 1950, the court has power to remove an arbitrator, or to set aside an award, where an arbitrator or umpire has misconducted himself or the proceedings. The powers conferred by these sections are very wide. What the court is primarily concerned with under this jurisdiction is whether the procedure that has been or is being followed is unacceptable as being in breach of:

(a)   the provisions of the Arbitration Acts;
(b)   the terms of the contract (usually in rent review, the lease); or
(c)   the rules of natural justice.

It is not necessary to show that the award was wrong. The power of the court to interfere with an award on the grounds that it is wrong have been severely limited by restrictions imposed by the Arbitration Act 1979, and the Court of Appeal has said that the jurisdiction under section 22 of the Arbitration Act 1950 is not to be used as a back-door method of circumventing those restrictions.[1]

15.2.2—*Cases in which the courts will intervene*

The cases in which the jurisdiction has been exercised in the past may be grouped under six heads:

(a) The arbitrator had no jurisdiction.

(b) The award is defective on its face. If on one possible interpretation the award is valid, the court will prefer that interpretation to one that would make the award defective.

(c) There is a mistake in the award (going beyond a mere clerical mistake or error) admitted by the arbitrator.

(d) Misconduct. The courts have always refused to give an exhaustive definition of what constitutes "misconduct": the word is used to cover a range extending from fraud or other grave malpractice at one extreme to a mere procedural error at the other.

(e) "Procedural mishap" where, through some misunderstanding, a party has failed to put the whole of his case before the arbitrator or has been unaware of material put before the arbitrator by his opponent.

(f) Fresh evidence. Just as the court will sometimes set aside a judgment if fresh evidence is found which could not with reasonable efforts have been put forward at the trial of an action, so it will, in a proper case, set aside an arbitration award in similar circumstances.

15.3—Appeals under the Arbitration Act 1979

15.3.1—*The statutory right of appeal*

A limited right of appeal is given by sections 1(2) and 2(1) of the Arbitration Act 1979. As interpreted by the courts those sections may be summarised thus:

(a) No appeal may be made to the court if the parties have made a

---

[1] *Moran v. Lloyds* [1983] 1 Lloyd's Rep. 472.

valid "exclusion agreement", *i.e.* an agreement excluding the right of appeal.

(b) A valid "exclusion agreement" may be entered into:

    (i) by any parties, if it is made after the dispute to which it relates has arisen;

    (ii) by parties of whom at least one is a national of, or habitually resident in any state other than the United Kingdom, or is a body corporate which is incorporated in, or whose central management and control is exercised in any state other than the United Kingdom, at any time whether before or after a dispute has arisen between them.

Where there is no valid exclusion agreement:

(c) No appeal may be made to the court except on a question of law arising out of an award.

(d) No appeal may be brought, even on a question of law, unless *either* all parties consent, *or* the court grants leave.

(e) The court cannot grant leave unless it considers that, having regard to all the circumstances, the determination of the question raised could substantially affect the rights of a party.

(f) In commercial cases the court will not grant leave if the point of law is "one-off", *i.e.* a point unlikely to arise in other cases, unless the decision of the arbitrator is obviously wrong.

(g) In commercial cases, even if the point of law is likely to arise in other cases, the court will not grant leave unless it considers that there is a strong prima facie case that the decision of the arbitrator on the point is wrong.

(h) The decision on whether to grant leave should be arrived at after brief argument only.

(i) In rent review cases there is no real equivalent to the standard printed forms of contract commonly incorporated into commercial contracts. Moreover, a decision of the court as to the legal effect of the rent review clause will be relevant to future reviews under the same lease, as well as to similar provisions in other leases.

(j) Even in rent review cases the judge should approach the application for leave with a bias towards finality, that is to say a bias towards upholding the arbitrator's award. So before leave will be given there must be a "strong" prima facie case that the arbitrator was wrong.

(k) If the court considers that the award fails, adequately or altogether, to set out reasons in such details as may be necessary to consider the question of law raised in the appeal, it may order the arbitrator to state further reasons.

If no reasons were given, the court will not order the arbitrator to give reasons unless:

(a) before the award was issued one of the parties gave notice to the arbitrator that a reasoned award would be required: or

(b) there is some special reason why such notice was not given.

There are restrictions, in section 1(6A) and (7) of the Arbitration Act 1979, on the right to appeal to the Court of Appeal against a judgment of the High Court given on an application under the section.

Chapter Sixteen: Control by the Court of the Determination of an Expert

16.1—There is no statutory right of challenge

The Arbitration Acts do not apply to determinations by experts. So little of what has been said in Chapter Fifteen applies. The concepts of "misconduct" and "procedural mishap" are not directly relevant. So if an expert, immediately after appointment under a lease which is silent as to procedure, were to issue his determination without asking the parties if they wished to make any representations to him, it is doubtful whether his determination would be set aside.[1] Likewise, there is no right of appeal as such, and the complicated questions as to when leave to appeal will be given do not arise. Nor is there any obligation upon the expert to give reasons for his determination.

16.2—When the court will set aside the determination of an expert

There are some circumstances in which the court may set aside an expert determination. They include:

(a) where his determination is tainted by fraud, collusion or corruption;

(b) where his determination goes beyond the jurisdiction conferred upon him by the contract;

(c) where his determination, or the way in which it was reached, contravenes some clear provision of the contract; and

(d) possibly, where he has arrived at his determination by a process which breaches the principles of natural justice.

---

[1] Acting in this way would not be in accordance with the R.I.C.S. Guidance Notes; see Section 4.2 in Appendix III below p. 201.

16.3—The principles of natural justice may apply

There is no authority on the questions whether the principles of natural justice apply to the determination of an expert. In general, those principles apply to the performance of a judicial or quasi judicial function, and a determination by an expert is neither judicial nor quasi judicial. But it is suggested that the procedure that he adopts may be such as to bring the principles into operation. Thus, if he announces that he will consider representations from the parties, and receives them from one party, but then makes his determination before the time limited for them has expired, and before the other party has delivered his representations, his award would probably be set aside.

16.4—Expert has no immunity from actions for negligence

The principle that a person discharging a judicial or quasi-judicial function is not liable for negligence does not apply to a person undertaking a valuation as an expert. But although he is not immune from being sued, the mere fact that his decision is not the "right" one is not of itself even evidence of negligence. The nature of valuation is such that there is necessarily a bracket of "right" figures; see *e.g.* the judgment of Phillips J. in *Banque Bruxelles Lambert S.A. v. Eagle Star Insurance Co. Ltd*[2].

---

[2] [1994] E.G. 68.

Chapter Seventeen:
Consequences of the Review

17.1—Memorandum of award or determination

Once a binding agreement as to the reviewed rent has been reached, or the arbitrator has made his award, or the expert has given his determination, the review process has, strictly speaking, been completed and the reviewed rent becomes payable in accordance with the lease. No deed of variation or other document under seal is required to give effect to it. However, many rent review clauses provide that the parties shall sign a formal rent review memorandum recording the fact that the rent has been agreed or determined at a particular figure.

17.2—Effect of the review as between the parties

Many leases provide that if the amount of the reviewed rent is not known by the review date, rent will continue to be paid at the old rate, but the reviewed rent will be payable retrospectively as from the review date, and the shortfall between the rent paid and the reviewed rent will become due and payable on the quarter day next following the review. Others make it payable as soon as the reviewed rent has been ascertained. In the absence of an express provision dealing with the matter, it appears that the obligation to pay the increased rent arises on the quarter day following the agreement or publication of the arbitrator's award, see *South Tottenham Lands Securities Limited v. R. & A. Millett (Shops) Limited*.[1] Most modern leases provide that interest shall be payable upon the shortfall at a stipulated rate.

17.3—Effect of the review on original lessee and sureties

The persons who are the landlord and the tenant at the date of review are not the only people who may be affected by it. If, since the lease was granted, there has been an assignment of the term, the original lessee nonetheless remains liable to pay the rent during the whole of the term (though not during any statutory extension of it),[2] his liability arising by privity of

---

[1] [1984] 1 W.L.R. 710.
[2] See *City of London v. Fell* [1994] 2 E.G.L.R. 131.

contract.[3] A surety, that is to say somebody who has guaranteed the obligations either of the original lessee or a subsequent assignee, is in a similar
position. Despite the fact that these third parties are vitally affected by the
amount of rent which the tenant agrees upon review, it is uncommon for
rent review provisions to allow the original tenant or any of the sureties to
take part in the rent review process. Nor is it usual for their position to be
safeguarded in any other way. One rare exception is to be found in the case
of *Cressey & Ors. v. Jacobs*,[4] where the rent review clause stated that the rent
could only be reviewed by agreement "between the parties". This was held to
include a surety, who had been one of the parties to the original lease, so that
any agreement made without his consent was not binding.

Whether an original tenant or surety is bound by an "irregular" review,
that is to say a review which is not operated in strict accordance with the
terms of the clause, is doubtful, see *e.g. Haslemere Estates v. British Oli-
vetti*.[5]

17.4—Effect of the review on future reviews

Issue estoppel is a principle which prevents a party to a dispute from
raising a point which has already been decided against him in previous
litigation. For example, if a landlord and a tenant had raised in court
proceedings the question whether a particular use of the premises was
permitted under the lease, and the court had ruled against the tenant, he
would not be able to defend subsequent forfeiture proceedings on the basis
that his use of the premises was permitted; the effect of the previous decision
would be to estop (*i.e.* debar) him from again raising that issue.

The doctrine also applies to rent review arbitrations. The arbitrator's
decision on, say, the first review on any specific issue of law raised before him
will be binding on the parties on all future reviews. But the limits of the
doctrine should be noted. First, it will only apply to an issue of law; the
decision of an arbitrator on a specific set of facts will not bind a future
arbitrator even if the facts before him are the same. Second, the doctrine will
only apply where the point has been specifically raised and has been the
subject of a specific decision by the arbitrator. Thus, where it is unclear
whether the point was really raised by the parties at all or where it is unclear
precisely what the arbitrator's decision on the point was—perhaps because
he did not give reasons for his award—no estoppel will arise. The House of
Lords has also held that, in very exceptional circumstances, no estoppel will
arise where it can be shown that the original decision was clearly wrong in
law, see *Arnold v. National Westminster Bank*.[6]

---

[3] See para. 2.2.6.
[4] (1977) unreported decision digested in the Handbook.
[5] (1977) unreported decision digested in the Handbook.
[6] [1991] 2 W.L.R. 1177.

Appendices

Appendix I: Glossary of Frequently Used Terms

Assign, assignment, assignor, assignee

The remaining term (or "residue") of an existing lease or tenancy may only be transferred to another person by a formal deed:

— the deed is called an assignment;

— the person who transfers it is the assignor; and

— the person to whom he assigns it is the assignee—for some purposes he may be called an assign.

Capitalisation

Valuer's treatment of a rental or other income payment to represent its capital equivalent.

Comparable

A comparable transaction is one which is considered to be, in some way, similar to, or capable of being usefully compared with, the subject matter of a valuation so as to provide evidence of the value of that subject matter. The phrase "comparable transaction" is often abbreviated to "comparable".

Covenant, implied covenant

A covenant is an express contractual obligation by a party to a lease or under-lease. The word covenant is inaccurately, but commonly, applied to a contractual obligation contained in a tenancy agreement which is not under seal and is therefore not a lease.

A few—very few—covenants are implied by law where a tenancy is created informally.

Decapitalisation

Valuer's treatment of a lump sum or capital payment to represent its income or rental equivalent.

Demise

A word, now archaic, meaning the grant of a leasehold interest.

Demised premises

The premises demised by a lease or under-lease.

Forfeit, forfeiture

Almost every lease and tenancy agreement contains a clause giving the lessor or landlord the right to bring it to a premature end if the lessee or tenant fails to comply with his covenants or obligations. The right to terminate is called a right of forfeiture, and the lessor or landlord who exercises the right is said to have forfeited the lease or tenancy.

Ground rent

A rent which is less than a rack rent (defined below), usually because the lessee undertakes some particularly burdensome obligation such as erecting a new building, or carrying out some extensive building operations.

Land

In English law anything built on or fixed to land becomes part of the land. So, *e.g.* a flat on an upper floor of a tower block is as much part of the land as are the foundations on which the block is built, or an underground garage beneath it.

Landlord, tenant, tenancy

Where a person entitled to the possession of land (which for this purpose includes buildings or anything fixed to the land) agrees expressly or by implication to allow some other person to have exclusive possession and use of the land either for a fixed period, or for a period automatically renewable, *e.g.* weekly or monthly or quarterly or annually:

— the person first mentioned is called a landlord;

— the other party to the agreement is called a tenant;

— the arrangement is called a tenancy; and

— if it is in writing, the agreement is called a tenancy agreement.

Leasehold, leaseholder

A word used to describe the interest of a lessee (see above).

Lessor, lessee, lease

If the agreement in embodied in a formal sealed document:

— the landlord may alternatively be called the lessor;

— the tenant may alternatively be called the lessee;

— the document is called a lease; and

— the interest granted is also called a lease.

Peppercorn rent

A notional rent where, in substance, no rent is payable by reason of the nature of the obligations undertaken by the lessee. It is nowadays more usual for the lease to reserve a low rent, so that the lessor keeps some form of contact with the lessee for the ultimate benefit of the reversion.

Premises

An imprecise word, technically meaning "what has gone before", but usually used to mean "the property the subject of this lease" (or "the property the subject of this tenancy").

Premium

Lump sum or capital payment made by tenant to landlord in consideration of the grant of a lease, where the rent will be less than a full (rack) rent and the term is a significant number of years.

Privity of Contract, Privity of Estate

See paragraphs 2.2.6 *et seq.*, page 14.

Rack rent

A rent equal to the full market rental value of the premises at the beginning of a lease, if offered for letting on the terms of the lease.

Rent

A periodic payment, usually in money, payable by a tenant to his landlord in return for his right to occupy the land.

Reverse premium

Lump sum or capital payment made by landlord to tenant to persuade him to take a lease, usually where market conditions for letting are poor, and/or the rent to be paid is above market level.

Reversion, reversioner

When a grantor has, by a lease under-lease or tenancy agreement, granted to another the right to possess and enjoy the land for a period shorter than the period for which the grantor is entitled to possess and enjoy it, he retains the right to possess and enjoy the land when the term for which he has granted the lease or tenancy ends. This right is called his reversion, and he is called the reversioner. If he is himself a lessee or tenant, his reversion may be as short as one day. But there can be no relationship of landlord and tenant without some reversion.

Stepped rent

A rent which rises by pre-determined amounts over a period.

Sub-lessor, sub-lessee, sub-lease

If the landlord is himself a tenant:

— the agreement is called a sub-tenancy;

— the tenant is called a sub-tenant;

— the landlord may for some purposes be called an inferior landlord; and

— the landlord's landlord may for some purposes be called the superior landlord.

If the landlord is himself a sub-tenant:

— the agreement is called a sub-sub-tenancy, and so on.

If the grant is embodied in a formal sealed document and the grantor is himself a lessee or tenant:

— the grant is called a sub-lease or under-lease;

— the document is also called a sub-lease or under-lease;

— the grantor is called the sub-lessor or under-lessor (though he may also be called the landlord—he is never called the sub-landlord); and

— the grantor is called the sub-lessee or under-lessee (though he may also be called the sub-tenant or just the tenant).

"Term"

This may mean *either* the interest granted by a lease *or* the duration of such an interest, *e.g.* 15 years. "The residue of the term" means the unexpired period of the interest granted by a lease.

"Time of the essence"

See paragraph 3.3.2

Appendix II: A Typical Shop Arbitration—a Worked Example

This worked example has been constructed to show a valuer's file that might come into existence in the course of a typical rent review of a High Street shop. The specimen letters should not be treated as precedents.

Setting the scene

14 High Street, Anytown is a ground floor lock-up shop in a small parade. It was let by the freeholders, Property Investments Limited, to Mr Andrew Tennant by a lease dated March 25, 1987 for a term of 21 years. The lease provides for upwards-only reviews at seven-yearly intervals. The rent review clause is in conventional terms, providing for review to "open market rental value" as there defined. The rent review machinery is as follows:

"The open market rental value shall be assessed as follows:

(i) it shall be such an amount as is proposed by the landlord in a notice in writing served on the tenant at any time before the rent review date; or

(ii) it shall be such alternative amount as the parties may agree before the expiration of three months after service of the said notice; or

(iii) it shall be such amount as is determined at the election of the tenant (to be made by a counter-notice in writing served by the tenant upon the landlord within the said three-month period) by an arbitrator appointed on the application of either party by the President of the Royal Institution of Chartered Surveyors, such arbitration to be conducted in accordance with the provisions of the Arbitration Acts 1950 and 1979."

It is further provided in the lease that "all stipulations as to time in the foregoing provisions shall be of the essence of the contract and shall not be capable of enlargement save by agreement in writing between the parties".

For the first review due at March 25, 1994 Property Investments Limited is represented by its in-house surveyor, Mr J. Snooks, A.R.I.C.S., and Mr Tennant is represented by a local agent, Mr M. Tonks.

The following are extracted from Mr Tonks' file.

The landlord's trigger notice specifying proposed rental figure

September 29, 1993

Dear Sir

Re: 14, High Street, Anytown

On behalf of your Landlords, Property Investments Limited, I hereby give you notice pursuant to clause 3 of the lease, dated March 25, 1987, that the amount of the open market rental value of the premises proposed by them to take effect as from the first review date, namely March 25, 1994, is £20,000 per annum.

Yours faithfully,

J. Snooks, A.R.I.C.S.
Deputy Estates Surveyor

Tenant's agent's initial response

WITHOUT PREJUDICE
SUBJECT TO CONTRACT
October 4, 1993

Dear Sir

Re: 14, High Street, Anytown

I have been instructed by Mr A. Tennant to act on his behalf in relation to the rent review due as at March 25, 1994.

I note the figure of £20,000 per annum specified in your letter of September 29, 1993 which I assume to be a negotiating figure. It certainly far exceeds my own opinion of rental value. Perhaps we could meet within the next week or so to discuss comparables and to reach a preliminary agreement as to the measurements of the subject property. Please ring this office to discuss arrangements.

Yours faithfully,

J. Tonks
Copy: A. Tennant, Esq.

Landlord's surveyor's reply

WITHOUT PREJUDICE
SUBJECT TO CONTRACT[1]
October 9, 1993

Dear Mr Tonks

Re: 14 High Street, Anytown

This is to confirm our arrangements made over the telephone to meet at the premises on October 14 at 08.30 to see if we can agree measurements.

It might help you to know that the figure of £20,000 was quoted on the basis of three recent transactions in which the landlords have been involved in this parade. They are:

(a)   the rent review determination by an independent expert at 12 High Street;

(b)   the open market letting of 36 High Street; and

(c)   the assignment at a premium of the lease of 37 High Street.

I enclose on a separate sheet[2] details of those transactions, together with my analysis of them.

I look forward to meeting you.

Yours sincerely,

J. Snooks, A.R.I.C.S.
Deputy Estates Surveyor

The tenant's surveyor's letter proposing a settlement

WITHOUT PREJUDICE
SUBJECT TO CONTRACT

October 27, 1993

Dear Mr Snooks

14, High Street, Anytown

I am glad that we were able to agree the measurements of the shop at our

---

[1] It is, strictly speaking, unnecessary for this to be written on every letter, since Mr Tonks' letter has already established that the correspondence (and indeed any oral discussions) will be on a without prejudice and subject to contract basis. Repeating the formula here emphasises the point and acts as a reminder to both parties.

[2] Not reprinted here.

recent meeting and to discuss details of the comparables, including the two which I put forward at 4 and 17 High Street.

I now have my client's instructions to offer to settle this review at £14,5000 per annum. If that is acceptable to the landlords, perhaps you can let me have a formal memorandum for signature by my client agreeing the rent at that figure. If not, the matter will have to be referred to arbitration.

Yours sincerely,

J. Tonks
Copy: A. Tennant, Esq.

[**Note:** *The landlords reject the offer and put forward their own compromise figure of £17,500. This is not acceptable to Mr Tennant.*]

Counter-notice served on behalf of the tenant electing for arbitration

December 5, 1993

Dear Mr Snooks

Re: 14 High Street, Anytown

Please treat this letter as a formal counter-notice on behalf of my client, Andrew Tennant Esq., electing under the terms of clause 1(c) of his lease dated March 25, 1987 to have the amount of the new rent payable as from March 25, 1994 determined by an arbitrator pursuant to the Arbitration Acts 1950–1979.

Please acknowledge receipt of this letter.

Yours faithfully,

J. Tonks
Copy: A. Tennant Esq.

[**Note:** *In order to protect his client's right to go to arbitration, Mr Tonks has served a formal counter-notice on his behalf. It was vital that he should do so within the three-month period specified in the rent review machinery, because time is expressly made "of the essence" of this limit. If the notice had been served out of time, even by a day, the right to seek arbitration would have been lost and Mr Tennant would have been bound to pay the figure of rent specified in the original trigger notice, unless he was able to obtain an extension of time from the court under section 27 of the Arbitration Act 1950. Such an extension would not*] *necessarily be granted by the court and the making of such an application would have involved a waste of time and expense.*

The counter-notice has not been marked "without prejudice". There is at least a risk that so marking it would lead to the consequence that the counter-notice would be invalidated. (The marking "subject to contract" would also be inappropriate and confusing if attached to a counter-notice), see paragraph 3.6.2 above.

Letter from the landlord's surveyor inviting agreement on identity of arbitrator

Dear Mr Tonks

Re: 14 High Street, Anytown

On behalf of my client, Property Investments Limited, I acknowledge due receipt of your client's counter-notice dated December 5, 1993.

Since your client has elected to go to arbitration, I am concerned that the appropriate procedures should be put into operation promptly. I suggest that it is in the interests of both parties that this rent review should be settled as soon as possible.

I therefore propose for your agreement the following three persons, each of whom would be equally acceptable to my client as arbitrator:

(a)   J. Soap F.R.I.C.S., 8 The Parade, Anytown;
(b)   W. Z. Solomon F.R.I.C.S., The Market House, Othertown; or
(c)   A. Snodgrass, 5 Railway Cuttings, Anytown.

I trust that you will find at least one of these names acceptable, and, if so, perhaps you would let me know accordingly. If not, could you please propose some alternative names for my consideration.

Yours faithfully,

A. Snooks, A.R.I.C.S.

Letter from the tenant's surveyor agreeing to appointment of Mr W.Z. Solomon, F.R.I.C.S. as arbitrator

December 15, 1993

Dear Mr Snooks

Re: 14 High Street, Anytown

Thank you very much for your letter proposing three names for appointment as our arbitrator. I am prepared to agree to the appointment of Mr W.Z. Solomon, F.R.I.C.S., who is known to me.

I am as anxious to save time as you are, and accordingly enclose for your comments and approval a draft letter which I propose we send jointly to Mr Solomon. Perhaps we could discuss this over the telephone.

Yours sincerely,

J. Tonks
Copy: A. Tennant Esq.

Joint letter to the prospective arbitrator

December 21, 1993

Dear Mr Solomon,

Re: Rent review dispute at 14, High Street, Anytown

This letter is written jointly by J. Snooks, A.R.I.C.S., estate surveyor to Property Investments Limited, the landlord of the above property and J. Tonks, the surveyor acting for A. Tennant Esq., the tenant.

The lease of the above property provides for a rent review as at March 25, next. We have been unable to reach agreement upon the amount of the reviewed rent, and have agreed to invite you to act as arbitrator.

We enclose a brief description of the property, a summary of the principal lease terms, and the rent review provisions extracted from the lease.[3] If you would like any further information before deciding whether you are willing to accept appointment, please let us know. Equally, before confirming your appointment, the parties would like to know your proposals as to fees.

We would be obliged if your reply to this letter could be sent to both of the signatories.

Yours sincerely,

J. Snooks, A.R.I.C.S.
J. Tonks

[3] None of which are reprinted here.

Letter from Mr Solomon, F.R.I.C.S., accepting appointment as arbitrator

Gentlemen

<u>Re: 14 High Street, Anytown</u>

Thank you for your joint letter of December 21, 1993. I have considered the relevant matters set out in the R.I.C.S. Guidance Notes, including those relating to potential conflicts of interest, and find none.

Some years ago I acted for Mr Peregrine Tennant, who I believe to be an uncle of Mr A. Tennant, in a dispute concerning a right of way over his farm outside Othertown. I do not think that this previous connection with another member of the Tennant family prevents me accepting appointment as your arbitrator, but I think it right to draw the fact to your attention.

As to the other matters mentioned in the R.I.C.S. Guidance Notes, I hereby confirm:

(a)　that the subject matter of the dispute falls within the sphere of my own normal professional practice;

(b)　that I am able to undertake the task with reasonable expedition;

(c)　that there is no other reason why I should not accept the appointment; and

(d)　that there are no special requirements of the lease with which I do not comply.

I am, therefore, willing to accept your invitation to act as arbitrator. My fees would be as set out on the attached sheet. On the assumption that they can be agreed, I would suggest that, as the next step, you should each write to me formally confirming my appointment.

Yours faithfully,

W.Z. Solomon, F.R.I.C.S.

Letter to Mr Solomon formally appointing him as arbitrator

January 10, 1994

Dear Mr Solomon

Re: 14 High Street, Anytown

Thank you for your letter of January 6, 1994. I do not consider that the previous connection with Mr P. Tennant described in your letter gives rise to any conflict of interest on your part, and on behalf of Property Investments Limited I formally confirm your appointment.

We await your directions.

Yours sincerely,

J. Snooks, A.R.I.C.S.

[**Note:** *The letter from Mr Tonks, in similar terms, is not reprinted here.*]

Letter proposing a preliminary meeting

January 14, 1994

Gentlemen

Re: 15 High Street, Anytown

Thank you for your letters formally appointing me as your arbitrator. I would find it helpful to hold a short and informal meeting at these offices to discuss what procedures to adopt.

In particular, it is necessary to consider:

(a) whether the dispute is one of value only, or whether there are disputes of another nature, such as legal or factual disputes, and if so, how best they are to be resolved; and

(b) whether the arbitration can be conducted on written submissions only, or whether there is any reason to hold an oral hearing.

My secretary will ring your secretaries to arrange the meeting. Any communications from each of you to me should be in writing and should be copied to the other party.

Yours faithfully,

W.Z. Solomon, F.R.I.C.S.
Arbitrator

The Arbitrator's letter to parties' representatives following the preliminary meeting

Gentlemen

<u>Re: 14 High Street, Anytown</u>

At the recent preliminary meeting attended by both parties, it was agreed that this matter should be determined by written representations. As discussed at that meeting, and with the consent of both parties, I now therefore direct as follows:

(a) As many facts as possible and in particular floor areas in terms of zone A and plans in respect both of the subject property and of any comparable property intended to be referred to in either party's written representations shall be agreed between the parties and their agreement recorded in a statement signed by each party.

(b) Unless both parties otherwise agree, no negotiations, whether or not contained in correspondence marked "without prejudice", shall be referred to in any way in the representations.

(c) Written representations, in duplicate, are to reach me by [March 30, 1994]. When I have received these from both parties, I will transmit the duplicate copy to the other party. Each party should then inform me not later than five working days after receiving it whether there is any objection to my reading the other party's representations. If I receive any such objection by that date, I will consider further how to proceed. If I receive no such objection by that date, I will read each party's representation.

(d) Each representation shall be made by a named surveyor and shall contain that surveyor's honest opinion of the rental value of the subject premises in accordance with the terms of the rent review provisions of the lease.

(e) Cross-representations, in duplicate, are to reach me 14 days after receipt of the opposing party's representations. Cross-representations should not include any evidence other than evidence in rebuttal of the opposing party's representations. When I have received both parties' cross-representations, I will transmit the duplicate copies to the opposing party. I will allow a further period of three working days, for the purpose of objections in the manner indicated above, before reading the cross-representations myself.

(f) Particulars of any comparable transaction included in any representations, or (by way of rebuttal) in any cross-representation, should contain the following details:

(i)   a brief description of the property, its age and its construction;

(ii)   the names of the parties and their representatives (if any);

(iii) a brief description of the amenities and ancillary services;

(iv) the agreed floor areas in terms of zone A;

(v)   the nature of the comparable transaction, *e.g.* whether it is a new letting or a rent review settlement;

(vi) the date of the lease, the date specified for commencement of the term, and the length of the term;

(vii) full details of all terms and conditions in the lease which might have an effect on rental value;

(viii) the rent review period or pattern;

(ix) any other circumstances or features of the transaction which might be relevant to its proper analysis; and

(x)   the figure which has been agreed in the open market or upon rent review.

Unless the said details, in respect of the comparable transaction in question have been agreed between the parties to this arbitration, the person making the representation should certify that he has personal knowledge of that transaction and can confirm those details, or should submit a signed statement to that effect from some other person who has such personal knowledge.

I reserve the right to call an oral hearing if at any stage it appears that it is necessary or appropriate to do so, and each party is at liberty to apply to me for any further directions required.

Arrangements will be made at some convenient time and date in the future for me to inspect the subject property and (insofar as necessary) the comparable properties, accompanied by representatives of both parties.

Yours faithfully,

W.Z. Solomon, F.R.I.C.S.
(Arbitrator)

Respondent's *Calderbank* letter.

February 22, 1994

Dear Mr Snooks

Re: 14 High Street, Anytown

I am just about to start preparing my submission for delivery to the arbitrator but, in order to avoid any further unnecessary costs, I am instructed by my client, the respondent, to make the following offer to settle the dispute which is the subject of the arbitration. My client proposes that:

(a)   the rent as from March 25, 1994 be agreed at £ 16,500 per annum; and

(b)   each party bear its own costs to date, together with one half of the arbitrator's fees and charges.

This offer is open for 21 days from your receipt of this letter. Thereafter it is withdrawn.

This offer is made without prejudice, save as to costs, with the intention that it may be referred to the arbitrator on the question of costs, after he has dealt with all matters other than costs, but not otherwise.

Yours sincerely,

J. Tonks
Copy: A. Tennant

Written representations on behalf of the tenant

IN THE MATTER OF AN ARBITRATION

BETWEEN:

PROPERTY INVESTMENT LIMITED   *Claimant*

–and–

ANDREW TENNANT   *Respondent*

RE: 14 HIGH STREET, ANYTOWN

WRITTEN REPRESENTATIONS of James Arnold Snooks, A.R.I.C.S. on behalf of the Claimant.

(a) *The Valuer preparing this submission*

My name is James Arnold Snooks. I work in the Estates Department of Great Property Holdings PLC, the parent company of the Claimant. The Estates Department's address is Greater Property House, The New Business Park, Southchester.

(b) *Qualifications and expertise*

I have a degree in Estate Management from Reading University, having graduated in 1987.

I am a Professional Associate of the Royal Institution of Chartered Surveyors.

From 1988 I was an Assistant Surveyor in the Property Department of Sundry Estates Limited, a company with a mixed portfolio of residential, office, industrial and retail premises. My main experience at that time was in the evaluation for acquisition of industrial property.

In 1991 Sundry Estates Limited was taken over by Greater Property Holdings PLC, when I moved to my present position in its Estates Department. I was put in charge of the management of the retail property within the portfolio of the Claimant. In that position, I have been responsible for, amongst other things, the negotiation of new lettings of numerous shop properties, together with various lease renewals, and a number of rent reviews. This recent experience, although concentrated upon the retail sector, is geographically widespread. Although the subject property is the Claimant's only property-holding in Anytown, the Claimant's portfolio includes property in most provincial towns in England, including a number of properties in the centre of Othertown.

141

Within my responsibilities is the management of the subject property, 14 High Street, Anytown, which is held under the terms of the Lease dated March 25, 1987 and made between the Claimant as Landlord and the Respondent as Tenant.

As I was aware that a Rent Review was due as at March 25, 1994 I served a Notice on behalf of the Claimant on the Respondent, specifying a rent of £20,000 per annum. This figure was not acceptable to the Respondent, whose Agent, Mr Tonks, duly served a Counter-Notice on his behalf calling for Arbitration. In the course of preparing this Submission pursuant to your Directions, I have carefully inspected and measured the subject property with Mr Tonks and have done the same in relation to each of the Comparables. I should note here that I have visited the property about a dozen times since taking over my present responsibilities in 1991, on two of which occasions I have carried out a detailed inspection.

(c) Location of Property

(i) **Specific** The subject property is located in the middle of a Parade of lock-up shops with separate self-contained residential flats above, occupying the block numbered 2–30 (even), High Street.

(ii) **General** As the Arbitrator will be aware, Anytown is a thriving market-town with a population of 155,000 according to the most recent figures. There is a British Rail Station on the western periphery of the town on the main line between London and Birmingham. The town is particularly well served by road connections, and the recent completion of the new by-pass has alleviated the traffic congestion which historically has affected the town-centre.

(iii) **Maps and Plans** I have agreed with Mr Tonks, and have included as part of the Statement of Agreed Facts, a general location plan and a retailer's plan of the town-centre. On the latter plan the subject premises has been outlined in red and each of the Comparables has been edged in green. That part of the High Street which is pedestrianised has been coloured yellow.

(d) Description of Property

The subject property consists of the ground floor retail part of a three-storey building standing in the middle of a Parade built in the mid-1930s. The shop-front was installed by the present Respondent. This was a replacement of the existing shop-front and, although the new shop-front falls to be disregarded as a tenant's improvement, I have agreed with Mr Tonks that, for the purposes of the present review, the subject property should be valued on the basis that the old shop-front still exists. The Arbitrator should accordingly note that the agreed floor plans included in the Statement of Agreed Facts show the old, not the existing, shop-front and entrance. As is expressly stated in the Statement of Agreed Facts, Mr Tonks and I have agreed that there are no other tenant's improvements to be disregarded.

Floor-areas have been agreed as recorded in the Statement of Agreed Facts. For convenience, I summarise that agreement here:

Frontage: 26 ft;
Depth: 37 ft;

All measurements in the Agreed Statement of Facts are in accordance with the current R.I.C.S./I.S.V.A. Standard Code of Measuring Practice.

(e) Lease Terms

A copy of the Lease dated March 25, 1987 has already been supplied to the Arbitrator and a further copy has, for the sake of convenience, been included in the Statement of Agreed Facts.

The principal terms are as follows:

[**Note:** *Mr Snooks here recites the principal terms of the lease, such as the original parties, the date, the term, the rent and the rent review pattern. He quotes in full that part of the rent review clause which contains the valuation formula (but not the rent review machinery) and any specific clause which in his view, affects the valuation. Clauses which are not considered to have a specific effect on value should not normally be quoted in full. They might be mentioned (if at all) thus:*

> *"The alienation provisions permit assignment or sub-letting of the whole of the subject property with the Landlord's consent which is not unreasonably to be withheld. Assignment or sub-letting of part only is absolutely prohibited. Similar alienation provisions are contained in each of the comparables and I consider them to be in the form that I would expect in a Lease of a High Street shop. They have no specific effect on value."*]

I have no reason to believe from my general discussions with Mr Tonks that there is any difference between us as to the true interpretation or legal effect of any of the Lease terms, but if any difference should emerge from my consideration of his Representations, I reserve the right to return to this matter in my Counter-Representations.

There are no sub-lettings or other matters relating to the title which might have an effect on the value of the subject property.

(f) Town Planning

The permitted use of the subject property is as a retail shop within Class A1 of the Town and Country Planning (Use Classes) Order 1987.

I am not aware of any redevelopment proposals or other matters which might have a bearing upon a valuation of the premises as at the review date, except the partial pedestrianisation of the High Street under the temporary scheme which came into effect in January 1992 and which was made permanent shortly after the review date in April 1994.

(g) Repair

Although there are some minor disrepairs of a cosmetic nature affecting the appearance of the Parade as a whole, I have ignored this in my valuation, since the Lease is a full-repairing Lease.

(h) Factors affecting Value

I now list the principal factors which, in my view, affect the valuation of the subject property under the terms of the Rent Review provisions of the Lease. These are as follows:

(i) the location of the premises in what I consider to be near the "prime pitch" in the High Street, opposite Marks & Spencer;

(ii) the pedestrianisation of this part of the High Street;

(iii) the proximity of the subject property to the intersection of High Street and Main Street;

(iv) the convenient shape of the subject property;

(v) the strength of the retail market in Anytown as at the review date, as indicated by the Comparables; and

(vi) the beneficial review pattern.

(i) Comparables

The factual details of all the comparable transactions have been agreed and are set out in the Agreed Statement of Facts. For convenience, I now set out, in tabular form, my analysis of each of those Comparables, arranged in date-order of transaction.
[TABLE THEN FOLLOWS]

I now comment on each of the Comparables in turn, adopting the same order as in the above Table.

[**Note:** Mr Snooks' detailed commentary on the comparables is extensive, and is not reproduced here.]

(j) Comments on Other Party's Case.

I will, of course, comment in detail upon Mr Tonks' Representations in my Counter-Representations, but I believe it would assist the Arbitrator if I were here to set out what I understand to be the principal areas of difference between us:

(i) Mr Tonks does not believe the subject property to be in as good a location as 10 High Street, and he believes its position to be no better than that of 37 High Street. I believe that this view gives insufficient weight to the presence (opposite) of Marks & Spencer and greatly underestimates the importance of the pedestrianisation scheme which comes into force in April 1994. Accordingly, I attach considerable weight to 10 High Street as providing direct evidence of the rental value appropriate to the subject property and would uplift significantly the value achieved at 37 High Street before applying it to the subject property.

(ii) Mr Tonks has suggested that there are considerable deficiencies in the layout of the subject property which justify a substantial discount. I disagree. The layout of the subject premises seems to me, on the contrary, to be ideally suited to the purposes of any hypothetical tenant who would use the subject property for retail purposes. Even if Mr Tonks were correct, the layout of the subject property is identical to that of all the Comparables situated within the same Parade and I do not see how it can possibly be argued that the other Comparables do not themselves suffer from excessive depth with consequent lack of flexibility.

(iii) Mr Tonks apparently considers that the market has fallen significantly between the date of the majority of the Comparables (December 1991) and the valuation date. I disagree and exhibit as Appendix "JAS1" to these Representations an extract from Messrs J.L. Wallis's Retail Survey of the United Kingdom to demonstrate that this view is mistaken.

(iv) I understand that Mr Tonks argues that no addition to the base value is justified because of the beneficial Rent Review pattern in view of the allegedly depressed state of the market. I believe that,

145

on the contrary, there was an expectation of rapid improvement in market conditions which fully justify my 10 per cent addition.

(k) Valuation

Accordingly, I present my valuation of the subject property in accordance with the terms of the Rent Review provisions of the Lease as at March 25, 1994 as follows:

... sq ft ITZA @ £ ... =	£ ....
Uplift for rent review pattern (10%)	£ ....
Total:	£ ....

I certify that the above valuation fully and truly represents my honest opinion of rental value and I ask the Arbitrator to award accordingly.

(Signed)

J.A. Snooks, A.R.I.C.S.

Dated: March 29, 1994

[**Note:** *In the normal course of the arbitration Mr Tonks would, of course, have put in his own full written representations to which Mr Snooks would have replied in his counter-representations. Mr Tonks would also have put in counter-representations.*]

Letter from the arbitrator after exchange of counter-representations

Gentlemen

Re: 14 High Street, Anytown

Having exchanged counter-representations and received no objections, I am now in a position to prepare my award. Neither party has asked me to give reasons for my award and I do not propose to do so, since it seems to me that the issues which are raised are matters of valuation involving no point of law.

As requested by both parties, I will make an interim award, final save as to costs. This will enable the parties either to agree how the costs should be borne once my interim award has been published, or to make further submissions to me on costs, thus enabling me to deal with that issue in a final award.

Yours faithfully,

W.Z. Solomon F.R.I.C.S.
Arbitrator

Interim award (final save as to costs)

IN THE MATTER OF AN ARBITRATION

BETWEEN:

PROPERTY INVESTMENT LIMITED   *Claimant*

–and–

ANDREW TENNANT   *Respondent*

WHEREAS:

INTERIM AWARD

(1)   I, WILLIAM ZEBEDEE SOLOMON, F.R.I.C.S., was appointed by agreement of the parties hereto as Arbitrator to determine a dispute arising as to the amount of rent payable pursuant to the terms of a Lease dated March 25, 1987 and made between the Claimant as Landlord and the Respondent as Tenant.

(2)   The Claimant and the Respondent by their respective representatives have put before me an Agreed Statement of Facts and have respectively made Representations and Counter-Representations in accordance with Directions by Consent which I made on February 15, 1994.

(3)   I have inspected the subject property and the Comparables referred to in the Agreed Statement of Facts and the Representations.

(4)   I have carefully considered all the evidence and arguments put before me.

NOW THEREFORE I, WILLIAM ZEBEDEE SOLOMON, F.R.I.C.S., Arbitrator, do Award and Determine as follows:

(1)   That the rent payable pursuant to the terms of the rent review provisions of the said Lease as from March 25, 1994 is the amount of £16,000 per annum.

(2)   That my fees and charges of and arising out of this reference to Arbitration are hereby taxed and settled by me in the sum of £1,050 plus Value Added Tax thereon.

This is my Interim Award, Final on all matters save Costs. I hereby give liberty to either party to apply to me as to the costs order which should be included in my Final Award.

(Signed)   (Date)

William Zebedee Solomon, F.R.I.C.S.
Arbitrator

148

Letter to both parties informing them the interim award is ready for collection

Gentlemen

Re: 14 High Street, Anytown

This is to inform you that I have now completed and hereby publish my interim award herein, which is final on all matters, save as to costs.

It is available at these offices upon payment of my total fees and charges which I have taxed and settled in the amount of £1,050 plus VAT. A formal VAT invoice is enclosed.

I invite the parties to write to me making submissions as to costs, alternatively informing me of how they have agreed that the question of costs should be dealt with in my final award.

Yours faithfully,

W.Z. Solomon F.R.I.C.S.
Arbitrator

Letter from the tenant's agent to the landlord's surveyor concerning costs

Dear Mr Snooks

Re: 14 High Street, Anytown

You have now no doubt had time to consider the arbitrator's award herein.

May I remind you that I submitted a *Calderbank* offer on behalf of my client on February 22, 1994 which was not accepted. In view of the arbitrator's award in the lesser figure of £ 16,000 I take the view that my client is entitled to be awarded his costs of the arbitration. I understand that your client has already paid the arbitrator's costs and charges in full upon taking up the interim award.

I invite your agreement to the above, and suggest that we write to the arbitrator informing him that the question of costs has been agreed and that there is no need for him to make a formal final award.

Yours sincerely,

J. Tonks
Copy: A Tennant Esq.

Letter from the landlord's surveyor replying to tenant's agent on costs

Dear Mr Tonks

Re: 14 High Street, Anytown

Thank you for your letter on the question of costs. I am reluctantly forced to agree that my client should pay your client's costs *as from the date of expiry of your Calderbank letter*. I cannot agree, however, to pay all your client's costs as you appear to be suggesting. Please inform me whether you are prepared to agree with my proposal and submit a note of any further costs incurred by your client from the relevant date. I hope that we can agree the proper amount of these, so as to avoid a further taxation by the arbitrator.

If this can be agreed between us, then we can write jointly to the arbitrator telling him that he need take no further action.

Yours sincerely,

J. Snooks, A.R.I.C.S.

And that is what happened . . . . .
And so came to an end this Typical Shop Arbitration.

Appendix III: Guidance Notes for Surveyors acting as Arbitrators or as Independent Experts in Rent Reviews

Sixth Edition

Note

These notes are R.I.C.S. Guidance Notes and not an R.I.C.S. Statement of Standard Practice. The R.I.C.S. accepts no liability for any use to which these Guidance Notes may be put. The law of Arbitration continues to evolve both as a result of statutory changes and case law. These Notes give guidance as at the date of publication and will be revised from time to time.

The Royal Institution of Chartered Surveyors reminds members that when they have been properly appointed to act as an Arbitrator, because of the very limited rights of appeal by the parties, they are vested with powers which are in some ways greater than those of a High Court Judge. Before accepting any such appointments, they must therefore be satisfied that they have a sufficient knowledge of the practice, procedures, the law of Arbitrations, the subject matter of the dispute and perhaps the locality to ensure that they are able to assess the relevance and quality of the evidence presented to them by which they arrive at their decision and Award.

It is equally important that a member invited to accept appointment as Expert should satisfy himself that he has sufficient knowledge and expertise to accept the appointment since the parties' rights of appeal are even more limited.

© R.I.C.S. April 1993

R.I.C.S. Guidance Notes (Sixth Edition)

4-5 THE DETERMINATION OF THE INDEPENDENT EXPERT

5-1 GENERAL COMMENTS

Guidance Notes

1-1 PART ONE: GENERAL INTRODUCTION

1.1.1. *Scope of Guidance Notes*

These Guidance Notes, together with a Commentary on them, are printed in the *Handbook of Rent Review* by Bernstein and Reynolds (1993 Revision).

They are designed primarily to assist those who are appointed either by the President of the R.I.C.S., or directly by the parties to a dispute, to act as Arbitrators or as Independent Experts.

They are also intended to assist the parties themselves and those acting for them by making them aware of the procedures likely to be followed, but these pages are not intended to be regarded as a treatise on the law and practice of arbitration generally. These Notes are based upon the law and practice in England and Wales; Scottish law and practice are somewhat different.

The majority of appointments made by the President are in landlord and tenant matters, notably rent review. Accordingly these Guidance Notes were specifically prepared for rent review Arbitrations and Independent Expert appointments to determine rents. Some of the procedures included in the Notes, and the principles of natural justice, apply to all arbitrations.

As regards agricultural holdings, however, it should be borne in mind that there are separate provisions to be found in the agricultural holdings legislation, concerning which the appropriate publications should be consulted.

While these Notes will provide adequate guidance for surveyors acting as Arbitrators in the great majority of cases it must be stressed that, in some cases, the surveyor Arbitrator will need to have a wider and deeper understanding of the law and procedure than it has been considered appropriate to provide in these pages. This is particularly so in construction industry arbitrations where the subject of the dispute is more likely to concern matters such as the necessity for or manner in which work should be carried out, or concerning the payment of a capital sum, for which it is unlikely that the "written representation" procedure set out hereafter would be appropriate and an arbitration hearing conducted on more formal lines would probably apply.

Any surveyor likely to be appointed as Arbitrator in references which may involve issues of law and procedure outside his normal experience would be well advised to attend one of the courses conducted from time to time by the

R.I.C.S., the Chartered Institute of Arbitrators and the College of Estate Management.

The standard legal textbooks on the subject are *Russell on Arbitration* (2nd ed., 1989, published by Stevens and Sons); Mustill and Boyd, *Commercial Arbitrations* (2nd ed., 1989, published by Butterworths). *The Handbook of Arbitration Practice* (2nd ed., published by Sweet & Maxwell and the Chartered Institute of Arbitrators) contains, *inter alia*, a general section by Ronald Bernstein Q.C., F.C.I.Arb. and Derek Wood Q.C., F.C.I.Arb., together with a section on "Practice in Rent Review Arbitrations" by W. G. Nutley, B.Sc., F.R.I.C.S.

An Arbitrator should have access to a library containing the standard legal textbooks.

RICS GUIDANCE NOTE

Throughout these Guidance Notes, references to the masculine include the feminine.

1.1.2 *Comparison of arbitration with determination by Independent Expert*

The duties and suggested procedures for both Arbitrators and Independent Experts are in some respects the same. The differences as regards rent reviews may be summarised as follows:

Arbitrator	*Independent Expert*
a. The Arbitrator acts (as does a judge) only on evidence and arguments submitted to him and bases his decision thereon. His award must lie between the extremes contended for by the parties. He is however expected to use his expertise in assessing the relevance and quality of the evidence and arguments submitted to him—but see also paragraph 1.1.8.	a. The Independent Expert has the duty of investigation to discover the facts and/ or relevant transactions (though he may receive evidence of facts and/or transactions from the parties).
b. The Arbitrator cannot decide without receiving evidence from the parties or (when proceeding *ex parte*) one of the parties.	b. The Independent Expert must decide upon his own knowledge and investigations, but he may be required by the instrument under which he is appointed to receive submissions from the parties.
c. The procedure for arbitration is regulated by the Arbitration Acts.	c. There is no legislation governing procedure for the Independent Expert.
d. A party to an arbitration can (through the courts) compel disclosure of documents or the attendance of witnesses—see paragraph 3.6.3	d. The Independent Expert has no such powers.
e. An Arbitrator may not delegate any of his duties, powers or responsibilities (see also paragraph 2.1.5).	e. During the course of his investigations the Independent Expert may seek assistance from any other person, who can undertake tasks on the Independent Expert's behalf. However, the Independent Expert has a duty to use his own knowledge and experience in arriving at his own decision (see also section 4–3).
f. In an arbitration the Arbitrator can order one party to pay all or part of the Arbitrator's fees and all or part of the other party's fees.	f. An Independent Expert has no power to make any orders as to his fees, or as to the costs of a party, unless such a power is conferred upon him by the lease or by agreement between the parties.

Arbitrator	*Independent Expert*
g. The Arbitrator's award may be enforceable as a judgment of the court. (This is not, however, of practical importance in rent review arbitrations. Enforcement of rent review awards is by separate action for arrears of rent, or forfeiture or by distress).	g. The Independent Expert's determination cannot be enforced as such; a separate action must be brought based on it.
h. The Arbitrator's fees can be taxed by the court under the Arbitration Act—see paragraph 3.9.6.	h. There is no procedure for taxation of an Independent Expert's fees.
i. There is some (albeit limited) right of appeal against the award of an Arbitrator on a point of law.	i. There is no right of appeal against the determination of an Expert, though in some circumstances the court might set it aside.
j. The Arbitrator is not liable for negligence.	j. The Independent Expert is liable in damages for any losses sustained by a party through his negligence. This is so notwithstanding that the court will not interfere with a final and binding determination that he has made.

1.1.3 Nature of appointment: interpretation of lease or agreement

Where a lease or agreement, with reference to the appointment of a surveyor, mentions "Arbitrator" or "arbitration" or the Arbitration Acts, even though it may also make reference to a "valuer," "Independent valuer," "Expert" or other such term, it is generally treated as calling for the appointment of an Arbitrator, unless it is clear that the parties intended otherwise.

1.1.4 Doubt as to nature of appointment

The rent review clause will not always be clear as to whether the appointment is to be of an Arbitrator or an Independent Expert. The appointee should, therefore, ensure that the nature of the appointment is explicitly stated in the letter or other instrument of appointment. If it is not, he should clarify the point with the parties before he proceeds with his reference.

If there is any doubt as to the correct interpretation of the lease or other document giving rise to his appointment, the parties may agree which interpretation is correct. However, there is a danger that third parties (such as the original lessee, or a surety) will be able subsequently to dispute that agreed interpretation. In case of doubt, the parties may wish to have the question decided by the court.

1.1.5. *Umpires*

By the Arbitration Act 1950, section 8, as amended by the Arbitration Act 1979, section 7, unless a contrary intention is expressed every arbitration agreement which provides for the appointment of two Arbitrators, one to be appointed by each party, shall be deemed to include a provision that the two Arbitrators may appoint an Umpire at any time after they are themselves appointed. If they fail to agree on their award, they must forthwith appoint an Umpire. The usual procedure is for the Arbitrators to attempt to agree on their award, and if they fail they notify the Umpire in writing that they cannot agree, whereupon their functions as Arbitrators cease and the Umpire in effect becomes sole Arbitrator in their place. Moreover, once an Umpire has been appointed, the High Court may, on the application of either party and notwithstanding anything to the contrary in the arbitration agreement, order that the Umpire shall enter upon the reference in place of the Arbitrators as if he were a sole Arbitrator. The appointment of an Umpire should be discussed with the parties as there could be advantages in appointing an Umpire at the beginning of the reference to avoid hearing evidence twice but this would involve extra costs of the Umpire. In any event a stenographer should be employed if hearings take place.

1.1.6. *The statutory framework: arbitration*

The principal Act governing the conduct of Arbitrators is the Arbitration Act of 1950 as amended by the Arbitration Act 1979 and Part V of the Courts and Legal Services Act 1990. There is, of course, special legislation relating to agricultural holdings. The person appointed to act as Arbitrator must therefore have regard to the provisions of these Acts and, whatever his view may be as to the desirability of conducting the hearing with a greater or lesser degree of informality, it is important that he should be careful not to infringe any express provision of these Acts or of the arbitration agreement, lest his award be set aside or remitted. (See paragraph 3.8.11).

1.1.7. *Independent Expert free to exercise his own judgment*

There is no legislation, and little case law, governing the appointment or conduct of a surveyor to act in this capacity; the person appointed must exercise his personal professional expertise and judgment. The notes in Part 4 of these Guidance Notes should afford general guidance.

1.1.8. *Fees and costs*

Sections 3–9 and 3–10 deal with fees and costs for Arbitrators and 4.4. with fees and costs for Independent Experts.

2–1 PART TWO: APPOINTMENT AND ACCEPTANCE

2.1.1. *Application to the President for appointment*

Application to the President for the appointment of an Arbitrator or Independent Expert should be in writing and preferably made on the form obtainable on application to the R.I.C.S..

2.1.2. *Document(s) and fee on application*

The application will not be processed until the appropriate non-refundable fee has been received together with a copy of the lease or other document conferring on the President power to make the appointment.

2.1.3. *Appointee should study document under which appointment made*

Whether he has been appointed by the President or privately, the Arbitrator or Independent Expert should study in detail the lease or other document under which he is appointed so that he is clear as to the precise nature of the dispute and any special provisions that may apply.

2.1.4. *Responsibility and disqualification*

The acceptance of an appointment as Arbitrator or Independent Expert carries with it a heavy responsibility, and every effort is made by the President to select a person suitable for appointment in accordance with his current policy statement on conflict of interest (see Appendix 1).

A person considered suitable for appointment is approached and asked to confirm:

    (*a*) that the subject matter of the dispute falls within the sphere of his own normal professional practice (not merely that of his firm);

    (*b*) that he will be able to undertake the task with reasonable expedition;

    (*c*) that there is no other reason why he should not accept the appointment;

163

(*d*) that he complies with any special requirements of the lease;

(*e*) that he is not currently engaged as Arbitrator or as Independent Expert in another case where his duties and functions to the parties would conflict with his duties and functions to the parties in the case;

(*f*) that he has appropriate professional indemnity insurance.

In deciding whether he should accept an appointment the prospective appointee should take into consideration and disclose all matters which might give rise to the possibility or appearance of bias. He must disclose every matter which could reasonably be considered to create a conflict of interest. If there is any doubt as to whether a connection with the property, a party or a representative of a party might give rise to a conflict of interest it must be disclosed. The test as to what constitutes a conflict of interest is an objective one. Disclosure of a possible conflict of interest does not mean that the surveyor will not be appointed by the President. The possible conflict may be disclosed to the parties prior to appointment and their views sought. If neither party objects then the appointment will be made. Where a surveyor wilfully fails to disclose a conflict of interest, or accepts an appointment and subsequently purports to resign on the basis that instructions accepted after appointment give rise to a conflict, the President may conclude that the surveyor is not suitable for future appointments.

2.1.5. *Arbitrator may not delegate without parties' consent*

The Arbitrator acts in a personal capacity and may not without the consent of the parties delegate any of his duties, powers or responsibilities. But where problems outside the range of his expertise arise (for example, where a valuation surveyor is asked to decide issues of structural engineering) the parties will usually accept any sensible proposals he may make for obtaining the assistance of an expert in that field. As to obtaining legal advice, see paragraph 3.2.7.

2.1.6. *When appointment takes effect*

The appointment takes effect from the date on which the President *makes* the appointment.

2.1.7. *After the appointment has been made*

Once the President has made an appointment, his jurisdiction in the matter is at an end unless the lease (or, in a relatively few cases, statute) itself provides to the contrary. If, therefore, after the appointment of the Arbitrator or Independent Expert, a party should bring to the attention of the appointee a matter claimed to constitute a real pecuniary or other interest in the outcome of the dispute or to give rise to a real danger of bias, the Arbitrator or Expert would be expected to:—

    (*a*) obtain full details of the objection in writing;

    (*b*) notify the other party in writing and invite his comments;

    (*c*) consider whether the matters disclosed might affect his mind in coming to a decision or would raise a real danger of bias in the eye of a reasonably-minded person;

    (*d*) if the answer to either of these questions is yes, retire unless both parties agree in writing that he should continue;

    (*e*) if the answer to each of these questions is no, continue.

Equally, if the Arbitrator or Independent Expert should discover a matter which might affect his mind in coming to a decision, or would raise a real possibility of bias in the eyes of a reasonably+minded person, he would be expected immediately to disclose it to the parties and then proceed as in (*d*) or (*e*) above.

2.1.8. *Acceptance of private appointments*

Some leases or other documents call for appointment of a surveyor (whether to act as an Arbitrator or an Independent Expert) by a person other than the President of the R.I.C.S. Or the parties themselves may agree to appoint him. In either case it is no less important that attention should be paid to the factors listed in paragraphs 1.1.7 and 2.1.4.

PART THREE: ARBITRATORS

3.1.1 POWERS AND DUTIES OF AN ARBITRATOR

3.1.1. *Deriving from contract*

Parties who include in any agreement a clause for settling by arbitration any dispute within the scope of that clause are thereby referring those disputes to private determination rather than to a court of law. Since in most cases the Arbitrator derives his authority from the contract between the parties they can also agree, as a matter of contract, the principles and procedure which he shall apply in any dispute which may arise, provided that these do not conflict with the Arbitration or other Acts. The first rule for the

Arbitrator is therefore to look at the arbitration agreement and other sources of his authority to see what is provided.

3.1.2. *Other sources of powers and duties*

When the Arbitrator has been duly appointed, his powers and duties stem from the following:

(*a*) the Arbitration Acts 1950 and 1979 and Part V of the Courts and Legal Services Act 1990;

(*b*) the provisions of any special legislation applying to the particular subject matter;

(*c*) the terms of the arbitration agreement (*e.g.* the rent review clause in the lease or the arbitration clause of a contract);

(*d*) the principles of natural justice.

Any problems arising in the arbitration that are not provided for expressly or implicitly in the arbitration agreement or the relevant Acts are matters for the Arbitrator's discretion. This must be exercised judicially, and in accordance with the rules of natural justice. Above all, it is the duty of an Arbitrator, as it is of a Judge, to hear both sides to the dispute (except when proceeding *ex parte*—see paragraph 3.6.13.) and to decide it according to the evidence and to the law. These Notes are intended to indicate to surveyors, in relation to problems commonly arising in arbitrations, the principles on which this discretion should be exercised. In general, if there is nothing in the Acts or in the arbitration agreement to indicate the contrary, the Arbitrator should proceed in whatever way seems to him to be the fairest.

3.1.3. *Liquidators/receivers and guarantors*

Although the usual parties to an arbitration are the landlord and the tenant, a properly appointed liquidator or receiver (for either of them) may take over the relevant role. An assignor or guarantor is not a party to the arbitration. He can be called by either party as a witness. He cannot attend or present his own case unless both parties agree, or one party consents to his having the conduct of that party's case in the arbitration. In such a case the Arbitrator should satisfy himself that the assignor or guarantor is properly authorised by the relevant party. Another possibility, if the lease seems likely to be revested in an assignor in a fairly short time, is to delay the proceedings until the revesting has occurred. But the Arbitrator must balance the desirability of doing this against prejudice to the other party caused by the delay.

3.1.4. *The nature of arbitration*

Arbitration procedure, like litigation procedure, is fundamentally adversarial. Each party decides what evidence and what contentions he wishes to put before the Arbitrator. An Arbitrator, like a judge, has no duty to make investigations or to ensure that all relevant information has been put before him.

But in most rent review arbitrations the Arbitrator has been appointed because of his professional qualifications and his knowledge and experience. Justice would not be done if he were obliged to put his knowledge and experience aside. He is entitled to prefer the opinion of one valuer, apparently unsupported by comparable transactions, to the opinion of another, apparently supported, if his judgment tells him to do so. So it is open to him, if the facts warrant it, to say:

> "Although the comparables cited to me appear to support the opinion of the landlord's surveyor rather than that of the tenant's surveyor, my judgment as a valuer makes me prefer the latter. I accept the evidence of the tenant's surveyor, and I determine the rent accordingly."

But any *particular* facts within the Arbitrator's knowledge should be treated as evidence given by him and should therefore be subject to the same scrutiny and the same rules of evidence as any other evidence. Thus he should be willing to be questioned by the parties on the facts that he has communicated to them. If he gives them such opportunity for scrutiny there is no reason to exclude any material which he considers to be important.

Similarly, if an Arbitrator, because of his experience, is minded to draw from the evidence an inference different from that drawn by an expert witness, he should say so and should give the expert (or the advocate, if separate) an opportunity of dealing with the matter. In practice, if this situation arises during a hearing he should wait to see if the opposing side raises the matter, before raising it himself.

3.1.5. *The bracket of the parties' contentions*

The Arbitrator should not award more than is finally sought by the landlord nor less than is finally submitted by the tenant. Likewise he should not award more or less than is suggested by the evidence before him. He should however use his professional skill in assessing the relevance and quality of the evidence.

167

3–2 ACTION BY THE ARBITRATOR ON BEING APPOINTED

3.2.1. *Informing the parties*

On appointment it is the Arbitrator's duty to proceed without delay. He should therefore notify the parties or their representatives of his appointment, and proceed with the arbitration unless requested by both parties to defer proceedings.

3.2.2. *Establishing the Arbitrator's fees or charges*

Unless already agreed at the time of accepting the appointment, the Arbitrator should at this stage state the amount of his fees or give an indication of the basis on which he intends to charge. Where appropriate the fee should be expressed to be exclusive of disbursements, particularly any legal costs the Arbitrator may incur. See further as to fees, Section 3–9, particularly paragraph 3.9.7.

3.2.3. *The possibility of compromise*

The Arbitrator should, at the outset, enquire of the parties whether there is any possibility of their reaching a negotiated settlement and, if so, whether they wish him to defer the arbitration. Either in the initial letter, or at the preliminary meeting if any, the parties should be reminded that they are at liberty to settle between themselves at any time prior to the award, but in this event will be liable for the Arbitrator's fees and disbursements to date.

3.2.4. *Award by consent*

If the parties compromise in the course of an arbitration their agreement may either be that their dispute is resolved upon the agreed terms, or that they will agree before the Arbitrator what award he should make. Technically, if the agreement is of the former nature its effect is to deprive the Arbitrator of his authority for there is no longer any dispute between the parties. Any award which he might subsequently make would be a nullity. In the latter case, the agreement is not technically a resolution of the dispute itself, but an agreement that the Arbitrator shall decide it in a particular way. In that case it will be an "award by consent." This distinction could be of importance if a question were to arise as to whether a third party was bound by an award. For this reason an award by consent is usually preferable to a compromise not incorporated in an award. An award by consent would be an award which incorporates the agreed terms of settlement and the apportionment between the parties of costs, including the fees and expenses of the Arbitrator. Leases, being documents under seal, necessitate any amendments also being under seal. Many leases provide that a memorandum of any agreed review rent is to be endorsed on the lease and counterpart. Where however this provision does not occur, the parties may prefer that the agreed review rent is incorporated in an award by consent, since an award is a legally binding document. Such an award would avoid the (admittedly remote) possibility of future arguments between the parties and/or subsequent assignees which might arise if the agreed review rent was only incorporated in an exchange of letters.

3.2.5. *Choice between hearing or written representations*

If the parties agree, before or immediately after the appointment, that they wish to proceed by written representations without a hearing, the Arbitrator should write to each of them setting out the procedure he proposes to adopt and inviting them to agree, or to suggest different directions. Otherwise, the Arbitrator should write asking the parties whether they wish him to proceed by way of written representations or by a hearing, pointing out that if one party so requires there must be a hearing.

However in most cases a preliminary meeting with the parties following his appointment should lead to more rapid identification and clarification of the matters which it is necessary for the Arbitrator to cover in his directions (see Section 3–3).

Obviously both parties must be invited and should attend any such preliminary meeting—but see paragraphs 3.6.11 to 3.6.15 on proceeding *ex parte*.

The questions whether there is any issue of law between the parties, and if so, how it is to be resolved, will often be material to the choice between a hearing and written representations only; see paragraphs 3.2.7 and 3.2.8.

3.2.6. *Written representation procedure often appropriate*

In view of the nature of the matters likely to concern surveyors, and their particular skill in the writing of reports, the written representation procedure is often more appropriate to a rent review dispute.

Even if this procedure is decided upon, the Arbitrator should reserve the right to call for a hearing. He may consider it necessary or desirable to have a hearing if matters of fact or evidence contained in the written representations require clarification, or if the difference between the parties' respective figures is so great as to require explanation. The prospect of an opinion expressed in writing being subjected to cross-examination under oath at a hearing may act as a deterrent to the inclusion of irresponsibly high (or low) figures.

3.2.7. *Disputes involving issues of law*

Although most rent review arbitrations involve only issues of valuation, some may raise one or more points of law, such as the meaning of the rent review clause or of other parts of the lease, or the admissibility of evidence.

When a point of law is raised the Arbitrator should require the party raising it to formulate it in writing, and to send a copy to the other party. The Arbitrator should then seek to agree with the parties the exact nature of the point of law, and how it can be best resolved. The following are the main possibilities:

(*a*) The parties may enter into an "exclusion agreement," thereby leaving the point for the sole decision of the Arbitrator without there being any possibility of a later appeal to the court. In practice parties rarely agree this.

(*b*) The parties may authorise the Arbitrator to take legal advice on the point before making his award. It is desirable that the Arbitrator should seek to agree with the parties the wording of the question or questions on which he is to take legal advice. If he wishes to seek the advice of counsel he may do so direct; see the *Guidance Notes to assist Chartered Surveyors in the use of Direct Access to Barristers in England and Wales* (published by Surveyors Publications).

(*c*) The Arbitrator may, with the parties' consent, appoint a legal assessor to sit with him and hear argument.

(*d*) A case may be stated jointly by the parties for the opinion of counsel, the parties agreeing to be bound by that opinion. This would have the same effect as an "exclusion agreement."

(*e*) The point may be decided by the court as a preliminary point of law—see paragraph 3.2.8.

(*f*) The point may be determined by the Arbitrator after considering submissions from both parties, without prejudice to any rights of appeal that may exist. If this course is adopted it is usually best for the Arbitrator to make an award in the alternative, stating what he would have awarded if he had decided the point of law the other way.

If the parties do not agree or consent to any of (*a*) to (*e*) above, the only course for the Arbitrator to adopt is to proceed under (*f*).

The tendency of the courts since the Arbitration Act 1979 to discourage appeals from Arbitrators, even on points on interpretation, places upon the Arbitrator who adopts procedure (*f*) a greatly increased responsibility. In cases of this kind the Arbitrator should refer to the *Handbook of Rent Review*, Part 10, and textbooks on arbitration.

3.2.8.   *The determination of a preliminary point of law*

It is sometimes convenient and economical to have a disputed question of interpretation of the lease decided as a preliminary point, *i.e.* before any evidence on the valuation issues is called. This would be in the form of an interim award. Such cases are relatively rare because in most instances the issues of valuation and interpretation are inextricably interwoven.

Where such a request by one party is opposed by the other the Arbitrator should not grant the request unless he considers that the balance of advantage to the parties is overwhelming. In this respect he must consider the possibility that the court may give leave to appeal against his decision on the point.

As an alternative to the preliminary point being decided by the Arbitrator, it may be decided by the court under section 2 of the Arbitration Act 1979. This is only possible if (a) the Arbitrator or all the parties consent, and (b) the High Court is satisfied that the determination might produce substantial savings in costs and that the point was one where leave to appeal would be likely to be given.

3.2.9.   *Procedural differences between written representations and hearing procedure*

Once the choice has been made, the procedure thereafter will vary according to which has been chosen. Section 3–4 deals with procedure by written representations and Section 3–5 with procedure by way of hearing. The remainder of Section 3 (dealing with evidence, the Award and fees and costs) is common to both procedures.

3.2.10.   *Arbitrations on overlapping issues—powers and limitations*

Where the same or a substantially similar issue arises in a "hierarchical" situation (*e.g.* between landlord and tenant and between tenant and subtenant); or in a "parallel" situation (*e.g.* between a landlord and his tenants of a row of identical shops), and the applications for the appointment of an Arbitrator are made to the President at or about the same time, the President may decide to appoint the same person as Arbitrator in both or all cases.

171

If he does so, the Arbitrator should consider in consultation with all the parties whether a procedure for a combined hearing or combined submissions can be devised which is acceptable to all of them.

The main attraction of a combined hearing is that of consistency of results, but saving in costs will also normally result.

If the Arbitrator is appointed in two or more related cases:

(*a*) he must follow any procedural requirements laid down in any of the leases, even if these vary from lease to lease;

(*b*) he has no power to order combined hearings or submissions unless all parties consent, such consent to extend to agreeing that the Arbitrator may act in each case on all the evidence and submissions given at the combined hearing or contained in the combined submissions;

(*c*) if there are separate hearings or submissions, he must not act in one on evidence or argument not given in that arbitration. He may raise matters which have arisen in a previous arbitration or probe the evidence in the light of such knowledge, but he must not base his award on a point not argued before him (or present in submissions) in the arbitration to which his award relates;

(*d*) all cases, whether dealt with by written representations or hearings, must be given individual consideration and separate awards must be issued in respect of each.

Sometimes a party or parties may claim that the only fair way of dealing with related cases, particularly in headlease/sublease disputes on the same property, is to have combined hearings or submissions, whilst another party or parties take the opposite view. Since the Arbitrator cannot order combined hearings against the wishes of one or more parties, he must decide whether he considers that the cases can fairly be dealt with separately. It is suggested that it will nearly always be possible to deal justly with such references separately if the principles listed at (*a*)-(*d*) are borne in mind.

3.2.11. *Arbitrations on overlapping issues—action on appointment*

When appointed the Arbitrator should:

(*a*) notify all parties in writing of all appointments;

(*b*) call all the parties to a preliminary meeting;

(*c*) at that meeting explain the nature of a consolidated hearing with particular reference to the matters set out in paragraph 3.2.10;

(*d*) give directions for the conduct of references bearing in mind the matters set out in paragraph 3.2.10;

(*e*) if one party claims that the only fair way to deal with related cases is to have combined hearings or submissions whilst another or others take the opposite view, the Arbitrator must decide whether the cases can fairly be dealt with separately, since he cannot order combined hearings against the wishes of any parties;

(f) the Arbitrator should not attempt to withdraw from one or more references on the sole grounds that the parties are opposed on the question of having combined hearings, as this will not assist in the resolution of the disputes. If he were to withdraw, one or more replacement Arbitrators would be faced with similar problems. The onus is on the party requesting combined hearings to apply to the court for a declaration as to how the Arbitrator should proceed, and the Arbitrator would be wise to allow a reasonable opportunity for such an application, but must be wary of delaying tactics.

3–3 PRELIMINARY MEETING

3.3.1. *Establishing the procedure*

In a relatively few cases, where it is clear that the sole issue is one of valuation and the parties have agreed that the arbitration shall be conducted by written representations, the parties are able to agree upon a timetable and to agree also that a preliminary meeting is necessary, it is possible to dispense with a preliminary meeting. In most cases it is important to hold a preliminary meeting before issuing directions. This enables the Arbitrator to establish (preferably by consent), the procedure to be followed, including many of the matters suggested in these Guidance Notes.

If either party intends to be represented at the hearing by a solicitor or counsel, it is highly desirable that the solicitor be present at the preliminary meeting and (if it has been decided to instruct counsel) that he discusses with counsel before the meeting the nature of the directions desired. It is often helpful to the parties if the Arbitrator, when convening the meeting, sends to them a draft showing the directions that he is minded to give. In this way the attention of the parties will be drawn to the points that have to be considered and they may be able to agree all or most of the directions necessary to prepare for the hearing. As a matter of courtesy and, more importantly, to avoid the costs and delay that would be caused by adjournments, a party who intends to be represented at the preliminary meeting by solicitor or counsel should notify the opposing party a sufficient time in advance to enable the opposing party, if so minded, to instruct solicitor or counsel.

3.3.2. *Directions*

Matters to be dealt with at the preliminary meeting should include the following:

(*a*) Who is to be the claimant and who the respondent? Thereafter the parties should be referred to as landlord and tenant as appropriate.

(*b*) The parties should seek to agree a set of documents and to supply them to the Arbitrator.

(*c*) What procedure do the parties wish to adopt? In particular, does either of them, at this stage, ask for a hearing?

(*d*) Is the representative attending the meeting on behalf of a party the person who will be representing him thereafter or is it intended to instruct someone else to act as advocate, *e.g.* a solicitor or barrister? If so, has the representative discussed the procedure with the designated advocate?

(*e*) The expert witnesses should be reminded that each of them has a duty to the arbitration tribunal which overrides his duty to his client. His evidence should reflect his fair and honest opinion, and not his client's negotiating stance.

(*f*) Is any question of law likely to arise? If so, which of the procedures mentioned in paragraph 3.2.7 is most appropriate? Should the Arbitrator be given express power to take legal advice, and if so, do the parties wish to agree upon the legal adviser to be consulted.

(*g*) Are pleadings necessary, or will the issues be sufficiently defined by lodging submissions and (in due course) counter-submissions?

(*h*) Should the submissions (and later the counter-submissions) be exchanged, or delivered consecutively?

(*i*) Does either party wish to apply for discovery?

(*j*) Do the parties wish to enter into an agreement under section 3 of the Arbitration Act 1979 excluding the right of appeal that they might otherwise have?

(*k*) What directions as to the timing of the various steps to be taken can best combine speed in obtaining an award with the need to give each party a fair opportunity to prepare its case.

If the parties agree that there should be a hearing, or if the Arbitrator decides that there should be one, the following additional matters may need to be considered:

(*l*) Should all the issues be dealt with together, or should they be split in some way?

(*m*) If expert witnesses (other than the advocates themselves) are to be called, by what date are their proofs to be exchanged?

(*n*) What rules of evidence are to apply to this arbitration? The assumption should be that strict rules of evidence apply unless the parties otherwise agree. The directions should either confirm this general rule or state any agreed alternative method of proof, *e.g.* a letter from a person with direct knowledge of a comparable, or a pro-forma signed by an agent involved in the transaction. See also paragraph 3.7.6.

(*o*) A date should be fixed by which the parties are to agree upon, and send to the Arbitrator, a list of the issues he has to decide. If they cannot agree, each should send to the Arbitrator his own list of the issues to be decided.

(*p*) A date should be fixed by which the claimant is to send to the Arbitrator a bundle or bundles of agreed documents, so that he can read them with the assistance of the list of issues.

(*q*) Where is the hearing to be held?

(*r*) Do the parties wish the Arbitrator to issue a final award dealing with all matters in issue including his award as to costs? Or do they wish him to issue an award final as to all matters except costs, and to give them an opportunity to make submissions as to costs before deciding how to deal with them?

(*s*) Will either party request the Arbitrator to give reasons for his award?

3.3.3. *Request to defer proceedings*

If both parties request the Arbitrator, in writing, not to take any action he should defer to their wish. He should inform the parties that he will proceed on the application of either party at any time.

3.3.4. *The unco-operative party*

It sometimes happens that one party (because he wants to delay, or for some other reason) fails or declines to co-operate in the holding of a preliminary meeting, or declines to co-operate in discussions as to how the arbitration should proceed. If this occurs the Arbitrator should notify both parties that unjustified delay in proceeding with the arbitration will be a matter to be considered when the Arbitrator comes to consider the costs of the arbitration. If no immediately satisfactory solution can be reached, the Arbitrator is advised to proceed as for a hearing.

175

3–4 PROCEDURE FOR WRITTEN REPRESENTATIONS

3.4.1. *Directions*

Whether or not a preliminary meeting is held, the Arbitrator should give directions dealing with the following matters:

(*a*) The parties should seek to agree a set of documents and supply them to the Arbitrator.

(*b*) The parties should if possible agree by a specified date upon the description of the building, its services and amenities, net floor areas, planning use rights, lease use rights, and (if applicable) any tenant's improvements that are to be disregarded. The agreement should be recorded in a statement signed on behalf of each party.

(*c*) If possible, the parties should also agree upon the like details with respect to each comparable property to which either wishes to refer. As to agreeing facts generally, see paragraph 3.6.9.

(*d*) Unless both parties otherwise agree, any "without prejudice" negotiations or offers whether oral or contained in correspondence should not be referred to in any way in the representations.

(*e*) Whether either party wishes to raise any point of law (*e.g.* as to the meaning of the rent review clause) affecting the dispute; if so, whether the parties wish the Arbitrator to decide the point after taking legal advice; if not, how the point is to be resolved. As to disputes involving issues of law see paragraphs 3.2.7 and 3.2.8.

(*f*) A date by which each party is to serve upon the Arbitrator two copies of his representations; when these have been lodged by each party the Arbitrator will send one copy to the opposing party (unless representations are to be exchanged in the Arbitrator's office). As a less favoured alternative, the Arbitrator may permit the parties to exchange submissions direct, sending the second copy of each to him. In either event the Arbitrator should state that he will allow a specified period, say five working days, to elapse before he examines the submissions, during which either party may object to the admissibility of any evidence. This gives each side the opportunity of checking the opposite side's representations to ensure that they do not disclose "without prejudice" negotiations.

(*g*) Unless the parties otherwise agree, the method of proof of a comparable is a letter from a person with direct knowledge of a comparable, or a pro-forma (to be drafted by the Arbitrator if not agreed) signed by an agent involved in the transaction. (But see also paragraph 3.7.6.)

(*h*) Each representation should contain the valuer's honest opinion of the rental value of the subject premises in accordance with the terms of the lease.

(*i*) A date by which each party shall submit to the Arbitrator two copies of his representations in reply (commonly referred to as "cross-representations"). Again, when these have been lodged by both parties the Arbitrator will send one copy to the opposing party unless they are to be exchanged in the Arbitrator's office.

(*Note*: Cross-representations should not contain representations or evidence other than in rebuttal of points made in the opposing party's initial representations).

(*j*) Expert witnesses should be reminded that their duty to the arbitration tribunal overrides their duties to their clients.

(*k*) The directions should specify whether the award will be a final award dealing with all matters in issue, including the costs of the arbitration or an interim award, final as to all matters except the costs of the arbitration—see Section G.3–10.

(*l*) The Arbitrator's intentions and requirements for inspecting the subject property and comparables. (See paragraphs 3.6.16 and 3.6.17.)

(*m*) Confirmation of the amount of, or the basis for calculating, the Arbitrator's fee. This should be expressed to be exclusive of disbursements, and where appropriate of the cost of taking legal or other specialist advice—see Section G.3–9.

(*n*) Save in emergency, all communications with the Arbitrator should be in writing and a copy sent direct to the other party.

(*o*) The Arbitrator should expressly reserve the right to call for a hearing if at any time he considers it necessary; see for example paragraph 3.2.6.

3.4.2. *Directions to be confirmed in writing*

When the procedural matters outlined above have been decided (whether by agreement or by decision of the Arbitrator) the Arbitrator should confirm them in writing. If no preliminary meeting has been held prior to the Arbitrator's giving directions, he should invite the parties to suggest amendments to them within a specified time limit, but the final decision as to directions remain with the Arbitrator.

3.4.3. *The unco-operative party*

If the parties have agreed to written representations being the appropriate procedure but a party then fails or refuses to co-operate, the Arbitrator should notify the parties that he will proceed on the basis of the evidence submitted. He should however before making his award pass a copy of the single submission to the defaulting party for comment.

As to extending the power of the Arbitrator, see paragraph 3.6.12.

3–5 PROCEDURE WHERE THERE IS TO BE A HEARING

3.5.1. *Drafting directions preliminary to a hearing*

(*a*) The parties should seek to agree a set of documents and supply them to the Arbitrator.

(*b*) The parties should if possible agree upon the description of the building, its services and amenities, net floor areas, planning use rights, lease use rights, and (if applicable) any tenant's improvements that are to be disregarded. The agreement should be recorded in a statement signed by or on behalf of each party.

(*c*) The parties should if possible agree upon the like details with respect to each comparable property to which either party wishes to refer. As to agreeing facts generally, see paragraph 3.6.9.

(*d*) If there is any issue as to tenant's improvements or other matters that are to be disregarded, directions should be given for identifying the issue and recording the contentions of each party upon it.

(*e*) If any issue of law is involved, directions should be given as to how to resolve it—see paragraphs 3.2.7 and 3.2.8.

(*f*) A date should be specified by which each party is to serve upon the Arbitrator two copies of a statement of his case; when these have been lodged by each party, the Arbitrator will send one copy to the opposing party. (*Note*: In a relatively straightforward case, these statements may be full presentations of the case equivalent to written representations, but in others, particularly where the parties are to be legally represented, they may wish to omit matters of detail which will be covered by the expert witnesses in their proofs of evidence to be exchanged before the hearing). Unless both parties otherwise agree, any "without prejudice" negotiations or offers whether oral or contained in correspondence should not be referred to in any way in the statements.

(*g*) Unless the parties otherwise agree, the method of proof of a comparable is by calling as a witness a person with direct knowledge of the transaction. The method usually agreed, however, is by a letter from a person with direct knowledge of a comparable, or by a pro-forma (to be drafted by the Arbitrator if not agreed) signed by an agent involved in the transaction.

(*h*) A date should be specified by which each party shall submit to the Arbitrator two copies of his reply to the other party's statement. Again when these have been lodged, the Arbitrator will send one copy to the opposing party. The Arbitrator should state that the cross representations should not contain representations or evidence other than in rebuttal of points made in the opposing party's initial representations.

(*i*) A date and procedure should be specified for the submission and exchange of proofs of evidence if applicable (*e.g.* when the initial statements do not constitute a full statement of the case).

(*j*) Each proof of evidence should contain the valuer's honest opinion of the rental value of the subject premises in accordance with the terms of the lease. Expert witnesses should be reminded that their duty to the arbitration tribunal overrides their duties to their clients.

(*k*) The directions should specify whether the award will be a simple award or if requested a reasoned award (see paragraphs 3.8.8 and 3.8.9) and that the award will either be a final award dealing with all matters at issue, including the costs of the arbitration, or will be an interim award, either on a preliminary point of law or final as to all matters except the costs of the arbitration (see section G.3–10).

(*l*) Save in emergency, all communications with the Arbitrator should be in writing and a copy sent to the other party.

(*m*) A date and place should be fixed for the hearing.

(*n*) The Arbitrator should state his intentions and requirements for inspecting the subject property and comparables—see paragraphs 3.6.16 and 3.6.17.

In particularly complicated cases it may be preferable instead of the directions outlined in (*f*) and (*g*) above to direct that the claimant delivers points of claim by a specified date, that the respondent delivers points of defence within a specified number of days thereafter, and the claimant deliver points of reply within a further specified period.

In one reported case (*Chapman v. Charlwood Alliance* (1981) 260 E.G. 1041) determination of a preliminary point in a rent review arbitration was sought with the Arbitrator's consent but with the other party opposing. The court refused to determine it because a substantial saving in costs was unlikely and the point was not one where leave to appeal would be likely to be given.

3-6 THE HEARING

3.6.1. *Hearing is private*

An arbitration is a private tribunal, and the only persons entitled to attend are the parties themselves and those whose attendance is required in order to assist the parties in presenting their cases whether as advocates, or witnesses.

3.6.2. *Procedure*

The usual procedure at a hearing is set out below:

(*a*) The Arbitrator opens the proceedings and announces the arrangements for the hearing.

(*b*) The claimant or his representative opens and presents his case and, where appropriate, his reply to any counter-claim, probably by summarising his case upon each.

(*c*) The claimant calls his first witness and examines him upon the evidence which he gives. (As to receiving written proof of evidence see paragraph 3.7.7).

(*d*) The respondent cross-examines the witness.

(*e*) The claimant may if he wishes re-examine the witness by asking further questions, but only on matters arising out of stages (*c*) and (*d*) above.

(*f*) The Arbitrator questions if necessary; see paragraph 3.6.4.

(*g*) The Arbitrator gives each party the opportunity to ask questions arising out of the witness' answers to the Arbitrator's questions.

(*h*) Stages (*c*) to (*g*) are repeated for each subsequent witness.

(*i*) The respondent outlines his case if he wishes.

(*j*) Stages (*c*) to (*g*) are repeated for this and for each subsequent witness called by the respondent.

(*k*) The Arbitrator raises any matter within his knowledge, not hitherto raised, that he considers to be relevant, and invites submissions on it.

(*l*) The respondent makes his final submissions.

(*m*) The claimant makes his final submissions.

(*n*) The Arbitrator closes the hearing and makes arrangements to inspect.

3.6.3. *Witnesses*

The Arbitrator has no power to call a witness but he may re-call a witness if he thinks fit.

3.6.4. *Conduct by Arbitrator of the hearing*

When an advocate is making a submission, it is helpful to him and can considerably shorten the time if the Arbitrator indicates, as each point is made, whether or not he understands it and whether or not he provisionally agrees with it. But if he has "stopped" the advocate on a point, by giving such an indication, he should not find against him on that point without giving him an opportunity of making further submissions on it—if necessary at a further hearing. The Arbitrator should always seek clarification of a point he does not understand. On the other hand, he should be careful not to interrupt the submission to such an extent that the advocate is prevented from putting a coherent case.

3.6.5. *Where a surveyor is both advocate and witness*

A major difficulty for the Arbitrator may arise in a hearing where a party is represented by a surveyor acting both as witness and as advocate. The Arbitrator and the parties' surveyors must at all times seek to distinguish between the two roles and to establish in which capacity the surveyor is acting at any one time. A surveyor will be acting as an advocate when opening his case, summing up, or when he is cross-examining the expert surveyor acting for the other party, but he will be acting as an expert witness when giving evidence or expressing an opinion, and will be subject to cross-examination when doing so. It will help both him and the Arbitrator if the surveyor occupies a different seat or position when giving evidence from that which he uses when making submissions.

3.6.6. *Note of evidence*

The Arbitrator must have a sufficiently full note of the evidence and arguments to enable him to make a reasoned award dealing with the substance of the case made by each party.

The Arbitrator should either himself make a note of evidence and argument or (with both parties' consent) arrange for a shorthand typist familiar with property terminology to record the proceedings. In very substantial matters it may be desirable to have a note taken by professional court reporters. Although this is an expensive course, the delay involved in slowing down the proceedings so that the Arbitrator himself may take a note may be more expensive than the cost of employing court reporters.

Even when a complete transcript is being made the Arbitrator should still take sufficient notes to remind himself of any material points that need clarification during the hearing.

3.6.7. *Note of issues argued or agreed*

It is important that a precise note be made of any facts or propositions of law that may be agreed during the hearing. Similarly, if a point of law is being argued, the propositions contended for should be recorded in writing.

3.6.8. *Oath or affirmation*

Section 12(2) of the Arbitration Act 1950 provides that evidence shall be taken on oath or affirmation if the Arbitrator sees fit. The administration of the oath depends upon the religious beliefs of the witness, and before the hearing the Arbitrator should enquire whether it will be sufficient for him to have separate copies of the New Testament (for Christians) and the Old Testament (for Jews). The witness should take the appropriate Testament in his uplifted hand and say or repeat after the Arbitrator:

> "I swear by Almighty God that the evidence I shall give touching the matters in difference in this reference shall be the truth, the whole truth and nothing but the truth."

If the witness has no religious belief, or if his religious beliefs prohibit the swearing of an oath in these circumstances, he is entitled to affirm. In such cases, he should say or repeat after the Arbitrator:

> "I solemnly, sincerely and truly affirm and declare that I will true answers make to all such questions as shall be asked of me touching the matters in difference in this reference."

If other religions are involved, the Arbitrator should ask the party or his representative concerned to make the appropriate arrangements in advance.

3.6.9. *Agreeing facts*

The presentation of oral evidence is time-consuming and therefore costly. Moreover, it may give rise to complex issues relating to the law of evidence. There are great advantages in persuading the parties at the preliminary meeting to agree facts, including the facts of comparables, to the greatest possible extent so that at the hearing the Arbitrator can concentrate on the presentation of argument and interpretation; see paragraph 3.7.5.

3.6.10. *Attendance of witnesses*

Under the Arbitration Act 1950, section 12(1), the Arbitrator has power, unless a contrary intention appears from the arbitration agreement, to make orders concerning the examination on oath of the parties, production of documents and other matters. Additionally, either party may apply to the High Court for a subpoena to compel witnesses to attend and to bring with them particular documents to be put in evidence—see section 12(4). Section 12(6) gives the court wide powers to make orders in relation to the production of documents and other matters. Moreover, the Arbitration Act 1979, section 5 enables the High Court to confer on the Arbitrator the same power to continue after non-compliance with a direction as the court would have in similar circumstances—see paragraph 3.6.13, below. If a party persistently fails to comply with the directions of the Arbitrator, or with an order under section 12, legal advice should be sought.

3.6.11. *The unco-operative party*

If neither party wishes the Arbitrator to proceed he should defer to their wishes. It sometimes happens that one of the parties has a motive for delay and fails or refuses to co-operate. If without reasonable excuse one party does not attend the preliminary meeting or the hearing, or fails to supply written submissions, the Arbitrator is entitled to proceed in his absence. Indeed, in view of the Arbitrator's duty to proceed expeditiously, proceeding *ex parte*, that is, in the absence of one party, may be the only option open to him. However, if there is any doubt it would be wise to adjourn the hearing to a later date. Great care must be taken before proceeding *ex parte* and the Arbitrator must ensure that notification of the date for the adjourned hearing is given to the party concerned. This is particularly important if either of the parties is not professionally represented.

Prepaid recorded delivery to the appropriate address is desirable.

3.6.12. *Extending the Arbitrator's powers*

If a party fails to comply with a direction given by the Arbitrator, the opposing party or the Arbitrator himself may apply to the High Court under the Arbitration Act 1979, s.5, to have the Arbitrator's powers extended. If

183

the High Court makes such an order, the Arbitrator will have the power to continue with the reference notwithstanding the default of the party, in the same way as the Judge of the High Court could continue after non-compliance with an order of the Court.

It is usually preferable for the application to be made by the party prejudiced by the defaults, rather than by the Arbitrator.

3.6.13. *Proceeding ex parte*

Even when an order has been obtained under section 5 of the 1979 Act, or the hearing is continued *ex parte*, the Arbitrator must conduct the reference with the same fair and impartial regard to the evidence placed before him as if the defaulting party were present. Thus he must assess the value of evidence put before him notwithstanding the fact that the opposing party is not present.

Nevertheless it is not the Arbitrator's duty to represent the defaulting party who is not in attendance. If from his own experience and knowledge he doubts the value or accuracy of any of the evidence presented to him by the attending party, he should voice this doubt and give his reasons, so that the attending party has the opportunity to present evidence and/or argument to him on the view he is minded to take. See particularly *Fox/Fisher v. P. G. Wellfair Ltd.* (1982) 263 E.G. 589, 657.

The defaulting party does not lose any right he may have to ask for a reasoned award or to challenge the award on the ground of misconduct or on a question of law—see paragraphs 3.8.9 and 3.8.11.

3.6.14. *Directions before proceeding ex parte*

It is suggested that before proceeding *ex parte* the Arbitrator should ensure that

- (*a*) the absent party has given either no reason, or a reason that the Arbitrator considers unacceptable, for his absence;
- (*b*) the Arbitrator has given the absent party notice that he intends to proceed on a specified date, and will do so whether or not that party attends;
- (*c*) he has taken steps to ensure that evidence of service of such a notice is available, *e.g.* a statutory declaration of personal service, or a duly completed post office acknowledgement of receipt form.

This is particularly important if the absent party is not professionally represented.

184

3.6.15. *The raising of legal issues as a means to delay*

The Arbitrator should bear in mind when a point of law is raised, or when he is asked to give an award containing reasons, that this may merely be an attempt to delay matters—see paragraph 3.8.8.

3.6.16. *Inspections*

An Arbitrator will usually find it of advantage to make a brief preliminary inspection before the hearing (if any hearing is to be held). He should make a more detailed inspection after having received all the evidence. The Arbitrator should inspect the subject property and the "comparables" submitted to him (or at least those which he considers relevant or important) as soon as the hearing or the written representations have been concluded, so that the relevant evidence and submissions are still fresh in his mind when he inspects.

Where a tenant is unco-operative, and refuses the Arbitrator access, the Arbitrator should request the other party to apply for an order of court that the tenant allow the Arbitrator access, such order to be enforced if necessary by court officials.

3.6.17. *Attendance at inspections*

The Arbitrator may often prefer and find it more convenient, with the agreement of the parties, to make inspections unaccompanied. Unless the Arbitrator is inspecting unaccompanied by the parties, inspections should be conducted in the presence of both parties or their representatives unless either party indicates in advance that he has no wish to be present and no objection to the inspection taking place in the presence of the other party. The inspection is not an appropriate occasion for re-opening the hearing.

It is unusual for the parties accompanying the Arbitrator on his inspection to address any comments to him. However if comments are made to the Arbitrator, they must be limited to drawing his attention during the inspection to factual matters covered in their evidence. Conversely the Arbitrator may put relevant questions to the parties during his inspection of any property.

3-7 EVIDENCE

3.7.1. *Evidence—factual or expert*

The courts recognise that evidence can be either factual or the opinion of an expert. The same applies in an arbitration. The weight to be attached to any piece of evidence, whether of fact or of opinion, is a matter of judgment for the Arbitrator. Where there is little or no factual evidence, the opinions of the expert may be unsupported by evidence of comparable lettings. In assessing the weight to be attached to an opinion, the Arbitrator should take into account the ability, experience and objectivity of the expert who expresses it.

Although the Arbitrator is bound to act on evidence, he has an important role to play in weighing the evidence. Indeed, one of the main reasons for the parties choosing to have their dispute determined by a chartered surveyor as Arbitrator is that he can be expected to have the appropriate expertise and experience to weigh the evidence properly. In some cases, both parties may put in inadequate submissions; for example, they may concentrate on the evidence of comparables which are out of date in relation to the review date, but contain little or no discussion or evidence of how the market has moved over the relevant period. The Arbitrator should not let himself be put in the position where he has insufficient evidence to enable him to reach a decision. If the submissions and evidence are inadequate in any way, the Arbitrator should encourage the parties to supplement them, indicating the nature of his concern about the evidence already before him; if necessary he should convene a hearing for this purpose under the powers he has reserved in his Directions (see paragraphs 3.1 and 3.4.1(*n*). See also paragraph 3.1.4 above.)

3.7.2. *The rules of evidence*

Unless the parties have expressly or implicitly agreed to the contrary, an Arbitrator is probably bound by the same rules of evidence as the courts of law. Those rules are too lengthy to be included in these Notes. Further guidance is given in Part 7 of the *Handbook of Rent Review* (1993 Revision); and see paragraph 1.1.1.

In practice the parties to an arbitration, like the parties to an action in court, will often agree to the admission of material which otherwise would not be strictly admissible as evidence, *e.g.* hearsay evidence of comparables. In commercial arbitrations, the court will often assume this even where no such agreement is specifically provided.

The recommendations in paragraphs 3.4.1(*c*) and 3.5.1(*c*) of these Guidance Notes are specifically included to enable the admission and presentation of what would otherwise be hearsay evidence of valid and material comparables, without incurring the sometimes considerable additional costs of calling the surveyors involved to give evidence of a particular transaction.

The following paragraphs attempt some guidance on points that often arise in rent review and other valuation arbitrations.

3.7.3. *Burden of proof*

The burden of proof of an assertion lies upon the party making the assertion.

3.7.4. *Hearsay evidence*

The rule against hearsay evidence can be stated as follows. A witness may give evidence only of matters within his own personal knowledge, and not of matters that he has been told either orally or by reading some document. The reason for this rule is practical rather than technical; for example, an apparently self-contained arms length market transaction may well have been affected by the surrender of an existing lease or by family or by other personal relationships. Only a witness who has first hand personal knowledge of the transaction will be able to give a full account of all relevant circumstances (see paragraph 3.7.10).

An Arbitrator, like a judge, may have a discretion whether to allow hearsay evidence to be presented under the Civil Evidence Act 1968. But clearly he would have to consider very carefully what weight could be given to such evidence. He should beware of allowing hearsay evidence to be given of a matter which appears essential to his decision.

3.7.5. *Evidence of comparables*

In rent review arbitrations, the rule against hearsay evidence is most likely to be relevant to evidence of comparable transactions.

The subject of hearsay evidence in relation to comparables is fully dealt with in the judgment of Megarry J. in *English Exporters (London) Ltd. v. Eldonwall Ltd.* [1973] 1 All E.R. 726 (a case under the Landlord and Tenant Act 1954, Part II). In that case the Judge said:—

  (1) "As an expert witness, the valuer is entitled to express his opinion about matters within his field of competence. In building up his opinions about values, he will no doubt have learned much from transactions in which he has himself been engaged and of which he

187

could give first-hand evidence. But he will also have learned much from many other sources, including much of which he could give no first-hand evidence. Textbooks, journals, reports of auctions and other dealings, and information obtained from his professional brethren and others, some related to particular transactions and some more general and indefinite, will all have contributed their share ... No question of giving hearsay evidence arises in such cases; the witness states his opinion from his general experience."

(2) "On the other hand, quite apart from merely expressing his opinion, the expert often is able to give factual evidence as well. If he has first-hand knowledge of a transaction, he can speak of that ... Basically, the expert's factual evidence on matters of fact is in the same position as the factual evidence of any other witness. Further factual evidence that he cannot give himself is sometimes adduced in some other way, as by the testimony of some other witness who was himself concerned in the transaction in question, or by proving some document which carried the transaction through, or recorded it; and to the transaction thus established, like the transactions which the expert himself has proved, the expert may apply his experience and opinions, as tending to support or qualify his views."

(3) "That being so, it seems to me quite another matter when it is asserted that a valuer may give factual evidence of transactions of which he has no direct knowledge, whether per se or whether in the guise of giving reasons for his opinion as to value ... I know of no special rule giving expert valuation witnesses the right to give hearsay evidence of facts."

(4) "When a list of comparables is being prepared for the trial as is usual and convenient, it is all too common to include in the list transactions upon which there will be no admissible evidence but only hearsay of a greater or lesser degree of reliability. If the parties exchange lists of comparables at an early date, often much time and money can be saved by the experts on each side agreeing such of the transactions in each list as, after any necessary enquiry, they feel they can accept as being reliably summarised; and in this way the additional expense of proving a favourable comparable not within an expert's own knowledge can be avoided. But if the other side will not accept the facts, then either the transaction must be proved by admissible evidence or it must be omitted as a comparable."

Apparently comparable transactions may have been affected by VAT and/or by the phasing of the Uniform Business Rate.

3.7.6. *Agreeing facts of comparables*

As was suggested by Megarry J., in most cases, if particulars of the comparable transactions intended to be referred to by the witnesses are exchanged well before the hearing, so as to give the opposite party an opportunity of verifying the details given, the relevant facts can be admitted. First hand evidence of transactions in which the witnesses themselves have been involved is the most satisfactory. If this is not available then, if the opposing party insists, particulars of the transaction must be proved by someone with personal knowledge of it, *e.g.* the person, party or agent who negotiated it. Production of a document admissible in evidence, *e.g.* the original lease would prove that a lease was granted in those terms, though it would not prove or disprove any associated transaction, *e.g.* that there was a side letter waiving the rent for an initial period. If the parties are able to reach agreement *on the terms of a particular transaction*, it is suggested that they should specifically set out in writing the facts which they agree under the following headings:—

- (*a*) Age of the property.
- (*b*) A brief description of the property and its construction.
- (*c*) A brief description of the amenities and ancillary services.
- (*d*) The agreed net floor areas.
- (*e*) The nature of the comparable transactions, *e.g.* whether it is a new letting or a rent review.
- (*f*) The date of the lease in question, the date specified for commencement of the term, and the length of term.
- (*g*) Full details of all terms and conditions in the lease which might have an effect on rental value.
- (*h*) The rent review period or pattern, and the review valuation date.
- (*i*) The names of the parties.
- (*j*) The figure which has been agreed in the open market or upon rent review.

In all cases where comparables are being relied upon, they should be accompanied by a specific statement from a person having first-hand knowledge thereof as to whether there are, or are not, any special aspects of the transaction which might affect the weight to be attached to it as a comparable.

3.7.7. *Arbitration awards as evidence*

In *Land Securities plc v. City of Westminster* (1992) 44 E.C. 193 Hoffmann J. decided that without the consent of both parties, the award of an Arbitrator in relation to a comparable property is not admissible in evidence.

The reasoning of the Judge would appear also to render inadmissible the decision of a county court. Commentators have disagreed as to whether the decision also applies to experts' determinations and as to whether it makes any difference if the Arbitrator's award was given before the review date and was known in the market place at that date. In practice, parties often agree to allow to be put before the Arbitrator material which, strictly speaking, is inadmissible as evidence. Where they do not an Arbitrator may have to decide for himself how far the *Land Securities* principle extends.

3.7.8. *Evidence of transactions occurring after the review date*

Evidence of transactions occurring after the review date is in general terms admissible. The weight to be given to such evidence is a matter for the Arbitrator to assess in the light of his experience and knowledge of the relevant market. The longer the period between the valuation date and the date of the transaction, the less weight the evidence is likely to carry with the Arbitrator. If there has been some political or economic or local event which has significantly affected market values, this too will reduce—perhaps to zero—the weight to be attached to the evidence.

3.7.9. *Written proofs*

In valuation disputes it is usually convenient for an expert witness to present his evidence in written form, which he will read and which he may elaborate in response to questions from the party calling him. However, this procedure is liable to abuse, *e.g.* the proof may contain inadmissible material such as hearsay or reference to "without prejudice" negotiations. For the procedure to work properly the proof should not contain such inadmissible matter. To safeguard against this a proof should not be placed before the Arbitrator (whether before or at the hearing) unless the opposing party has been given a copy and has said that he does not object to its being read. Directions for a hearing should specify a date for exchange of proofs intended to be placed before the Arbitrator.

3.7.10. *Duty when giving evidence of comparables*

A surveyor representing a party should remember that, when giving evidence of comparables, he is acting as an expert witness and not as an advocate. He must therefore disclose any relevant details of the transaction of which he is aware, whether such details assist his client's case or not.

Failure to do so may be taken into account by the Arbitrator when considering his award as to costs. It could also amount to professional misconduct.

3.7.11. *Oral evidence as to the contents of a document*

Strictly speaking this is not acceptable; unless otherwise agreed, the original document or (in practice) what purports to be a photostat or certified copy of it, should be put in evidence.

3.7.12. *The Arbitrator's general approach to the strict rules of evidence*

Notwithstanding the points made above, the Arbitrator is in practice allowed considerable latitude in relation to the law of evidence. A submission to arbitration is a private judicial proceeding intended to be of a less formal nature than a court hearing. It will often be appropriate for the Arbitrator, with the agreement of the parties, to relax the strict rules of evidence. And the Arbitrator should not refuse to hear evidence tendered by one party unless the other party objects to it, in which case he must rule as to its admissibility. If the reason put forward is technically sound, but of no real merit, the Arbitrator may order the party taking the objection to pay the increased costs caused by the need to observe the technicalities.

3.7.13. *Hearsay and the Civil Evidence Act 1968*

It is open to the parties to take certain procedural steps under the Civil Evidence Act 1968 in order to make evidence of hearsay admissible.

A party who wishes to adduce hearsay evidence must serve notice on the other party, giving details of the hearsay statement. The party in receipt of the notice may serve a counternotice objecting to the hearsay and requiring direct evidence of the hearsay statement, but if no objection is made to the hearsay, it becomes admissible. Disputes regarding the admission of hearsay evidence should be settled by the Arbitrator before the hearing. The party wishing to call hearsay evidence may resist a counternotice requiring him to call direct evidence on certain statutory grounds, *e.g.* that the witness is dead, unfit to attend or cannot be found. If one of these grounds applies the Arbitrator must allow the admission of the hearsay's evidence.

The Arbitrator has a discretion to admit hearsay evidence at the hearing, even though the requisite notices have not been served on the other party.

Further information is provided in Section 7–7 of the *Handbook of Rent Review* (1993 Revision).

3.7.14. *Discovery—the principles*

Discovery is an important feature of the English adversarial legal system. These Guidance Notes can give only a bare outline of the process. A full account can be found in the *Supreme Court Practice 1993*, (see under Order 24). Part 7 of the *Handbook of Rent Review* (1993 Revision) deals with discovery in rent review arbitrations. But whereas in litigation discovery is automatic, in arbitration it is subject to the discretion of the Arbitrator.

Discovery is a two stage process. The first stage is for one party to identify documents which he believes are, or are likely to be, in the possession, power or control of the other party; which are relevant to some issue in the arbitration; and which might assist him in presenting his case. The second stage of which is the production of documents (or copies of them). An example might be documents, in the possession of the other party or his agents, showing completed lettings of or attempts to let comparable properties owned by or let to the other party.

If one party asks the Arbitrator to make an order for discovery, and identifies a document or a class of documents to be discovered, *that seems likely to be relevant to an issue in the arbitration*, the Arbitrator should order that they be disclosed unless the party in possession or control of them can show reason why they should not be disclosed.

Once a document is listed the onus is on the party wanting the production of the document to show why this is required. If a party requests discovery the Arbitrator should ask him to identify the document or documents he requires and his reasons for wanting it or them to be produced. The other party should then be given an opportunity to comment or object.

The two grounds on which applications for discovery are most commonly resisted are (i) irrelevance and (ii) privilege. The Arbitrator should reject an application for discovery if he considers the documents called for are irrelevant to any issue in the dispute. Privilege is discussed below.

If a party fails to comply with an Arbitrator's direction for discovery, the party seeking discovery may apply to the court under section 5 of the 1979 Act for an order giving the Arbitrator power to continue with the reference in like manner as a judge of the High Court might continue with proceedings in that court where a party fails to comply with an order or requirement of that court. If an order under section 5 has been made the Arbitrator should be able, for example, to strike out a points of claim (if the claimant has failed to comply with an order) or a points of defence (if the respondent has failed to comply).

3.7.15. *Discovery—general or special*

The Arbitrator can order either:—

(a) General discovery. This requires a party to disclose all documents relating to matters in question in the arbitration.

(b) Specific discovery. This requires a party to disclose specified documents or classes of documents.

In litigation general discovery is automatic. In arbitration it is discretionary, and in rent review arbitration it is suggested that the Arbitrator should not order general discovery unless he considers that for some reason an order for specific discovery would not meet the case.

The order for discovery should specify first a date by which a list of documents must be delivered and then a date by which the opposing party must be allowed to inspect and take copies.

3.7.16. *Documents privileged from discovery*

A document is privileged if it falls within one of the recognised classes of privilege. The class most relevant to rent review arbitrations is legal professional privilege.

3.7.17. *Legal professional privilege*

Correspondence and other communications between a client and his solicitor is almost always privileged. As a general rule an expert's report provided for a client will be privileged if it is provided with the primary purposes of assisting in the preparation of a contemplated arbitration, but not otherwise. Thus a valuation made for a proposed acquisition of a property may have to be disclosed in a subsequent rent review arbitration concerning that property. But once an arbitration reference has started, all discussions and correspondence concerned with the accumulation of evidence for the case are privileged, no matter between whom the communications take place.

The mere fact that a document is confidential or commercially sensitive does not of itself make it privileged so as to prevent it from being the subject of a direction for disclosure. But even if a document is not privileged, the Arbitrator should refuse discovery if he considers that to direct disclosure would be oppressive in that it would impose on the party concerned a disadvantage or detriment disproportionate to any assistance that it is likely to give to the Arbitrator in arriving at a just decision.

It is submitted that where a party instructs a surveyor to conduct an arbitration for him, communications between the party and the surveyor-advocate should be privileged in the same way as communications between the party and a lawyer-advocate. But there is no authority on this point.

The Arbitrator may be asked to decide whether a document is privileged or not.

3.7.18. *Enforcing a direction for discovery*

If a party fails to comply with an Arbitrator's direction for discovery, the party seeking discovery may apply to the court under section 5 of the 1979 Act for an order giving the Arbitrator power to continue with the reference in like manner as a judge of the High Court might continue with proceedings in that court where a party fails to comply with an order or requirement of that court. If an order under section 5 has been made the Arbitrator should be able, for example, to strike out points of claim (if the claimant has failed to comply with an order) or points of defence (if the respondent has failed to comply).

In practice disobedience to a direction of an Arbitrator is rare, and section 5 is seldom invoked.

3.7.19. *Without prejudice correspondence and discussions*

Correspondence or discussions between the parties to a contemplated or pending arbitration will be privileged from discovery (whether before or at a hearing) if they concern an attempt to compromise the dispute. Such correspondence or discussions are said to have been "without prejudice." It cannot however automatically be assumed that a letter marked "without prejudice" is privileged; it will only be so if it genuinely is part of negotiations pending with a view to achieving a compromise. Conversely, correspondence not marked "without prejudice" may still be privileged if it is part of a genuine attempt to settle a dispute. A letter not itself marked "without prejudice," which is part of continuing correspondence between the parties initially marked "without prejudice," almost certainly would be privileged.

A chartered surveyor who intentionally submits "without prejudice" information risks disciplinary action by the Professional Practice Committee of the Institution.

3-8 THE AWARD

3.8.1. *Award: time and minimum requirements*

The award of an Arbitrator should be addressed to or otherwise refer to the parties to the dispute; as a minimum it should contain a clear finding on the subject of the dispute, directions as to costs and be signed and dated by the Arbitrator.

The Arbitrator should proceed with his inspections and award as soon as the hearing or the written representations have been concluded.

3.8.2. *Award: suggested contents*

For completeness, it is suggested that the award should cover the following:

(a) a heading, naming the parties to the dispute and the subject property;

(b) reference to the Arbitrator's appointment, covering
   (i) the document containing the parties' agreement to submit to arbitration;
   (ii) the date of appointment;
   (iii) the method of appointment (*e.g.* whether by the President of the R.I.C.S. or by the parties direct);
   (iv) the instrument of appointment;

(c) the subject matter of the dispute;

(d) his decisions or findings on the subject matter of the dispute;

(e) his decision as to costs (or reservation to determine liability as to costs);

(f) signature and date.

It may also be desirable to include one or more of the following:

(g) a reference to the preliminary meeting, if held, and the procedures adopted;

(h) a reference to a statement of agreed facts, claimant's pleadings and the respondent's reply;

(i) the date and place of the hearing;

(j) the attendance of the parties or their representatives at the hearing or the submission, in lieu of a hearing, of written representations and cross-representations;

(k) a reference to the Arbitrator's inspection of the subject matter and any "comparables" submitted by the parties.

195

3.8.3. *Mistakes*

Except for the correction of slips, for which section 17 of the Arbitration Act 1950 provides, the award once published cannot be altered.

3.8.4. *Splitting the difference*

The Arbitrator should in general avoid giving the false impression that the amount in his award is determined by splitting the difference. To do so would be to fail in his duty to decide upon the evidence. If, however, after due consideration of the evidence his view is that the figure lies exactly between the rival contentions of the parties, it is his duty so to find, notwithstanding that his award might wrongly be thought to have been arrived at by splitting the difference.

3.8.5. *Issue of the Award*

When the interim or final award is ready for issue the Arbitrator should notify both parties that it is available to be taken up on payment of his total fee (including costs and VAT). If one party pays the full amount the award should be issued to him and a signed and dated duplicate should be sent to the other party at the same time. This is important because there is a limited time during which to appeal (paragraph 3.8.11.). Thereafter either party has the right to obtain reimbursement in respect of costs in accordance with the terms of the award by ordinary court proceedings. If the party who has paid the full fee in this way is not required by the terms of the award to bear total responsibility for the Arbitrator's fee, he may obtain appropriate re-imbursement in accordance with the terms of the award. It frequently happens that the parties agree that, in order that the award should be issued, each should pay half the fees subject to any necessary adjustment later. This practice is undesirable, for it causes complications in the publication of the award and in the running of time for appealing against the award and in extreme cases a party may be shut out from appealing altogether. In the unlikely event that, having been advised that it is available, neither party takes up the award within a reasonable time the Arbitrator should issue the award to both parties and if eventually necessary, sue for recovery of his fees in accordance with the award.

3.8.6. *Award not stating reasons*

Unless required by the terms of his appointment or by an order of the court made under the Arbitration Act 1979 an Arbitrator is not obliged to give any reasons for his decision. In simple cases there will probably be no need for a "speaking" award (*i.e.* one that gives reasons) and an award is binding and enforceable notwithstanding that it does not give reasons.

3.8.7. *Court's power to require reasons*

If the Arbitrator is asked to give an award supported by reasons he should consider it in the light of the provisions of the Arbitration Act 1979, s.1. This section abolished the old "special case" procedure (s.21 of the 1950 Act) and substituted a system of appeal "on any question of law arising out of the award." It also gives the High Court a discretionary power to order an Arbitrator to "state the reasons for his award in sufficient detail to enable the court, should an appeal be brought under this section, to consider any question of law arising out of the award." The High Court will make this order, on an application with the consent of both parties or failing such consent or agreement by leave of the High Court, only where:

(a) it appears to the High Court that the award does not set out any or any sufficient reasons for the award, and

(b) either (i) at least one of the parties gave notice to the Arbitrator before the award was made that he required a reasoned award or (ii) there is some special reason why notice was not given.

3.8.8. *When a reasoned award is requested*

It is suggested that the Arbitrator approach the question whether or not to give reasons in the following way:

(a) If neither party asks him to give reasons he should not do so.

(b) If both parties ask him to give a reasoned award, or if one party asks and the other does not oppose, he should comply.

(c) If one party asks him to give reasons and the other party opposes, then if a question of law is likely to arise, or a point of principle (not amounting to a point of law) likely to recur in future dealings between the parties, he should give reasons; but otherwise he need not.

3.8.9. *What a reasoned award should contain*

The requirements of a reasoned award have been the subject of judicial guidance, and may be summarised:
The Arbitrator should:

(*a*) explain why the arbitration came about;

(*b*) recount the facts as agreed between the parties;

(*c*) as regards the controversial issues, first set out the alternative versions both in relation to points of law and matters of fact and value;

(*d*) give his decision on each such issue, and the reasons why the alternatives have been rejected;

(*e*) end with his conclusion and his determination as to costs.

3.8.10. *Award must be final*

Although not all of the points mentioned in paragraphs 3.8.2 to 3.8.9 need to be covered in an award, it is always essential that the Arbitrator makes an unequivocal decision on the amount of the rent. The wording of his findings and award and his directions as to costs must therefore be clear and unambiguous. Where as suggested in paragraph 3.2.7(*f*) the Arbitrator makes alternative findings, it is of course necessary to say which of the alternatives he accepts. As to awards final on all matters except costs, see paragraph 3.10.7.

3.8.11. *Challenging or setting aside the award*

The High Court has power to set aside, vary or remit an award if either there is an error of law which substantially affects the rights of one of the parties (Arbitration Act 1979, s.1) or the Arbitrator has been guilty of "misconduct" (Arbitration Act 1950, s.23(2)). "Misconduct" in this context is conduct which is not according to law and this can range from serious breaches such as accepting bribes to mere procedural error such as wrongly refusing to allow an adjournment, or by the Arbitrator using personal knowledge investigations or expertise without disclosing it or them to the parties, see *Fisher v. P. G. Wellfair Ltd.* (1982) 263 E.C. 589, 657; *Top Shop Estates v. Danino* (1985) 273. E.G. 197. The procedure for applying to the High Court is outside the scope of these Notes (see paragraph 1.1.1). However, it is important to note that an appeal against an award must be lodged within 21 days of the date of publication of the award (or such other time as the Court may allow). The date of publication is the date when both parties are notified that the award is ready for collection and in many cases is earlier than the date on which the award is received by either party.

3.8.12. *Application to challenge or set aside the award*

A party aggrieved by the award of an Arbitrator can seek to have it set aside or varied only by making a formal application to the High Court.

An aggrieved party can challenge the award in one or more of three ways:

(*a*) He can ask the court to remit the award to the Arbitrator under section 22 of the Arbitration Act 1950 for his reconsideration. Normally, if the court remits an award under this section it will give directions or guidance to the Arbitrator on the matters which justify the remission.

(*b*) He can apply to have the award set aside under section 23 of the Arbitration Act 1950. Upon being set aside, the award ceases to have effect, and the court will then decide how the arbitration is to proceed, possibly before a different Arbitrator.

(*c*) He can seek leave to appeal on a point of law under section 1 of the Arbitration Act 1975.

The procedure for applying to the High Court is outside the scope of these Guidance Notes. As to the time limit for applying, see the previous paragraph.

The Arbitrator will not normally be involved in applications of this kind, nor will he usually be made a party to the proceedings. Often, however, he will be served with notice of the proceedings and supporting documents either where the Rules of Court require it or as a matter of courtesy. In normal circumstances it is appropriate for the Arbitrator to stand back, to take no part in the proceedings, and to await the outcome of any application. If the appeal is against an interim award, it will usually be sensible to defer making a final award until the outcome of the application is known.

If the Arbitrator has reason to believe that the application involves a challenge to his integrity or conduct, he may wish to be more closely informed of the course of proceedings, and may ask to be supplied with copies of all relevant documents. It would not normally be appropriate for the Arbitrator to take part in, or to attend the proceedings but in rare cases where his personal conduct is being attacked he may wish to be represented. In any circumstances which suggest to the Arbitrator that he ought to consider taking an active role, he is strongly recommended to take legal advice, even though he may not be able subsequently to recoup his expenses from either party.

3-9 FEES

3.9.1. *Fees to be agreed or fixed by Arbitrator*

Unless the Arbitrator has agreed with the parties the amount of his fee (or more usually the basis on which it will be calculated), the amount is a matter for his discretion subject to the right of either party to apply to the High Court for taxation of the fees under the Arbitration Act 1950, s.19(1). Thus it is prudent for the Arbitrator to state in writing to the parties at an early stage following his appointment, the amount of his fee or the basis on which it is to be calculated. This is a matter which together with many other procedural matters could properly be settled at a preliminary meeting, and emphasises the advantages of holding a preliminary meeting. If there is to be no preliminary meeting the Arbitrator's intention as to fees should be notified in writing to the parties when he indicates his intended procedure and their written agreement should be obtained.

Where an Arbitrator is charging on a time basis, he should from appointment onwards keep a full log of the time spent and disbursements so as to be able to justify his fees ultimately charged if either party challenges them. Once the Arbitrator has accepted the appointment, as a general rule he should not demand payment of fees in advance. But in exceptional circumstances it might be reasonable to call for security for his fees and/or disbursements.

3.9.2. *Percentage based fees*

Before the abolition of most of the R.I.C.S. scale fees on March 1, 1982 following the investigation by the Monopolies Commission and discussions with the Office of Fair Trading, it was common practice for an Arbitrator to quote a bracket of percentages between which his fee would lie, *e.g.* $1/\frac{1}{4}$ or $1/\frac{1}{2}$ times the *ad valorem* R.I.C.S. valuation scale charge.

While such a fee basis, because of its uncertainty, was not totally related to the amount of the award, the R.I.C.S. have been advised that any such fee basis might perhaps be capable of challenge in the Courts, and thereby might result in the award being set aside. This basis should not be used.

3.9.3. *The basis of charge*

In fixing his fee the Arbitrator may properly have regard to the complexity and importance of the matter in dispute, the degree of responsibility, skill and specialised knowledge involved, the amount of time involved, the level of the representation and the amount or value in dispute. These are the criteria likely to be applied by the Taxing Masters if the Arbitrator's fees have to be taxed by the Court.

In many cases it will be impossible for him to name a precise fee at the outset though as stated in paragraph 3.2.2 he should give an indication as early as possible as to the basis he is going to adopt.

Where the amount or rental value of the subject property is small, a fee based on a normal hourly or daily rate of charging may be large in relation to the amount involved. In such cases it is common for the surveyor Arbitrator to charge a lower fee as part of the service that members of the R.I.C.S. traditionally give to the public.

It is therefore suggested that the Arbitrator should

(*a*) start with the hourly or daily rate that he would charge for routine professional work;

(*b*) adjust this rate as he would in any case for the importance of the matters in dispute, the degree of responsibility, skill and specialised knowledge involved, the level of representation and the amount or value in dispute;

(*c*) he should then look at the resultant figure and consider whether it is a fair amount to charge, having regard to the interests of the parties who have to pay it, and to the interests of the profession in providing the rent review service to the public;

(*d*) the time rate will be applied to the time spent outside the hearing as well as in it, but the time spent must be reasonable;

(*e*) the parties should be made aware that the shorter and clearer the submissions, the less will be the time required to peruse and understand them, with the consequent cost savings. Likewise, the smaller the number of comparables referred to, the less will be the time required;

(*f*) the Arbitrator's fee may also vary according to whether or not a reasoned award is required. The increase in the fee should reflect the amount of additional time taken to provide the reasoned award.

3.9.4. *Fees where a negotiated settlement is reached before the award is taken up*

Whilst it is impossible to make specific recommendations (because the appropriate fee must depend on the circumstances of each individual case) the following, read in conjunction with paragraphs 3.9.2 and 3.9.3 of these Notes, may provide some guidance.

Time of Settlement	*Appropriate Fee*
(*a*) After appointment and before (*b*) below.	Nominal charge, if any.
(*b*) After perusal of documents and/or preliminary meeting and issue of directions, but before proceedings in accordance with those directions are commenced.	Quantum meruit (based on time) plus disbursements.

(c) After action in (b) above together with submission of statement of agreed facts and delivery of pleadings, representations, and cross-representations, perusal by the Arbitrator, preliminary inspection and general preparation for hearing.

A fee of $\frac{1}{4}$ to $\frac{1}{2}$ of the full fee which would have been charged had the arbitration/expert valuation proceeded to finality.

(d) After action in (b) and (c) above, and holding the hearing, or giving detailed consideration to the representations and cross-submissions and detailed inspections of the subject property and comparables, but before preparation of the award determination.

A fee of say $\frac{2}{3}$ to $\frac{3}{4}$ of the full fee as above.

(e) After action in (b), (c) and (d) above and completion of the award/determination and notification to the parties that it is available to be taken up.

The full fee plus disbursements.

3.9.5. *Repetitive work*

Where an Arbitrator is appointed to determine a series of similar disputes, *e.g.* several units in a parade of shops, or as regards the same premises, between a head lessor, head lessee and under-lessee, or where the work is repetitive, a fee on the previously mentioned basis might be appropriate for a selected test unit, with reduced fees for the allied and subsequent arbitrations concerning the adjacent properties or under-let parts of the property.

3.9.6. *Objections to the basis of charge*

If both parties object to the Arbitrator's proposed fee basis and the matter cannot be resolved by agreement, the Arbitrator can inform the parties that he will proceed and his fees will be subject to taxation. Alternatively, the Arbitrator may offer to withdraw to enable the parties to proceed to the appointment of a replacement Arbitrator.

The procedure for replacement is as follows:

(a) The parties can agree upon a replacement Arbitrator, or
(b) Either party may apply to the Court to appoint a replacement under section 10 of the Arbitration Act 1950, or
(c) The parties may jointly apply to the President of the R.I.C.S. to appoint a replacement Arbitrator.

If the Arbitrator's fee basis remains unagreed he can proceed without any agreement as to the basis of his charge. In this case he would be entitled to receive a reasonable amount which, if the parties still do not agree it, would be taxed by the High Court, upon the criteria mentioned in paragraph 3.9.3.

The courts have held that it is improper for an Arbitrator, after appointment, to make an agreement as to fees with one party if the other party objects. It is therefore suggested that the Arbitrator should merely state the amount which (or the basis on which) he proposes to charge. If one party objects, the Arbitrator should reply that the objection is noted.

It cannot be over-emphasised that Presidential appointments as Arbitrators are regarded as important matters carrying a high degree of responsibility on the part of the member so appointed, whose ability to act with impartiality is of paramount consideration. It is therefore unthinkable that an Arbitrator would be prejudiced against a party because of an objection to the basis of charge proposed by the Arbitrator.

3.9.7. *Fees:costs incurred by Arbitrator*

The Arbitrator's fees and disbursements will on occasion include also the cost of taking legal or other specialist advice and these costs form part of the costs of the reference. It will be wise for the Arbitrator to include these in his decision as to costs which forms part of his award.

However, where such ancillary specialist costs seem likely to arise, the Arbitrator would be wise to obtain the parties' agreement to their payment at the outset and this is a matter which is best dealt with at the preliminary meeting.

3–10 COSTS

3.10.1. *Responsibilities for costs*

Under section 18 of the Arbitration Act 1950, any agreement entered into before a dispute has arisen to the effect that each party shall pay his own costs in arbitration proceedings is void. Thus the provision often found in leases and other arbitration agreements, stipulating an equal division between the parties of the costs of any arbitration proceedings, is void, but there is nothing to prevent the parties reaffirming their acceptance of this provision, after a dispute has arisen.

Unless an arbitration agreement contains valid provisions concerning division of costs (*i.e.* agreed after the dispute has arisen giving rise to the reference to arbitration) the Arbitrator has both power and the duty to

203

include in his award his decision as to how the costs of the arbitration are to be borne.

3.10.2. *Meaning of costs*

In many cases where the award lies in between the parties' submissions, the award as to costs will be limited to the Arbitrator's own fees and disbursements, including any fees for legal advice which he may have taken. However, the Arbitrator has a duty to deal with his award with the costs incurred by a party in preparing and presenting his case, including the fees of expert witnesses, solicitors and counsel. There is no clear authority on the circumstances in which a judge or Arbitrator can award as part of the costs of the action or arbitration costs incurred before the commencement of the action or arbitration. It is suggested that in making an order for costs an Arbitrator can, if so minded, order that the costs should include all costs that would have been incurred if the expert witness had been instructed for the first time at the moment when the arbitration commenced. Such costs would include costs of preparing an initial valuation, which would be the starting point of a proof of evidence.

Where the arbitration is conducted under the written representation procedure, the parties often request or agree, at the preliminary meeting, that the Arbitrator's award as to fees and costs shall be limited to covering the Arbitrator's fees and costs only.

3.10.3. *Costs: the award must include directions as to costs*

In the absence of any express provision to the contrary the costs of an arbitration are, under the Arbitration Act 1950, s.18, in the discretion of the Arbitrator who may direct to and by whom and in what manner those costs are to be paid, and may tax and settle the amount of them. If the parties have not agreed upon how the costs shall be borne and the Arbitrator fails to deal with the matter of costs in his final award (see paragraphs 3.10.7 and 3.10.8 as to interim award excluding costs) the award is defective for want of finality, and can be challenged by either party in court on that ground. In such an instance, if there were no other ground for challenging the Arbitrator's award the court would probably refer the award back to the Arbitrator for amendment by including in his award his decision on the matter of costs.

Where the Arbitrator has omitted to deal with costs, a more practical course is for either party to apply to the Arbitrator to amend his award so as to deal with the question of costs. This application should be made within fourteen days (s.18(4)) of the publication of the award, but the court has power to extend this time limit.

3.10.4. *Costs: exercise of Arbitrator's discretion*

The Arbitrator's discretion as to costs must be exercised judicially. That means it must be exercised according to the rules of reason and justice, not according to the private opinion of the Arbitrator nor from motives of (for example) benevolence, or sympathy, or annoyance.

Whilst there are many factors affecting the exercise of the discretion as to costs, one of the most important is whether it can fairly be said that one party or the other has "won."

It is the settled practice of the court that in the absence of special circumstances a successful litigant should receive his costs.

In rent review disputes, a party can be said to have "been successful" if his figure is substantially nearer the award than that of his opponent. In such a case in the absence of other factors it is open to the Arbitrator, if he thinks fit, to award him a substantial proportion or even the whole of his costs (including the Arbitrator's fees): see paragraph 3.10.2.

An Arbitrator should in his award give reasons for any departure from these principles. The following are examples where he might consider himself justified in so doing:

(*a*) A party has made an offer in the nature of a *Calderbank* offer to settle the dispute; see paragraph 3.10.6 below.

(*b*) A party has behaved in an obstructive or unco-operative manner and has thereby increased the costs of the arbitration.

(*c*) A party has produced an unnecessary volume of submissions or evidence having little or no bearing on the subject matter, or has unreasonably extended the work involved in the reference.

3.10.5. *Costs: where the truth lies in-between*

In rent review or other valuation disputes it is seldom that either party is wholly successful in that the Arbitrator awards one party the figure contended for. In such a case where neither party can be said in substance to have won it would be proper for the Arbitrator to award that there should be

> " ... no order as to costs save that the Arbitrator's fees and disbursements shall be borne equally by the parties."

3.10.6. *Offers to settle*

A party may seek to protect himself against liability for costs by making an unconditional written offer to settle on specified terms, expressly reserving the right to refer such an offer to the Arbitrator after he has made his award as to all issues other than costs. Such an offer is known as a *Calderbank* offer;

see *Calderbank v. Calderbank* (1975) 3 All E.R. 333, and see also *Cutts v. Head* (1984) 1 All E.R. 597. To be effective it should contain the following:

(*a*) An unconditional written offer to settle the rent review at a specified rental figure.

(*b*) A reasonable offer to pay the other party's costs incurred up to the date of the offer. In rent review disputes it is usually appropriate to offer to propose that each party bears its own costs plus one-half of the Arbitrator's fees.

(*c*) The offer should state that it is made "without prejudice save as to costs."

Such an offer may be made by either or both parties. If the procedure is to be effective, the party making the offer, or both parties, should ask the Arbitrator to make an interim award which will be final as to all matters except costs. It will be too late to produce a *Calderbank* letter after publication of an award which deals with costs.

If the offer states a time within which it must be accepted the time allowed must be reasonable.

If the landlord makes a *Calderbank* offer, and the tenant does not accept it, and the Arbitrator determines a rent equal to or higher than the landlord's offer, then in the absence of special circumstances the Arbitrator should order the tenant to pay the landlord's costs, and the Arbitrator's fees, incurred after the date when the offer ought reasonably to have been accepted. Conversely where the tenant has made a *Calderbank* offer which is equal to or higher than the figure awarded. If the Arbitrator for special reasons departs from the usual order he should explain, in his award, why he has done so.

The notional date for acceptance should take into account a reasonable time for the party receiving the offer to take advice and consider it. Ten days is often taken to be an appropriate period for this purpose.

If the rent determined is lower than the landlord's offer, or higher than the tenant's offer, the decision on costs should be the same as it would have been had no offer been made.

If a party makes a second *Calderbank* offer, the Arbitrator must consider each in relation to the date at which it was given and the costs up to that date.

3.10.7 *Award final on all matters except costs*

A party who has made a *Calderbank* offer should request the Arbitrator to issue his award as an award final on all matters save as to costs. After the issue of the award the party or parties may, if they cannot agree, request the

Arbitrator to issue a final award dealing with the matter of costs, in the light of the *Calderbank* offer or offers which are then submitted to the Arbitrator.

However, neither party may refer, without the consent of the other, to any discussion or letter written on a "without prejudice" basis, where the right has not been expressly reserved to refer to it in connection with costs.

In his final award determining liability as to costs, in addition to the amount specified in any *Calderbank* offers the Arbitrator may have regard to other factors; examples are whether either party has won or lost a distinct issue in the proceedings which ought to be dealt with separately in relation to costs, or whether a party has been obstructive, such as by refusing to comply with a notice to admit material facts which are later proved at the hearing, or by wasting time in the reference.

3.10.8   *Open offers*

In the relatively unusual case where the Arbitrator is told that a party has made an open offer, the offer will not normally be relevant to any issue that the Arbitrator has to decide except that of costs. In some circumstances however it could be relevant to the credibility of the valuation witness.

3.10.9.   *Parties agreeing to disclosure of "without prejudice" material*

As an alternative procedure the parties may agree at the preliminary meeting that the Arbitrator should issue an interim award as to the rent, and reserve the question of costs to be dealt with in a final award. With the parties' agreement, this final award could be based on a further hearing to enquire into the conduct of the negotiations, including "without prejudice" offers and correspondence, notes of telephone calls, etc.

3.10.10.   *Where the above procedures have not been adopted*

If none of the procedures in paragraphs 3.10.6 to 3.10.9 has been adopted the Arbitrator must himself decide on what he considers to be a just award as to the parties' respective liabilities for costs, which is likely to follow his decision as to the dispute and merits of the parties' submissions to him, and include that decision in his award.

3.10.11. *Costs: determining the amount payable*

The Arbitrator should encourage the parties to agree costs between themselves. If the parties are unable to reach agreement, the Arbitrator should consider providing for the taxation of costs in one of the following ways:

(*a*) If no lawyer is involved, the Arbitrator should tax costs himself as he is likely to be fully conversant with the costs of the surveyor experts employed by the parties.

(*b*) If lawyers are involved, the Arbitrator should give the parties a choice of:
  (i) taxation by the Arbitrator with a costs assessor, or
  (ii) taxation by the High Court or county court.

3-11 OTHER MATTERS ARISING OUT OF THE AWARD

3.11.1. *Enforcement*

The Arbitration Act 1950, s.26 provides that an award is enforceable, by leave of the High Court, in the same manner as a judgment or order of the High Court. However, this provision does not apply to the normal rent review arbitration because in such an arbitration the Arbitrator's powers extend only to determining the amount of the rent payable under the lease, and do not extend to ordering the payment by one party to the other of a sum of money.

Accordingly once the award has been made the remedy of the landlord whose tenant does not thereafter pay whatever sums may be due is to proceed for the recovery of arrears of rent in the usual way.

3.11.2. *Supplementary award for amount due*

It is however open to the parties, if they so wish, to enter into a supplementary reference to arbitration conferring upon the Arbitrator who has been appointed under the rent review clause power to make an award for the payment by the tenant to the landlord of any arrears of rent that may be payable at the date when the primary rent review award is made. Such a supplementary award can be enforced under section 26 of the Arbitration Act 1950 in the same manner as a judgment or order of the High Court.

3.11.3. *Award of interest on rent*

The usual form of rent review clause refers to the Arbitrator only the question of what should be the rent payable under the lease. Under such a clause the Arbitrator has no power to award interest. Although modern leases usually provide for the payment of interest where the review rent is determined after the date on which it is payable, they rarely confer power on an Arbitrator to make an order for payment of such interest. In the absence of such power the Arbitrator cannot make any order as to interest.

The new section 19A, inserted in the Arbitration Act 1950 by section 15 and Schedule 1 to the Administration of Justice Act 1982, does not apply to a determination of rent under a rent review clause.

4–1 PART FOUR: THE INDEPENDENT EXPERT

4.1.1. *The Independent Expert*

Where parties to a lease intend that disputes as to rental value shall be determined not by arbitration but by a surveyor exercising his own professional expertise and judgment, they may call him "independent valuer," "independent surveyor," "third surveyor" or even "umpire." In these notes the single expression "Independent Expert" is used. There is no legislation, and little case law, governing the appointment or conduct of a surveyor acting in this capacity.

4.1.2. *To be distinguished from Arbitrator*

Although surveyors appointed to act as "Independent Experts" will find much that is of value to them in the earlier sections of these Notes, it is vital that they recognise that there are important differences between an Arbitrator and an Independent Expert. These are summarised in paragraph 1.1.5 but there are two which should be stressed again.

First, an Independent Expert is appointed in order to provide an impartial rental valuation based on his own investigations, knowledge and experience.

Secondly, an Independent Expert may be liable in damages if either party is able to show that he has been negligent, either in the assembly of material

209

relevant to the valuation or in the application of professional skill and judgment to that material.

4.1.3. *The duty to assemble information*

The parties, through their surveyors or otherwise, may jointly agree to submit to the Independent Expert an agreed statement of facts covering, for example, such matters as floor areas, the existing use of the various parts of the premises, etc. Each party may also decide to send to the Independent Expert details of transactions of which they wish him to be aware, representations as to the matters which he should take into account, or even their own valuations. Nevertheless, it is still the duty of the Independent Expert to ensure that he has any additional information that is necessary for him to arrive at his own conclusions based on his own opinions and calculations. In a valuation dispute this may include data relating to planning restrictions, restrictive covenants, the condition of the premises as found and as they are to be valued under the terms of the lease, the adequacy and efficiency of the services and all allied matters.

4-2 CONDITIONS ATTACHED TO APPOINTMENTS

4.2.1. *Terms of reference*

The terms of the appointment of an Independent Expert may consist of nothing more than a direction that he is to carry out an independent valuation. But it is essential that he establishes clearly his terms of reference and appointment, including the basis of his fee. If he does not, he increases both the risk of losing his fee and the risk of a claim against him for negligence. The possibility of a claim for negligence is higher where a surveyor is acting for two parties with conflicting interests than where he is acting for a single client. It is therefore particularly important that he should incorporate into the procedure which he agrees with the parties terms appropriate to define the extent of the obligations he is undertaking. In this context reference should be made to the model conditions of engagement for the valuation of commercial and industrial property.

When he is privately appointed the appointment may include a variety of conditions. These may direct that he is to hold an enquiry or to receive representations from the parties' representatives.

Even when he is appointed by the President the appointment may inferentially incorporate conditions contained in the rent review provisions under which he is appointed.

4.2.2. *Challenge to validity of appointment*

An Independent Expert has no power to decide a challenge to the validity of his appointment, and he should invite the parties to resolve the challenge before proceeding. He does however have a duty to proceed with the reference if the appointment is valid, and any delay should be brief unless the court orders him to stop. In particular, he should conform to any mandatory time limits in the lease unless the court otherwise orders.

4.2.3. *Preliminary meeting*

A preliminary meeting is the best way of identifying the scope of the valuation, agreed matters, the procedures and format for submissions (if any) which the parties may wish to make including a timetable. Thus, unless all terms of his appointment have been clearly established in writing, or the parties agree between them that a preliminary meeting is not necessary, the Independent Expert should call the parties or their advisers to a preliminary meeting.

See Section 4-4 in relation to fees, and paragraph 4.5.3 in relation to points of law. It is important that the Independent Expert's terms of engagement should provide for the parties to bear the costs of taking legal advice and for the possibility of the Independent Expert through no fault of his own being unable to proceed further. If no such provision has been made, he may have to bear such costs himself or face the prospect of an action for breach of contract for failing to complete the reference.

4.2.4. *Independent Expert not bound by representations*

Unless his terms of reference stipulate that the appointee is both to receive and to be bound by written representations it follows from the nature of his task that he could be justified in finding a figure outside those which may have been put before him by the parties. If there is a direction in the lease that he is to be bound by written representations it is possible that he may be regarded by the court as acting as an Arbitrator even if not described as such. In such circumstances, the appointed surveyor should seek to establish by agreement with the parties the nature of his appointment.

4.2.5 *Independent Expert: Unconditional appointments*

In most appointments however, whether by the President of the R.I.C.S. or by the parties themselves, there are no conditions laid down by the parties attaching to the appointment other than those that may be set out in the lease. In such cases, the appointee is free to agree with the parties his conditions of engagement (see paragraph 4.2.1) and thereafter he may proceed wholly in accordance with his own judgment.

4–3 PROCEDURE AND CONDUCT FOR DETERMINATION BY AN INDEPENDENT EXPERT

4.3.1. *Procedure should be appropriate for the circumstances*

The procedure to be adopted by the Independent Expert should be appropriate for the nature of the property, the wishes of the parties and the amount of the rent.

4.3.2. *The role of the Independent Expert*

A chartered surveyor appointed as Independent Expert should not treat the procedure as being identical to that of an arbitration. He should regard his task as being that of carrying out a valuation in the ordinary way, with the difference that he is jointly instructed by the parties and that the parties may put before him additional information. The procedure the Independent Expert will adopt should be appropriate for the nature of the property, the wishes of the parties and the amount of rent.

4.3.3. *At the preliminary meeting*

At the meeting, the Independent Expert will explain that its purpose is to settle procedural matters and emphasise that no negotiations must be mentioned at that meeting. The matters on which he will require confirmation or need to obtain decisions will include the following:

(*a*) The name of the present landlord and tenant and who is representing each.

(*b*) Confirmation that the lease documents provided to the Independent Expert are the relevant ones and that there are no supplemental deeds of variation, etc.

(*c*) Confirmation that there is no dispute on the procedures relating to the notices/counter notices implementing the rent review and those leading to the appointment of the Independent Expert.

(*d*) Confirmation that he has been correctly appointed and that no objection is then raised.

(*e*) Agreement on the rent review valuation date.

(*f*) Whether the parties want more time to negotiate a settlement. If so, he should record the request in his directions and should say that he will suspend the reference with liberty for either party to apply at any time for him to proceed.

(g) His terms of service and who will be responsible for his fees (see paragraph 4.4.2).

(h) Whether or not the parties wish to make representations to the Independent Expert and, if so, agree the detailed procedure and timetable.

(i) Whether or not there appears to be any dispute on the interpretation of the lease or any other legal matter and if so, how they propose the Independent Expert should deal with this.

(j) Whether there are any other matters relevant to the valuation and if so, how they are to be dealt with.

Before closing the meeting, he should enquire whether the parties have any questions or further points to raise. All the above matters should be confirmed to the parties in writing.

4.3.4. *Receiving information and representations from the parties*

It is desirable to invite the parties to make available to the Independent Expert any relevant factual information known to them, as this may produce evidence of which the Independent Expert himself is not aware, and is often of assistance in difficult cases. Whether the Independent Expert should invite representations (that is to say, arguments) as distinct from factual information is a matter for his discretion. In some circumstances—for example where the parties are grossly unequal in financial or technical resources, and the weaker party asserts that he does not wish to incur the expense of a professional valuation—it might be justifiable for him to invite factual information only, and to say that he will pay no attention to valuations, submissions or other representations. But he should not refuse to accept factual information that either party wishes to put before him. As to how far he should rely upon factual information put before him by an obviously interested party, this is a problem that may face any surveyor making a valuation, whether for a single client or as an Independent Expert, and it clearly calls for great caution in ensuring that the full facts have been disclosed to him and that they were wholly accurate, *e.g.* seeing the correspondence and lease or agreed rent review confirmation concerning the comparable under discussion. This is because he has a duty to make his own investigations into details of all transactions which he considers might be relevant and all matters of fact affecting the rental value of the property, including such matters as the incidence of VAT and the phasing of the Uniform Business Rate.

In most cases, the parties themselves like the opportunity of submitting an agreed statement of facts and representations (and sometimes also cross-representations). The Independent Expert should appreciate that, subject to any special terms attached to his appointment, he is not constrained by the limits set by the parties' representations and must still carry out his own investigation and calculations as his final decision must be his own independent solution. There is no duty upon the Independent Expert to inspect all properties said to be comparable, if he does not consider them relevant.

He should not enter into correspondence with the parties on the merits or otherwise of their evidence other than to establish the correctness of the information presented. All correspondence from the Independent Expert should be sent to both parties, and a copy of any document received by the Independent Expert from one party should be sent to the other. He should as far as possible avoid any oral discussion with one party in the absence of the other.

4.3.5. *Representations by one party only*

If only one party wishes to make representations or to submit facts and the other party refuses or is silent, then (unless the terms of the lease plainly preclude them) the Independent Expert should make it plain he will still be prepared to receive representations. In this case, a copy should be sent to the other party to give him the opportunity to comment thereon. If he does so, then the party making the original representations should be offered an opportunity to respond. Thereafter no further representations should be allowed unless in response to a request by the Independent Expert.

If one party remains silent throughout, the Independent Expert must use great care in ensuring that any relevant facts disclosed to him by the other are both full and accurate. This may require him to see any correspondence relied upon, or to have confirmation of the rental evidence cited.

4.3.6. *Dual function*

Thus an Independent Expert has a dual function. In the first place, he must assemble all the information material to a decision on the issue in respect of which he has been appointed. In the second place, he must arrive at a determination upon that material by applying his own professional judgment.

4.3.7. *Limited power to enforce agreed procedure*

The Independent Expert has no sanction to compel the parties if they both fail to honour the terms of the agreed procedure for determining the dispute. In these circumstances he should point out that there is an agreed contract between himself and the parties and that failure to comply with the agreed procedure would be in breach of that contract. In practice if one party or both parties fail to co-operate the Independent Expert will proceed with his determination after due notice to both parties but without the assistance of information from him or them.

4.3.8. *Evidence in determinations by an Independent Expert*

The rules of law as to the admissibility of evidence do not apply to determinations by an Independent Expert, and he can pay attention to any information he thinks relevant. But there is reason underlying most of them, and before flouting any rule he should ask himself whether it is sensible to do so.

4.3.9. *Disclosure of documents*

An Independent Expert has no power to direct any party to disclose documents. But he can of course request a party to supply documents or any other information. If his request is refused he can consider what inference can properly be drawn from the refusal.

4-4 FEES AND DISBURSEMENTS OF THE INDEPENDENT EXPERT

4.4.1. *General guidance*

The Independent Expert must decide his fee on the merits of each particular case. In view of his duty to assemble information and his potential liability in negligence, the Independent Expert may be justified in charging a fee higher than if he were acting as an Arbitrator. His fee should not be fixed as a percentage of his rental determination.

He has no authority to apportion the responsibility for his own fees and disbursements or the costs of the parties unless the terms of the lease or of his appointment expressly confer power on him to do this.

If he is required to deal with "costs" or "the costs of the determination" he should establish at a preliminary meeting (see paragraph 4.2.2) whether this embraces only his own fees and disbursements or alternatively whether he is required to decide also on the division of responsibility for the parties' costs. In either case, the principles outlined in Section 3-10 will usually prove helpful.

4.4.2. *Establishing the right to and amount of payment*

An Independent Expert who, after appointment, proceeds to a determination without any agreement of the parties (whether in the lease or separately) as to the payment of his fees and costs, may have a right in law to be paid a quantum meruit fee for work done at the implied request of both parties. However, he would be most unwise to proceed on this assumption. He should immediately upon appointment, or at latest at the preliminary meeting (if one is held), not only establish the basis of his fees and costs but also obtain an express agreement by one or both parties to pay them.

Current practice is for an Independent Expert to quote a fee higher than he would charge if acting as a valuer for either party alone.

The fee basis should be sufficiently flexible to cover disbursements for, *e.g.* legal advice.

4.4.3. *Fees where a negotiated settlement is reached before determination is issued*

It is impossible to make specific recommendations because the appropriate fee must depend on the circumstances of each individual case, but the following, read in conjunction with paragraph 4.4.2, may provide some guidance.

Time of Settlement	*Appropriate Fee*
(*a*) After appointment and/or perusal of documents and/or preliminary meeting and/or issue of directions but before the Independent Expert has done any further work.	No charge or if work has been done, a fee based on the amount of that work, plus disbursements.
(*b*) After the steps in (*a*) above, and the receipt and perusal of representations but before the Independent Expert has done any further work.	A fee of $\frac{1}{4}$ to $\frac{1}{2}$ of the full agreed fee plus disbursements.
(*c*) After the steps in (*a*) and (*b*) and the inspection of the premises, and assembly by an Independent Expert of his own material, and all further work except the completion and issue of the determination.	The full fee, subject to a reduction in respect of work not done, plus disbursements.
(*d*) After the determination has been finalised and notification has been finalised and notification to the parties that it is available to be taken up.	The full fee, plus disbursements.

216

4.4.4. *Excessive fees and disbursements*

As the Independent Expert's fees and disbursements are not directly subject to the court's control (as are those of an Arbitrator) they cannot be taxed. But a party who has paid would be entitled to bring an action to recoup an excessive payment if the amount or basis of the fees or disbursements has not been agreed and the payment has been made under protest.

4–5 THE DETERMINATION OF THE INDEPENDENT EXPERT

4.5.1. *The clarity of his decision*

When his determination on the matter is made, the Independent Expert should set it down clearly in writing and make it available to the parties once his fees have been paid. It is suggested that the determination should cover the following:

(a) A heading, naming the parties to the dispute and subject property.
(b) Reference to the Independent Expert's appointment covering:
   (i) the document (usually the lease) containing the parties' agreement to submit the dispute to an Independent Expert;
   (ii) the method of the appointment (*e.g.* whether by the President of the R.I.C.S. or by the parties direct);
   (iii) the date of the appointment;
   (iv) the terms attaching to the appointment and any adopted procedure.
(c) The subject matter of the dispute.
(d) His decision on the subject matter of the dispute.
(e) Fees and disbursements if appropriate.
(f) His signature and date.

4.5.2. *Slips and clerical errors*

If the Independent Expert becomes aware of a slip or clerical error in his determination, he should rectify it and immediately inform both parties.

4.5.3. *A point of law*

If a point of law arises which is likely to affect his determination and which he considers to be a difficult one, the Independent Expert should ask the parties to consider whether:–

(a) they will agree what is the correct answer to the point of law, or one of them will commence proceedings in the courts to decide it, before he proceeds with his determination;

(b) they would instead prefer him to take, and proceed on the basis of, legal advice on the point, which he incorporates in his determination. If he wishes to seek the advice of counsel he may now do so direct (see the *Guidance Notes to assist Chartered Surveyors in the use of Direct Access to Barristers*, published by Surveyors' Publications).

(c) he should continue to deal with the reference, but (by their written consent) as an Arbitrator, with or without a legal assessor: he should then proceed as indicated in paragraph 3.2.7.

(d) he should decide the point, state his decision and state his determination based upon it.

If all these courses are rejected, it is suggested that the Independent Expert is entitled to refuse to proceed further in the matter.

4.5.4. *A request for reasoned determination*

A determination by an Independent Expert, unless required under the terms of his appointment, should not normally include reasons or the basis of calculations. Nor is there any obligation to respond to a later request for them. However, since the Independent Expert is liable in negligence, it will be prudent for him to make, and retain for an appropriate period, notes on the material that he has used in the course of arriving at his valuation.

5-1 GENERAL COMMENTS

5.1.1. A chartered surveyor may also be called upon by parties to a lease or other similar agreement to determine other matters in dispute, such as the assessment of service charges or a valuation in connection with an option to purchase.

5.1.2. These notes are not intended to cover all such matters but in general terms the basic principles set out in the previous paragraphs of these Guidance Notes apply whether the reference is to Arbitrator or Independent Expert.

Index to Guidance Notes

Appendix IV: Part II of the Landlord and Tenant Act 1954

SCHEDULE 1

[NOTE: For convenience the relevant sections of Part II of the Act of 1954 (and not only the sections contained in Schedule 1 to the Act of 1969) are printed as amended by the Act of 1969, the Land Compensation Act 1973, the Rent Act 1977, the Housing Act 1980, the Local Government, Planning and Land Act 1980 and S.I. 1981 No. 69. Amendments are in square brackets.]

PART II

Tenancies to which Part II applies

Tenancies to which Part II applies

23.—(1) Subject to the provisions of this Act, this Part of this Act applies to any tenancy where the property comprised in the tenancy is or includes premises which are occupied by the tenant and are so occupied for the purposes of a business carried on by him or for those and other purposes.

(2) In this Part of this Act the expression "business" includes a trade, profession or employment and includes any activity carried on by a body of persons, whether corporate or unincorporate.

(3) In the following provisions of this Part of this Act the expression "the holding", in relation to a tenancy to which this Part of this Act applies, means the property comprised in the tenancy, there being excluded any part thereof which is occupied neither by the tenant nor by a person employed by the tenant and so employed for the purposes of a business by reason of which the tenancy is one to which this Part of this Act applies.

(4) Where the tenant is carrying on a business, in all or any part of the property comprised in a tenancy, in breach of a prohibition (however expressed) of use for business purposes which subsists under the terms of the tenancy and extends to the whole of that property, this Part of this Act shall

not apply to the tenancy unless the immediate landlord or his predecessor in title has consented to the breach or the immediate landlord has acquiesced therein.

In this subsection the reference to a prohibition of use for business purposes does not include a prohibition of use for the purposes of a specified business, or of use for purposes of any but a specified business, but save as aforesaid includes a prohibition of use for the purposes of some one or more only of the classes of business specified in the definition of that expression in sub-section (2) of this section.

Continuation of tenancies to which Part II applies and grant of new tenancies

24.—(1) A tenancy to which this part of this Act applies shall not come to an end unless terminated in accordance with the provisions of this Part of this Act; and, subject to the provisions of section 29 of this Act, the tenant under such a tenancy may apply to the court for a new tenancy—

(a) if the landlord has given notice under [section 25 of this Act] to terminate the tenancy, or

(b) if the tenant has made a request for a new tenancy in accordance with section 26 of this Act.

(2) The last foregoing subsection shall not prevent the coming to an end of a tenancy by notice to quit given by the tenant, by surrender or forfeiture, or by the forfeiture of a superior tenancy, [unless—

(a) in the case of a notice to quit, the notice was given before the tenant had been in occupation in right of the tenancy for one month; or

(b) in the case of an instrument of surrender, the instrument was executed before, or was executed in pursuance of an agreement made before, the tenant had been in occupation in right of the tenancy for one month.]

(3) Notwithstanding anything in subsection (1) of this section,—

(a) where a tenancy to which this Part of this Act applies ceases to be such a tenancy, it shall not come to an end by reason only of the lease, but if it was granted for a term of years certain and has been continued by subsection (1) of this section then (without prejudice to the termination thereof in accordance with any terms of the tenancy) it may be terminated by not less than three nor more than six months' notice in writing given by the landlord to the tenant;

(b) where, at a time when a tenancy is not one to which this Part of this Act applies, the landlord gives notice to quit, the operation of the notice shall not be affected by reason that the tenancy becomes one to which this Part of this Act applies after the giving of the notice.

[24A.—(1) The landlord of a tenancy to which this Part of this Act applies may,—

(*a*) if he has given notice under section 25 of this Act to terminate the tenancy; or

(*b*) if the tenant has made a request for a new tenancy in accordance with section 26 of this Act;

apply to the court to determine a rent which it would be reasonable for the tenant to pay while the tenancy continues by virtue of section 24 of this Act, and the court may determine a rent accordingly.

(2) A rent determined in proceedings under this section shall be deemed to be the rent payable under the tenancy from the date on which the proceedings were commenced or the date specified in the landlord's notice or the tenant's request, whichever is the later.

(3) In determining a rent under this section the court shall have regard to the rent payable under the terms of the tenancy, but otherwise sub-sections (1) and (2) of section 34 of this Act shall apply to the determination as they would apply to the determination of a rent under that section if a new tenancy from year to year of the whole of the property comprised in the tenancy were granted to the tenant by order of the court.]

Termination of tenancy by the landlord

25.—(1) The landlord may terminate a tenancy to which this Part of this Act applies by a notice given to the tenant in the prescribed form specifying the date at which the tenancy is to come to an end (hereinafter referred to as "the date of termination"):

Provided that this subsection has effect subject to the provisions of Part IV of this Act as to the interim continuation of tenancies pending the disposal of applications to the court.

(2) Subject to the provisions of the next following subsection, a notice under this section shall not have effect unless it is given not more than twelve nor less than six months before the date of termination specified therein.

(3) In the case of a tenancy which apart from this Act could have been brought to an end by notice to quit given by the landlord—

(*a*) the date of termination specified in a notice under this section shall not be earlier than the earliest date on which apart from this Part of this Act the tenancy could have been brought to an end by notice to quit given by the landlord on the date of the giving of the notice under this section; and (*b*)   where apart from this Part of this Act more than six months' notice to quit would have been required to bring the tenancy to an end, the last foregoing subsection shall have effect with the substitution for twelve months of a period six months longer than the length of notice to quit which would have been required as aforesaid.

(4) In the case of any other tenancy, a notice under this section shall not specify a date of termination earlier than the date on which apart from this Part of this Act the tenancy would have come to an end by effluxion of time.

(5) A notice under this section shall not have effect unless it requires the tenant, within two months after the giving of the notice, to notify the landlord in writing whether or not, at the date of termination, the tenant will be willing to give up possession of the property comprised in the tenancy.

(6) A notice under this section shall not have effect unless it states whether the landlord would oppose an application to the court under this Part of this Act for the grant of a new tenancy and, if so, also states on which of the grounds mentioned in section thirty of this Act he would do so.

Tenant's request for a new tenancy

26.—(1) A tenant's request for a new tenancy may be made where the tenancy under which he holds for the time being (hereinafter referred to as "the current tenancy") is a tenancy granted for a term of years certain exceeding one year, whether or not continued by section twenty-four of this Act, or granted for a term of years certain and thereafter from year to year.

(2) A tenant's request for a new tenancy shall be for a tenancy beginning with such date, not more than twelve nor less than six months after the making of the request, as may be specified therein:

Provided that the said date shall not be earlier than the date on which apart from this Act the current tenancy would come to an end by effluxion of time or could be brought to an end by notice to quit given by the tenant.

(3) A tenant's request for a new tenancy shall not have effect unless it is made by notice in the prescribed form given to the landlord and sets out the tenant's proposals as to the property to be comprised in the new tenancy (being either the whole or part of the property comprised in the current tenancy), as to the rent to be payable under the new tenancy and as to the other terms of the new tenancy.

(4) A tenant's request for a new tenancy shall not be made if the landlord has already given notice under the last foregoing section to terminate the current tenancy, or if the tenant has already given notice to quit or notice under the next following section; and no such notice shall be given by the

landlord or the tenant after the making by the tenant of a request for a new tenancy.

(5) Where the tenant makes a request for a new tenancy in accordance with the foregoing provisions of this section, the current tenancy shall, subject to the provisions of subsection (2) of section thirty-six of this Act and the provisions of Part IV of this Act as to the interim continuation of tenancies, terminate immediately before the date specified in the request for the beginning of the new tenancy.

(6) Within two months of the making of a tenant's request for a new tenancy the landlord may give notice to the tenant that he will oppose an application to the court for the grant of a new tenancy, and any such notice shall state on which of the grounds mentioned in section thirty of this Act the landlord will oppose the application.

Termination by tenant of tenancy for fixed term

27.—(1) Where the tenant under a tenancy to which this Part of this Act applies, being a tenancy granted for a term of years certain, gives to the immediate landlord, not later than three months before the date on which apart from this Act the tenancy would come to an end by effluxion of time, a notice in writing that the tenant does not desire the tenancy to be continued, section 24 of this Act shall not have effect in relation to the tenancy, [unless the notice is given before the tenant has been in occupation in right of the tenancy for one month.]

(2) A tenancy granted for a term of years certain which is continuing by virtue of section 24 of this Act may be brought to an end on any quarter day by not less than three months' notice in writing given by the tenant to the immediate landlord whether the notice is given [after the date on which apart from this Act the tenancy would have come to an end […] or before that date, but not before the tenant has been in occupation in right of the tenancy for one month.]

Renewal of tenancies by agreement

28.—Where the landlord and tenant agree for the grant to the tenant of a future tenancy of the holding, or of the holding with other land, on terms and from a date specified in the agreement, the current tenancy shall continue until that date but no longer, and shall not be a tenancy to which this Part of this Act applies.

Application to court for new tenancies

Order by court for grant of a new tenancy

29.—(1) Subject to the provisions of this Act, on an application under subsection (1) of section twenty-four of this Act for a new tenancy the court shall make an order for the grant of a tenancy comprising such property, at such rent and on such other terms as are hereinafter provided.

(2) Where such an application is made in consequence of a notice given by the landlord under section twenty-five of this Act, it shall not be entertained unless the tenant has duly notified the landlord that he will not be willing at the date of termination to give up possession of the property comprised in the tenancy.

(3) No application under subsection (1) of section twenty-four of this Act shall be entertained unless it is made not less than two nor more than four months after the giving of the landlord's notice under section twenty-five of this Act or, as the case may be, after the making of the tenant's request for a new tenancy.

Opposition by landlord to application for new tenancy

30.—(1) The grounds on which a landlord may oppose an application under subsection (1) of section 24 of this Act are such of the following grounds as may be stated in the landlord's notice under section 25 of this Act or, as the case may be, under subsection (6) of section 26 thereof, that is to say:—

(*a*) where under the current tenancy the tenant has any obligations as respects the repair and maintenance of the holding, that the tenant ought not to be granted a new tenancy in view of the state of repair of the holding, being a state resulting from the tenant's failure to comply with the said obligations;

(*b*) that the tenant ought not to be granted a new tenancy in view of his persistent delay in paying rent which has become due;

(*c*) that the tenant ought not to be granted a new tenancy in view of other substantial breaches by him of his obligations under the current tenancy, or for any other reason connected with the tenant's use or management of the holding;

(*d*) that the landlord has offered and is willing to provide or secure the provision of alternative accommodation for the tenant, that the terms on which the alternative accommodation is available are reasonable having regard to the terms of the current tenancy and to all other relevant circumstances, and that the accommodation and the time at which it will be available are suitable for the tenant's requirements (including the requirement to preserve goodwill) having regard to the nature and class of his business and to the situation and extent of, and facilities afforded by, the holding;

(*e*) where the current tenancy was created by the sub-letting of part only of the property comprised in a superior tenancy and the landlord is the owner of an interest in reversion expectant on the termination of that superior tenancy, that the aggregate of the rents reasonably obtainable on separate lettings of the holding and the remainder of that property would be substantially less than the rent reasonably obtainable on a letting of that property as a whole, that on the termination of the current tenancy the landlord requires possession of the holding for the purpose of letting or otherwise disposing of the said property as a whole, and that in view thereof the tenant ought not to be granted a new tenancy;

(*f*) that on the termination of the current tenancy the landlord intends to demolish or reconstruct the premises comprised in the holding or a substantial part of those premises or to carry out substantial work of construction on the holding or part thereof and that he could not reasonably do so without obtaining possession of the holding;

(*g*) subject as hereinafter provided, that on the termination of the current tenancy the landlord intends to occupy the holding for the purposes, or party for the purposes of a business to be carried on by him therein, or as his residence.

(2) The landlord shall not be entitled to oppose an application on the ground specified in paragraph (*g*) of the last foregoing subsection if the interest of the landlord, or an interest which has merged in that interest and but for the merger would be the interest of the landlord, was purchased or created after the beginning of the period of five years which ends with the termination of the current tenancy, and at all times since the purchase or creation thereof the holding has been comprised in a tenancy or successive tenancies of the description specified in subsection (1) of section 23 of this Act.

[(3) Where the landlord has a controlling interest in a company any business to be carried on by the company shall be treated for the purposes of subsection (1)(*g*) of this section as a business to be carried on by him.

For the purposes of this subsection, a person has a controlling interest in a company if and only if either—

(a) he is a member of it and able, without the consent of any other person, to appoint or remove the holders of at least a majority of the directorships; or

(b) he holds more than one-half of its equity share capital, there being disregarded any shares held by him in a fiduciary capacity or as nominee for another person;

and in this subsection "company" and "share" have the meanings assigned to them by section 455(1) of the Companies Act 1948 and "equity share capital" the meaning assigned to it by section 154(5) of that Act.']

Dismissal of application for new tenancy where landlord successfully opposes

31.—(1) If the landlord opposes an application under subsection (1) of section twenty-four of this Act on grounds on which he is entitled to oppose it in accordance with the last foregoing section and establishes any of those grounds to the satisfaction of the court, the court shall not make an order for the grant of a new tenancy.

(2) Where in a case not falling within the last foregoing subsection the landlord opposes an application under the said subsection (1) on one or more of the grounds specified in paragraphs (d), (e) and (f) of subsection (1) of the last foregoing section but establishes none of those grounds to the satisfaction of the court, then if the court would have been satisfied of any of those grounds if the date of termination specified in the landlord's notice or, as the case may be, the date specified in the tenant's request for a new tenancy as the date from which the new tenancy is to begin, had been such later date as the court may determine, being a date not more than one year later than the date so specified,—

(a) the court shall make a declaration to that effect, stating of which of the said grounds the court would have been satisfied as aforesaid and specifying the date determined by the court as aforesaid, but shall not make an order for the grant of a new tenancy;

(b) if, within fourteen days after the making of the declaration, the tenant so requires the court shall make an order substituting the said date for the date specified in the said landlord's notice or tenant's request, and thereupon that notice or request shall have effect accordingly.

[31A.—(1) Where the landlord opposes an application under section 24 (1) of this Act on the ground specified in paragraph (f) of section (30) (1) of this Act the court shall not hold that the landlord could not reasonably carry out the demolition, reconstruction or work of construction intended without obtaining possession of the holding if—

(*a*)   the tenant agrees to the inclusion in the terms of the new tenancy of terms giving the landlord access and other facilities for carrying out the work intended and, given that access and those facilities, the landlord could reasonably carry out the work without obtaining possession of the holding and without interfering to a substantial extent or for a substantial time with the use of the holding for the purposes of the business carried on by the tenant; or

(*b*)   the tenant is willing to accept a tenancy of an economically separate part of the holding and either paragraph (*a*) of this section is satisfied with respect to that part or possession of the remainder of the holding would be reasonably sufficient to enable the landlord to carry out the intended work.

(2) For the purposes of subsection (1) (*b*) of this section a part of a holding shall be deemed to be an economically separate part if, and only if, the aggregate of the rents which, after the completion of the intended work, would be reasonably obtainable on separate lettings of that part and the remainder of the premises affected by or resulting from the work would not be substantially less than the rent which would then be reasonably obtainable on a letting of those premises as a whole.]

Property to be comprised in new tenancy

32.—(1) Subject to the following provisions of this section, an order under section 29 of this Act for the grant of a new tenancy shall be an order for the grant of a new tenancy of the holding; and in the absence of agreement between the landlord and the tenant as to the property which constitutes the holding the court shall in the order designate that property by reference to the circumstances existing at the date of the order.

[(1A) Where the court, by virtue of paragraph (*b*) of section 31A(1) of this Act, makes an order under section 29 of this Act for the grant of a new tenancy in a case where the tenant is willing to accept a tenancy of part of the holding, the order shall be an order for the grant of a new tenancy of that part only.]

(2) The foregoing provisions of this section shall not apply in a case where the property comprised in the current tenancy includes other property besides the holding and the landlord requires any new tenancy ordered to be granted under section 29 of this Act to be a tenancy of the whole of the property comprised in the current tenancy; but in any such case—

(*a*)   any order under the said section 29 for the grant of a new tenancy shall be an order for the grant of a new tenancy of the whole of the property comprised in the current tenancy, and

(*b*)   references in the following provisions of this Part of this Act to the holding shall be construed as references to the whole of that property.

(3) Where the current tenancy includes rights enjoyed by the tenant in connection with the holding, those rights shall be included in a tenancy ordered to be granted under section 29 of this Act, [except as otherwise agreed between the landlord and the tenant or, in default of such agreement, determined by the court.]

Duration of new tenancy

33.—Where on an application under this Part of this Act the court makes an order for the grant of a new tenancy, the new tenancy shall be such tenancy as may be agreed between the landlord and the tenant, or, in default of such an agreement, shall be such a tenancy as may be determined by the court to be reasonable in all the circumstances, being, if it is a tenancy for a term of years certain, a tenancy for a term not exceeding fourteen years, and shall begin on the coming to an end of the current tenancy.

Rent under new tenancy

34.—[(1)] The rent payable under a tenancy granted by order of the court under this Part of this Act shall be such as may be agreed between the landlord and the tenant or as, in default of such agreement, may be determined by the court to be that at which, having regard to the terms of the tenancy (other than those relating to rent), the holding might reasonably be expected to be let in the open market by a willing lessor, there being disregarded—

(a) any effect on rent of the fact that the tenant has or his predecessors in title have been in occupation of the holding,

(b) any goodwill attached to the holding by reason of the carrying on thereat of the business of the tenant (whether by him or by a predecessor of his in that business),

[(c) any effect on rent of an improvement to which this paragraph applies,]

(d) in the case of a holding comprising licensed premises, any addition to its value attributable to the licence, if it appears to the court that having regard to the terms of the current tenancy and any other relevant circumstances the benefit of the licence belongs to the tenant.

[(2) Paragraph (c) of the foregoing subsection applies to any improvement carried out by a person who at the time it was carried out was the tenant, but only if it was carried out otherwise than in pursuance of an

234

obligation to his immediate landlord and either it was carried out during the current tenancy or the following conditions are satisfied, that is to say,—

(*a*) that it was completed not more than twenty-one years before the application for the new tenancy was made; and

(*b*) that the holding or any part of it affected by the improvement has at all times since the completion of the improvement been comprised in tenancies of the description specified in section 23(1) of this Act; and

(*c*) that at the termination of each of those tenancies the tenant did not quit.

(3) Where the rent is determined by the court the court may, if it thinks fit, further determine that the terms of the tenancy shall include such provision for varying the rent as may be specified in the determination.]

Other terms of new tenancy

35.—The terms of a tenancy granted by order of the court under this Part of this Act (other than terms as to the duration thereof and as to the rent payable thereunder) shall be such as may be agreed between the landlord and the tenant or as, in default of such agreement, may be determined by the court; and in determining those terms the court shall have regard to the terms of the current tenancy and to all relevant circumstances.

Carrying out of order for new tenancy

36.—(1) Where under this Part of this Act the court makes an order for the grant of a new tenancy, then, unless the order is revoked under the next following subsection or the landlord and the tenant agree not to act upon the order, the landlord shall be bound to execute or make in favour of the tenant, and the tenant shall be bound to accept, a lease or agreement for a tenancy of the holding embodying the terms agreed between the landlord and the tenant or determined by the court in accordance with the foregoing provisions of this Part of this Act; and where the landlord executes or makes such a lease or agreement the tenant shall be bound, if so required by the landlord, to execute a counterpart or duplicate thereof.

(2) If the tenant, within fourteen days after the making of an order under this Part of this Act for the grant of a new tenancy, applies to the court for the revocation of the order the court shall revoke the order; and where the order is so revoked, then, if it is so agreed between the landlord and the tenant or determined by the court, the current tenancy shall continue, beyond the date

at which it would have come to an end apart from this subsection, for such period as may be so agreed or determined to be necessary to afford to the landlord a reasonable opportunity for reletting or otherwise disposing of the premises which would have been comprised in the new tenancy; and while the current tenancy continues by virtue of this subsection it shall not be a tenancy to which this Part of this Act applies.

(3) Where an order is revoked under the last foregoing subsection any provision thereof as to payment of costs shall not cease to have effect by reason only of the revocation; but the court may, if it thinks fit, revoke or vary any such provision or, where no costs have been awarded in the proceedings for the revoked order, award such costs.

(4) A lease executed or agreement made under this section, in a case where the interest of the lessor is subject to a mortgage, shall be deemed to be one authorised by section ninety-nine of the Law of Property Act, 1925 (which confers certain powers of leasing on mortgagors in possession), and subsection (13) of that section (which allows those powers to be restricted or excluded by agreement) shall not have effect in relation to such a lease or agreement.

Compensation where order for new tenancy precluded on certain grounds

37.—(1) Where on the making of an application under section 24 of this Act the court is precluded (whether by subsection (1) or subsection (2) of section 31 of this Act) from making an order for the grant of a new tenancy by reason of any of the grounds specified in paragraphs (*e*), (*f*) and (*g*) of subsection (1) of section 30 of this Act and not of any grounds specified in any other paragraph of that subsection, [or where no other ground is specified in the landlord's notice under section 25 of this Act or, as the case may be, under section 26(6) thereof, than those specified in the said paragraphs (*e*), (*f*) and (*g*) and either no application under the said section 24 is made or such an application is withdrawn,] then, subject to the provisions of this Act, the tenant shall be entitled on quitting the holding to recover from the landlord by way of compensation an amount determined in accordance with the following provisions of this section.

(2) The said amount shall be as follows, that is to say,—

(*a*) where the conditions specified in the next following subsection are satisfied it shall be [the product of the appropriate multiplier[1] and] twice the rateable value of the holding,

(*b*) in any other case it shall be [the product of the appropriate multiplier and the rateable value of the holding.]

---

[1] As at the date of publication, the "appropriate multiplier" is one.

(3) The said conditions are—

(*a*)   that, during the whole of the fourteen years immediately preceding the termination of the current tenancy, premises being or comprised in the holding have been occupied for the purposes of a business carried on by the occupier or for those and other purposes;

(*b*)   that, if during those fourteen years there was a change in the occupier of the premises, the person who was the occupier immediately after the change was the successor to the business carried on by the person who was the occupier immediately before the change.

(4) Where the court is precluded from making an order for the grant of a new tenancy under this Part of this Act in the circumstances mentioned in subsection (1) of this section, the court shall on the application of the tenant certify that fact.

(5) For the purposes of subsection (2) of this section the rateable value of the holding shall be determined as follows:—

(*a*)   where in the valuation list in force at the date on which the landlord's notice under section 25 or, as the case may be, subsection (6) of section 26 of this Act is given a value is then shown as the annual value (as hereinafter defined) of the holding, the rateable value of the holding shall be taken to be that value;

(*b*)   where no such value is so shown with respect to the holding but such a value or such values is or are so shown with respect to premises comprised in or comprising the holding or part of it, the rateable value of the holding shall be taken to be such value as is found by a proper appointment or aggregation of the value or values so shown;

(*c*)   where the rateable value of the holding cannot be ascertained in accordance with the foregoing paragraphs of this subsection, it shall be taken to be the value which, apart from any exemption from assessment to rates, would on a proper assessment be the value to be entered in the said valuation list as the annual value of the holding;

and any dispute arising, whether in proceedings before the court or otherwise, as to the determination for those purposes of the rateable value of the holding shall be referred to the Commissioners of Inland Revenue for decision by a valuation officer.

An appeal shall lie to the Lands Tribunal from any decision of a valuation officer under this subsection, but subject thereto any such decisions shall be final.

(6) The Commissioners of Inland Revenue may by statutory instrument make rules prescribing the procedure in connection with references under this section.

237

(7) In this section—

the reference to the termination of the current tenancy is a reference to the date of termination specified in the landlord's notice under section 25 of this Act or, as the case may be, the date specified in the tenant's request for a new tenancy as the date from which the new tenancy is to begin:

the expression "annual value" means rateable value except that where the rateable value differs from the net annual value the said expression means net annual value;

the expression "valuation officer" means any officer of the Commissioners of Inland Revenue for the time being authorised by a certificate of the Commissioners to act in relation to a valuation list.

[(8) In subsection (2) of this section "the appropriate multiplier" means such multiplier as the Secretary of State may by order made by statutory instrument prescribe.

(9) A statutory instrument containing an order under subsection (8) of this section shall be subject to annulment in pursuance of a resolution of either House of Parliament.]

The appropriate multiplier (subss. (2), (8)) has been fixed at 3 by S.I. 1990 No. 363.

Restriction on agreements excluding provisions of Part II

38.—(1) Any agreement relating to a tenancy to which this Part of this Act applies (whether contained in the instrument creating the tenancy or not) shall be void [(except as provided by subsection (4) of this section)] in so far as it purports to preclude the tenant from making an application or request under this Part of this Act or provides for the termination or the surrender of the tenancy in the event of his making such an application or request or for the imposition of any penalty or disability on the tenant in that event.

(2) Where—

(a) during the whole of the five years immediately preceeding the date on which the tenant under a tenancy to which this Part of this Act applies is to quit the holding, premises being or comprised in the holding have been occupied for the purposes of a business carried on by the occupier or for those and other purposes, and

(b) if during those five years there was a change in the occupier of the premises, the person who was the occupier immediately after the change was the successor to the business carried on by the person who was the occupier immediately before the change,

any agreement (whether contained in the instrument creating the tenancy or not and whether made before or after the termination of that tenancy) which purports to exclude or reduce compensation under the last foregoing section shall to that extent be void, so however that this subsection shall not affect any agreement as to the amount of any such compensation which is made after the right to compensation has accrued.

(3) In a case not falling within the last foregoing subsection the right to compensation conferred by the last foregoing section may be excluded or modified by agreement.

[(4) The court may—

(a) on the joint application of the persons who will be the landlord and the tenant in relation to a tenancy to be granted for a term of years certain which will be a tenancy to which this Part of this Act applies, authorise an agreement excluding in relation to that tenancy the provisions of sections 24 to 28 of this Act; and

(b) on the joint application of the persons who are the landlord and the tenant in relation to a tenancy to which this Part of this Act applies, authorise an agreement for the surrender of the tenancy on such date or in such circumstances as may be specified in the agreement and on such terms (if any) as may be so specified;

if the agreement is contained in or endorsed on the instrument creating the tenancy or such other instrument as the court may specify; and an agreement contained in or endorsed on an instrument in pursuance of an authorisation given under this subsection shall be valid notwithstanding anything in the preceding provisions of this section.]

General and supplementary provisions

39.—(1) [*Repealed by the Land Compensation Act 1973, s.86 and Sched. 3.*]

(2) If the amount of the compensation which would have been payable under section thirty-seven of this Act if the tenancy had come to an end in circumstances giving rise to compensation under that section and the date at which the acquiring authority obtained possession had been the termination of the current tenancy exceeds the amount of [the compensation payable under section 121 of the Lands Clauses Consolidation Act 1845 or section 20 of the Compulsory Purchase Act 1965 in the case of a tenancy to which this Part of the Act applies,] that compensation shall be increased by the amount of the excess.

(3) Nothing in section twenty-four of this Act shall affect the operation of the said section one hundred and twenty-one.

Duty of tenants and landlords of business premises to give information to each other

40.—(1) Where any person having an interest in any business premises, being an interest in reversion expectant (whether immediately or not) on a tenancy of those premises, serves on the tenant a notice in the prescribed form requiring him to do so, it shall be the duty of the tenant to notify that person in writing within one month of the service of the notice—

(*a*)   whether he occupies the premises or any part thereof wholly or party for the purposes of a business carried on by him, and

(*b*)   whether his tenancy has effect subject to any sub-tenancy on which his tenancy is immediately expectant and, if so, what premises are comprised in the sub-tenancy, for what term it has effect (or, if it is terminable by notice, by what notice it can be terminated), what is the rent payable thereunder, who is the sub-tenant, and (to the best of his knowledge and belief) whether the sub-tenant is in occupation of the premises or of part of the premises comprised in the sub-tenancy and, if not, what is the sub-tenant's address.

(2) Where the tenant of any business premises, being a tenant under such a tenancy as is mentioned in subsection (1) of section twenty-six of this Act, serves on any of the persons mentioned in the next following subsection a notice in the prescribed form requiring him to do so, it shall be the duty of that person to notify the tenant in writing within one month after the service of the notice—

(*a*)   whether he is the owner of the fee simple in respect of those premises or any part thereof or the mortgagee in possession of such an owner and, if not,

(*b*)   (to the best of his knowledge and belief) the name and address of the person who is his or, as the case may be, his mortgagor's immediate landlord in respect of those premises or of the part in respect of which he or his mortgagor is not the owner in fee simple, for what term his or his mortgagor's tenancy thereof has effect and what is the earliest date (if any) at which that tenancy is terminable by notice to quit given by the landlord.

(3) The persons referred to in the last foregoing subsection are, in relation to the tenant of any business premises,—

(*a*)   any person having an interest in the premises, being an interest in reversion expectant (whether immediately or not) on the tenant's, and

(*b*)   any person being a mortgagee in possession in respect of such an interest in reversion as is mentioned in paragraph (*a*) of this subsection;

and the information which any such person as is mentioned in paragraph (*a*) of this subsection is required to give under the last foregoing subsection shall include information whether there is a mortgagee in possession of his interest in the premises and, if so, what is the name and address of the mortgagee.

(4) The foregoing provisions of this section shall not apply to a notice served by or on the tenant more than two years before the date on which apart from this Act his tenancy would come to an end by effluxion of time or could be brought to an end by notice to quit given by the landlord.

(5) In this section—

the expression "business premises" means premises used wholly or partly for the purposes of a business;

the expression "mortgagee in possession" includes a receiver appointed by the mortgagee or by the court who is in receipt of the rents and profits, and the expression "his mortgagor" shall be construed accordingly;

the expression "sub-tenant" includes a person retaining possession of any premises by virtue of [the Rent Act 1977] after the coming to an end of a sub-tenancy, and the expression "sub-tenancy" includes a right so to retain possession.

Trusts

41.—(1) Where a tenancy is held on trust, occupation by all or any of the beneficiaries under the trust, and the carrying on of a business by all or any of the beneficiaries, shall be treated for the purposes of section twenty-three of this Act as equivalent to occupation or the carrying on of a business by the tenant; and in relation to a tenancy to which this Part of this Act applies by virtue of the foregoing provisions of this subsection—

(*a*) references (however expressed) in this Part of this Act and in the Ninth Schedule to this Act to the business of, or to carrying on of business, use, occupation or enjoyment by, the tenant shall be construed as including references to the business of, or to carrying on of business, use, occupation or enjoyment by, the beneficiaries or beneficiary;

(*b*) the reference in paragraph (*d*) of [subsection (1) of] section thirty-four of this Act to the tenant shall be construed as including the beneficiaries or beneficiary; and

(*c*) a change in the persons of the trustees shall not be treated as a change in the person of the tenant.

(2) Where the landlord's interest is held on trust the references in paragraph (*g*) of subsection (1) of section thirty of this Act to the landlord shall be construed as including references to the beneficiaries under the trust or any of them; but, except in the case of a trust arising under a will or on the

intestacy of any person, the reference in subsection (2) of that section to the creation of the interest therein mentioned shall be construed as including the creation of the trust.

[41A.—(1) The following provisions of this section shall apply where—

(a)   a tenancy is held jointly by two or more persons (in this section referred to as the joint tenants); and

(b)   the property comprised in the tenancy is or includes premises occupied for the purposes of a business; and

(c)   the business (or some other business) was at some time during the existence of the tenancy carried on in partnership by all the persons who were then the joint tenants or by those and other persons and the joint tenants' interest in the premises was then partnership property; and

(d)   the business is carried on (whether alone or in partnership with other persons) by one or some only of the joint tenants and no part or the property comprised in the tenancy is occupied, in the right of the tenancy, for the purposes of a business carried on (whether alone or in partnership with other persons by the other or others.)

(2) In the following provisions of this section those of the joint tenants who for the time being carry on the business are referred to as the business tenants and the others as the other joint tenants.

(3) Any notice given by the business tenants which, had it been given by all the joint tenants, would have been—

(a)   a tenant's request for a new tenancy made in accordance with section 26 of this Act; or

(b)   a notice under subsection (1) or subsection (2) of section 27 of this Act;

shall be treated as such if it states that it is given by virtue of this section and sets out the facts by virtue of which the persons giving it are the business tenants; and references in those sections and in section 24A of this Act to the tenant shall be construed accordingly.

(4) A notice given by the landlord to the business tenant which, had it been given to all the joint tenants, would have been a notice under section 25 of this Act shall be treated as such a notice, and references in that section to the tenant shall be construed accordingly.

(5) An application under section 24(1) of this Act for a new tenancy may, instead of being made by all the joint tenants, be made by the business tenants alone; and where it is so made—

(a)   this Part of this Act shall have effect, in relation to it, as if the references therein to the tenant included references to the business tenants alone, and

(b)   the business tenants shall be liable, to the exclusion of the other joint tenants, for the payment of rent and the discharge of any

242

other obligation under the current tenancy for any rental period beginning after the date specified in the landlord's notice under section 25 of this Act or, as the case may be, beginning on or after the date specified in their request for a new tenancy.

(6) Where the court makes an order under section 29(1) of this Act for the grant of a new tenancy on an application made by the business tenants, it may order the grant to be made to them or to them jointly with the persons carrying on the business in partnership with them, and may order the grant to be made subject to the satisfaction, within a time specified by the order, of such conditions as to guarantors, sureties or otherwise as appear to the court equitable, having regard to the omission of the other joint tenants from the persons who will be the tenant under the new tenancy.

(7) The business tenants shall be entitled to recover any amount payable by way of compensation under section 37 or section 59 of this Act.]

Groups of companies

42.—(1) For the purposes of this section two bodies corporate shall be taken to be members of a group if and only if one is a subsidiary of the other or both are subsidiaries of a third body corporate.

In this subsection "subsidiary" has the meaning given by s. 736 of the Companies Act 1985.[2]

(2) Where a tenancy is held by a member of a group, occupation by another member of the group, and the carrying on of a business by another member of the group, shall be treated for the purposes of section 23 of this Act as equivalent to occupation or the carrying on of a business by the member of the group holding the tenancy; and in relation to a tenancy to which this Part of this Act applies by virtue of the foregoing provisions of this subsection—

(*a*)   references (however expressed) in this Part of this Act and in the Ninth Schedule to this Act to the business of or to use occupation or enjoyment by the tenant shall be construed as including references to the business of or to use occupation or enjoyment by the said other member;

(*b*)   the reference in paragraph (*d*) of [subsection (1) of] section 34 of this Act to the tenant shall be construed as including the said other member; and

(*c*)   an assignment of the tenancy from one member of the group to another shall not be treated as a change in the person of the tenant.

[(3) Where the landlord's interest is held by a member of a group—

(*a*)   the reference in paragraph (*g*) of subsection (1) of section 30 of

---

[2] As amended by the Companies Consolidation (Consequential Provisions) Act 1985.

this Act to intended occupation by the landlord for the purposes of a business to be carried on by him shall be construed as including intended occupation by any member of the group for the purposes of a business to be carried on by that member; and

(b) the reference in subsection (2) of that section to the purchase or creation of any interest shall be construed as a reference to a purchase from or creation by a person other than a member of the group.]

Tenancies excluded from Part II

43.—(1) This Part of this Act does not apply—

(a) to a tenancy of an agricultural holding or a tenancy which would be a tenancy of an agricultural holding if subsection (3) of s. 2 of the Agricultural Holdings Act 1986 did not have effect or, in a case where approval was given under subsection (1) of that section,[3] if that approval had not been given.

(b) to a tenancy created by a mining lease;

(c) [...]; or

(d) to a tenancy of premises licensed for the sale of intoxicating liquor for consumption on the premises, other than—

(i) premises which are structurally adapted to be used, and are bona fide used, for a business which comprises one or both of the following, namely, the reception of guests and travellers desiring to sleep on the premises and the carrying on of a restaurant, being a business a substantial proportion of which consists of transactions other than the sale of intoxicating liquor;

(ii) premises adapted to be used, and bona fide used, only for one or more of the following purposes, namely, for judicial or public administrative purposes, or as a theatre or place of public or private entertainment, or as public gardens or picture galleries, or for exhibitions, or for any similar purpose to which the holding of the licence is merely ancillary;

(iii) premises adapted to be used, and bone fide used, as refreshment rooms at a railway station.

(2) This Part of this Act does not apply to a tenancy granted by reason that the tenant was the holder of an office, appointment or employment from the grantor thereof and continuing only so long as the tenant holds the office,

---

[3] As amended by the Agricultural Holdings Act 1986.

appointment or employment, or terminable by the grantor on the tenant's ceasing to hold it, or coming to an end at a time fixed by reference to the time at which the tenant ceases to hold it:

Provided that this subsection shall not have effect in relation to a tenancy granted after the commencement of this Act unless the tenancy was granted by an instrument in writing which expressed the purpose for which the tenancy was granted.

(3) This Part of this Act does not apply to a tenancy granted for a term certain not exceeding [six months] unless—

(a) the tenancy contract provision for renewing the term or for extending it beyond [six months] from its beginning; or

(b) the tenant has been in occupation for a period which, together with any period during which any predecessor in the carrying on of the business carried on by the tenant was in occupation, exceeds [twelve months.]

[43A. Where the rateable value of the holding is such that the jurisdiction conferred on the court by any other provision of this Part of this Act is, by virtue of section 63 of this Act, exercisable by the county court, the county court shall have jurisdiction (but without prejudice to the jurisdiction of the High Court) to make any declaration as to any matter arising under this Part of this Act, whether or not any other relief is sought in the proceedings.]

Meaning of "the landlord" in Part II and provisions as to mesne landlords etc.

44.—(1) Subject to the next following subsection, in this Part of this Act the expression "the landlord", in relation to a tenancy (in this section referred to as "the relevant tenancy"), means the person (whether or not he is the immediate landlord) who is the owner of that interest in the property comprised in the relevant tenancy which for the time being fulfils the following conditions that is to say—

(a) that it is an interest in reversion expectant (whether immediately or not) on the termination of the relevant tenancy, and

[(b) that it is either the fee simple or a tenancy which will not come to an end within fourteen months by effluxion of time and, if it is such a tenancy, that no notice has been given by virtue of which it will come to an end within fourteen months or any further time by which it may be continued under section 36(2) or section 64 of this Act,]

and is not itself a reversion expectant (whether immediately or not) on an interest which fulfils those conditions.

(2) References in this Part of this Act to a notice to quit given by the

landlord are references to a notice to quit given by the immediate land-lord.

(3) The provisions of the Sixth Schedule to this Act shall have effect for the application of this Part of this Act to cases where the immediate landlord of the tenant is not the owner of the fee simple in respect of the holding.

45. [*Repealed*]

46. [Interpretation]

Appendix V: A Simple Form of Tenancy Agreement

This form includes, with some adaptations, the form of rent review clause agreed in 1985 by a joint working party of The Law Society and the R.I.C.S. The remainder of the agreement has been included to give readers some idea of the context in which a rent review clause is found, and *not* for the purpose of being used as a precedent; its brevity is quite untypical of a modern English lease.

1. THIS AGREEMENT

is made the   day of   1995
BETWEEN:

....
of..
(WHO IS IN THIS DOCUMENT CALLED "THE LANDLORD")

AND

....
of..
(WHO IS IN THIS DOCUMENT CALLED "THE TENANT")

FOR LETTING THE PROPERTY

....
....
(Postcode)..
(WHICH IS IN THIS DOCUMENT CALLED "THE PROPERTY")

for a period commencing on the...
and ending on the..
(WHICH PERIOD IS IN THIS DOCUMENT CALLED "THE TERM")

at the Rent of .... per annum payable (without any setoff or deduction) by equal monthly instalments of £ .... on the first day of each month

2. Obligations of the Tenant to the Landlord

The Tenant AGREES

Payment of Rent

(1) To pay the Rents at the times and in the manner above stated and not to exercise or seek to exercise any right or claim to withhold Rent or any right or claim to legal or equitable set-off

Payment of outgoings

(2) To pay punctually and to indemnify the Landlord against:

(*a*) all rates taxes charges duties assessments outgoings and imposi-tions (whether or not in the nature of those now in being) now or at any time during the Term payable in respect of the Property

(*b*) all charges for electricity gas and other services consumed or used at or in relation to the Property (including meter rents)

Decoration

(3) (*a*) In every seventh year and in the last year of the Term however determined to paint in a proper and workmanlike manner with two coats of good quality and suitable paint all parts of the interior of the Property usually painted and at such times other-wise to treat well and appropriately all other parts thereof previously or usually treated

(*b*) In every third year and in the last year of the Term however determined to paint in a proper and workmanlike manner with two coats of good quality and suitable paint all parts of the exterior of the Property usually painted and at such times other-wise to treat well and appropriately all other parts thereof previously or usually treated.

Repair

(4) To keep in good and substantial repair and condition the Property the Landlord's Fixtures and all drainage soil sanitary water gas electricity tele-phone and other service pipes wires cables and apparatus in and outside the Property so far as the same serve only the Property (damage by fire and other insured risks excepted)

Alterations

(5) (*a*) Not to erect any new buildings or structures upon the Property

(*b*) Except with the licence in writing of the Landlord and in accordance with plans elevations and specifications which shall have been previously submitted to and approved by it and to its satisfaction not to:

   (i) make any structural alteration or addition in or to the Property

   (ii) cut or remove (except for the purpose of making good any defect) the main walls or timbers or structural members of the Property

   (iii) make any non-structural alteration or addition in or to the Property nor make any alteration in the dimensions construction or architectural appearance thereof

(*c*) In any such licence granted by the Landlord to enter into such covenants as to the execution of the works the subject of the licence and as to the reinstatement of the Property on the expiration or sooner determination of the Term as the Landlord shall require

Use

(6) (*a*) Not to use the Property except as a retail shop for the sale of..... or any other use within Class A1 of the Town and Country Planning (Use Classes) Order 1987 to which the Landlord may subsequently consent such consent not to be unreasonably withheld

(*b*) To keep open the Property for business during the usual shopping hours of the locality and to maintain a window display of a high class nature at all times and to keep the windows suitably lit during hours of darkness

(*c*) Not to do on the Property anything which is noisy or which may be or become an annoyance nuisance or inconvenience to the Landlord or to the owners or occupiers of adjoining or neighbouring premises

(*d*) Not to use the Property for any illegal or immoral act or purpose

(*e*) Not to do anything whereby any policy of insurance on the Property may become void or voidable or the rate of premium thereon may be increased and to repay to the Landlord on demand all sums paid by way of increased premium and expenses incurred by the Landlord in or about the renewal of any such policy rendered necessary by a breach of this covenant

Alienation

(7) (*a*) Not to assign or underlet part only of the Property
    (*b*) Not without the previous written consent of the Landlord (which will not be withheld unreasonably) to assign or underlet the whole of the Property

Payment of costs

(8) To pay all costs charges disbursements and expenses (including without prejudice to the generality of the above those of Solicitors Counsel Surveyors Architects and Bailiffs) reasonably incurred by the Landlord in connection with or incidental to or in contemplation of:

    (*a*) the recovery or attempted recovery of arrears of rent or other moneys due from the Tenant
    (*b*) the preparation and service of any notices or proceedings under sections 146 or 147 of the Law of Property Act 1925 notwithstanding that forfeiture is avoided otherwise than by relief granted by the Court
    (*c*) any application for a consent or licence under this Lease whether such consent or licence is granted or properly refused or the application therefor is withdrawn; and
    (*d*) the preparation and service of a schedule of dilapidations during or after the expiration of the Term

Payment of interest

(9) In the case of any Rent or other money payable hereunder by the Tenant to the Landlord which is not paid within 14 days after the same is due and payable to pay to the Landlord on demand from the due date until the date of actual payment in addition to such Rent or other money interest (calculated on a daily basis) upon the amount thereof for the time being unpaid (as well after as before any judgment) at the rate of   per cent above National Westminster Bank PLC Base Lending Rate (or any similar lending rate which may replace the same) from time to time in force

Payment of V.A.T.

(10) To pay to the Landlord in addition to the Rents fees and other payments which may be payable by the Tenant pursuant to this Lease all Value Added Tax (and any additional or substituted tax of a similar nature)

250

at the rate from time to time in force which may at any time be payable or chargeable in respect of such Rents fees and other payments

Redelivering the Property to the Landlord when the Term Ends

(11) When the Term ends (in whatever manner) quietly to yield up to the Landlord the Property and the Landlord's Fixtures in accordance in all respects with the Tenant's covenants herein contained and with all locks keys and fastenings complete and to make good all damage caused to the Property by the removal of any Tenant's or trade fixtures

3. Obligations of the Landlord to the Tenant

The Landlord AGREES throughout the Term:

Quiet Enjoyment

(1) That the Tenant paying the Rents and performing and observing the Tenant's covenants and the conditions and agreements herein contained may peaceably hold the Property during the Term without any interruption by the Landlord or any person rightfully claiming under or in trust for it

Insurance

(2) To insure and (unless the insurance effected becomes void or voidable by reason of the act neglect or default of the Tenant) keep insured the Property the Landlord's Fixtures and the fixed plate glass and on demand to produce to the Tenant or its agents a copy of the policy or policies or sufficient details thereof and the receipt for the current premium or other sufficient evidence that the same is or (as the case may be) are subsisting and in case of destruction or damage by fire or such other risks as the Landlord may from time to time reasonably deem necessary as soon as is reasonably practicable and subject to being able to obtain all necessary consents therefor to apply all policy moneys received by virtue of such insurance in rebuilding and reinstating the same and (except in so far as the same is caused by the act neglect or default of the Tenant or of anyone at the Demised Premises

expressly or by implication with the Tenant's authority) to make up any deficiency out of its own moneys

4. Proviso for re-entry

If the Rents or any part thereof shall be unpaid for 21 days after becoming payable (whether formally demanded or not) or if the Tenant fails to perform or observe any of the covenants on its part or any of the conditions and agreements herein contained then and in any such case it will be lawful for the Landlord or any person or persons duly so authorised by it to re-enter upon the Property or any part thereof in the name of the whole and thereupon this demise will absolutely determine but without prejudice to any right of action or remedy of the Landlord in respect of any breach of the covenants on the Tenant's part or of the conditions and agreements herein contained

5. Terms as to revising the Rent payable under this agreement

(1) In this Lease "review date" means the .... day of .... in the year 19 .... and in every .... year thereafter and "review period" means the period starting with any review date up to the next review date or starting with the last review date up to the end of the term hereof
(2) The yearly Rent shall be:

> until the first review date the Rent of £ .... and
> during each successive review period a Rent equal to the Rent previously payable hereunder or such revised Rent as may be ascertained as herein provided whichever be the greater

(3) Such revised Rent for any review period may be agreed at any time between the Landlord and the Tenant or (in the absence of agreement) determined not earlier than the relevant review date by an Arbitrator such Arbitrator to be nominated in the absence of agreement by or on behalf of the President for the time being of the Royal Institution of Chartered Surveyors on the application of the Landlord or the Tenant made not earlier than six months before the relevant review date and so that in the case of such Arbitration the revised Rent to be awarded by the Arbitrator shall be such as he shall decide is the yearly Rent at which the demised premises might reasonably be expected to be let at the relevant review date

> (A)   On the following assumptions at that date:
>   (i)   That the Property

(a) is available to let on the open market without a fine or premium with vacant possession by a willing Landlord to a willing Tenant for a term of [10] years or the residue then unexpired of the Term of this Lease (whichever be the longer)

(b) is to be let as a whole subject to the Terms of this Lease (other than the amount of the Rent hereby reserved but including the provisions for review of that Rent)

(c) is fit and available for immediate occupation

(d) may be used for any of the purposes permitted by this Lease as varied or extended by any licence granted pursuant thereto

(ii) That the covenants herein contained on the part of the Tenant have been fully performed and observed

(iii) That no work has been carried out to the Property which has diminished the rental value and that in case the Property has been destroyed or damaged it has been fully restored

(iv) That no reduction is to be made to take account of any rental concession which on a new letting with vacant possession might be granted to the incoming Tenant for a period within which its fitting out works would take place

(B) But disregarding:

(i) Any effect on Rent of the fact that the Tenant its Sub-tenants or their respective predecessors in title have been in occupation of the Property

(ii) Any goodwill attached to the Property by reason of the carrying on thereat of the business of the Tenant its Sub-tenants or their predecessors in title in their respective businesses and

(iii) Any increase in rental value of the Property attributable to the existence at the relevant review date of any improvement to the Property or any part thereof carried out with consent where required otherwise than in pursuance of an obligation to the Landlord or its predecessors in title except obligations requiring compliance with statutes or directions of Local Authorities or other bodies exercising powers under statute or Royal Charter either (a) by the Tenant its Sub-tenants or their respective predecessors in title during the said Term or during any period of occupation prior thereto arising out of an agreement to grant such Term or (b) by any Tenant or Sub-tenant of the Property before the commencement of the Term hereby granted so long as the Landlord or its predecessors in title have not since the improvement was carried out had vacant possession of the relevant part of the Property

(4) IT IS HEREBY FURTHER PROVIDED in relation to the ascertainment and payment of revised Rent as follows:

(A)   The Arbitration shall be conducted in accordance with the Arbitration Acts 1950 and 1979 or any statutory modification or re-enactment thereof for the time being in force with the further provision that if the Arbitrator nominated pursuant to Clause 3 hereof shall die or decline to act the President for the time being of the Royal Institution of Chartered Surveyors or the person acting on his behalf may on the application of either the Landlord or the Tenant by writing discharge the Arbitrator and appoint another in his place

(B)   When the amount of any Rent to be ascertained as hereinbefore provided shall have been so ascertained memoranda, thereof shall thereupon be signed by or on behalf of the Landlord and the Tenant and annexed to this Lease and the counterpart thereof and the Landlord and the Tenant shall bear their own costs in respect thereof

(C)   (i)   If the revised Rent payable on and from any review date has not been agreed by that review date Rent shall continue to be payable at the rate previously payable and forthwith upon the revised Rent being ascertained the Tenant shall pay to the Landlord any shortfall between the Rent and the revised Rent payable up to and on the preceding quarter day together with interest on any shortfall at the seven-day deposit rate of ....BANK such interest to be calculated on a day-to-day basis from the relevant review date on which it would have been payable if the revised Rent had then been ascertained to the date of actual payment of any shortfall and the interest so payable shall be recoverable in the same manner as Rent in arrear

       (ii)   for the purposes of this proviso the revised Rent shall be deemed to have been ascertained on the date when the same has been agreed between the Landlord and the Tenant or as the case may be the date of the award of the Arbitrator

(D)   If either the Landlord or the Tenant shall fail to pay any costs awarded against it in an Arbitration under the provisions hereof within twenty-one days of the same being demanded by the Arbitrator the other shall be entitled to pay the same and the amount so paid shall be repaid by the party chargeable on demand

6. Arbitration of disputes

Any dispute arising under or connected with this agreement (other than a dispute as to whether the agreement has been ended) shall be decided by Arbitration. If the parties do not agree upon an Arbitrator either of them may apply to the Chairman of the Chartered Institute of Arbitrators to appoint one.

Appendix VI:
Books for Further Study

Beaumont, *Arbitration and Rent Review*, Estates Gazette

Bernstein, Reynolds and Fetherstonhaugh, *Handbook of Rent Review*, Sweet & Maxwell (looseleaf; updated half-yearly)

Bernstein and Wood, *Handbook of Arbitration Practice*, Sweet & Maxwell [2nd Edition, 1993] (especially Part VII—Rent Review—by W.G. Nutley F.R.I.C.S.)

Clarke, *The Surveyor in Court*, Estates Gazette

Clarke and Adams, *Rent Review and Variable Rents*, Longmans

Royal Institution of Chartered Surveyors, *Rent Review—A Simple Guide*, RICS Bookshop 0171–222–7000

Index